Management Accounting Innovations

Innovations

the Case of ABC
in Poland

Second Edition

WYDAWNICTWO
UNIWERSYTETU
ŁÓDZKIEGO

TOMASZ WNUK-PEL

Management Accounting Innovations

the Case of ABC in Poland

Second Edition

Łódź–Kraków 2014

Tomasz Wnuk-Pel – University of Łódź, Faculty of Management
22/26 Matejki St, 90-237 Łódź
e-mail: tomwnuk@uni.lodz.pl

Published by Łódź University Press & Jagiellonian University Press

Second edition, Łódź–Kraków 2014
W.06611.14.0.M

ISBN 978-83-7969-271-2 paperback Łódź University Press

ISBN 978-83-233-3811-6 paperback Jagiellonian University Press

ISBN 978-83-7969-270-5 electronic version Łódź University Press

ISBN 978-83-233-9100-5 electronic version Jagiellonian University Press

ISBN 978-83-7969-159-3 hard cover Łódź University Press

Łódź University Press
8 Lindleya St, 90-131 Łódź
www.wydawnictwo.uni.lodz.pl
e-mail: ksiegarnia@uni.lodz.pl
phone +48 (42) 665 58 63, fax +48 (42) 665 58 62

WYDAWNICTWO
UNIWERSYTETU
ŁÓDZKIEGO

Distribution outside Poland
Jagiellonian University Press
9/2 Michałowskiego St, 31-126 Kraków
phone +48 (12) 631 01 97, +48 (12) 663 23 81, fax +48 (12) 663 23 83
cell phone +48 506 006 674, e-mail: sprzedaz@wuj.pl
Bank: PEKAO SA, IBAN PL 80 1240 4722 1111 0000 4856 3325
www.wuj.pl

JAGIELLONIAN
UNIVERSITY PRESS

To my beloved wife Renata

CONTENTS

INTRODUCTION

At the turn of 1980s and 1990s management accounting was criticized (e.g. Johnson, Kaplan, 1987; Bromwich, Bhimani, 1989; Innes, Mitchell, 1990). The usefulness of methods used from the beginning of the century was questioned. It was claimed that the methods were inadequate in terms of the changing business environment, which was mainly influenced by technological development, global competition and development of IT. In the monograph *Relavance Lost* Johnson and Kaplan (1987) proved that new times demanded new methods of management accounting, and these methods included activity-based costing – ABC.

Activity-based costing emerged in the United States in the late 1980s and, subsequently, after a series of articles by Cooper and Kaplan, spread among companies all over the world. In the nineties, both practitioners dealing with the implementation of ABC and researchers studying the implementations observed that activity-based costing was something more than just an improved cost evaluation system. They additionally noted that ABC may be a basis for activity-based management – ABM. In the late eighties, but also in the nineties, numerous questionnaire research and research in the form of case studies (among them *action research*) were carried out. They aimed to analyze the process of activity-based costing implementation mainly in North American and European countries. Some of the research analyzed factors which influence activity-based costing implementation. Anderson (1995), Gosselin (1997) and Krumwiede (1998) studied factors which influence ABC implementation at different stages of the implementation process. Shields (1995), Swenson (1995), Foster and Swenson (1997), McGovan and Klammer (1997) as well as Anderson and Young (1999) analyzed the problem of the perception of ABC implementation satisfaction. Kennedy and Affleck-Graves (2001), Cagwin and Bouwman (2002) as well as Ittner *et al.* (2002) studied the influence of activity-based costing on the companies' performance.

Since the popularization of activity-based costing and activity-based management in the 1990s, the two concepts have become extremely popular among companies all over the world. However, implementation of the ABC system proved not to be a simple task. Implementation of activity-based costing is regarded to be technically complex and it requires adequate human and financial resources. Research carried out by Innes and Mitchell (2000) proved that a great amount of labour input needed for activity-based costing implementation is a significant factor at the stage of decision-making about implementation, but it is additionally one of the five key problems raised by companies in which activity-based costing is used (the remaining problems are: difficulties in collecting data about resource and activity drivers, the necessity to treat costs in the cross-section of processes going through numerous internal organizational units, other priorities and the great amount of labour from the financial section). A lot of research on activity-based costing has proved that information generated in companies by the system is used in decision-making processes in such areas as pricing, activity-based budgeting, product and service development, customer profitability analysis and cost modelling. Research on activity-based costing diffusion in different countries (e.g. Ask, Ax, 1992; Lukka, Granlund, 1996; Cinquini *et al.*, 1999; Innes, Mitchell, 2000; Bescos *et al.*, 2002; Pierce, 2004) enables a statement to be formulated that the percentage of companies which use ABC varies, however, in most of the research it is between zero and more than 20% (it should be noted that majority of the research studied medium-sized and large companies). The differences between countries in the percentage of companies using activity-based costing stems from the difference in the development of management accounting methods in those countries, the way the research sample was selected (large and small companies, production and non-production companies, financial institutions etc.) but most of all from the time of collecting information (in general, earlier studies show a significantly lower percentage of companies using ABC).

Due to historical conditions, the development of management accounting in Poland was less intense and delayed in comparison to the theory and practice in highly-developed countries[1], this trend is also noticeable in the case of activity-based costing implementation. Polish companies mainly use different traditional systems of cost accounting, whereas modern systems, including ABC, are used sporadically. The diffusion of ABC in Poland is lesser than in the United States, Great Britain or in other highly-developed countries, and despite the fact that the gap is closing, it still remains significant. The first study which proved that ABC is present in the practice of Polish companies was carried out by Sobańska and Wnuk (2000a). Studies conducted by other authors revealed single cases of activity-based costing or the use its elements (Jarugowa, Skowroński, 1994; Szychta, 2001, 2002; Karmańska, 2003; Januszewski, Gierusz, 2004; Januszewski, 2005d; Wnuk-Pel,

---

[1] Modern concepts of management accounting were known in Poland among academics, and what is more, there were cases of their practical use. However their use in theory and in practice was significantly lesser than in the western countries (see: Jarugowa, Skowroński, 1994; Sobańska, Szychta, 1995, 1996; Sobańska, Wnuk, 1999a).

2006a; Szychta, 2006a, 2007a), sometimes they signalled that the researched companies were implementing or were considering implementation of ABC (Dyhdalewicz, 2000, 2001; Szychta, 2001, 2002; Karmańska, 2003; Januszewski, Gierusz, 2004; Januszewski, 2005d; Szychta, 2006a, 2007a). Some of the studies up to that point did not notice a single company which used activity-based costing or was considering its implementation. Yet, it should be stressed that such findings came mainly from earlier studies (Kinast, 1993; Sobańska, Szychta, 1995, 1996; Gierusz *et al.*, 1996; Radek, Schwarz, 2000; Szadziewska, 2002, 2003).

A more detailed research on the use of activity-based costing in Polish practice was carried out by Karmańska (2003), Januszewski and Gierusz (2004), Januszewski (2005d) and by the author of this work (Wnuk-Pel, 2006b). The studies analyzed such issues as knowledge of ABC, benefits ensuing from ABC implementation, problems connected with the process of implementation anticipated by companies considering implementation and companies which quit implementation and problems that occurred during implementation.

In Poland, research on activity-based costing implementation in the form of case studies are becoming more frequent (including action research). The pioneer case studies carried out by means of surveys and interviews were conducted in 2000 (Wnuk, 2000; Kujawski, Ossowski, 2000) and the first action research was conducted in 2001 (Świderska, Pielaszek, 2001). In the course of time, the amout of such research grew, and it especially intensified from 2004 when the number of companies using or implementing or considering the implementation of activity-based costing systematically increased. Empirical research provided valuable information on the practice of activity-based costing in Polish companies. The research dealt with various problems and they mainly embraced the issues of activity-based costing implementation and the use of information generated by the system.

As far as activity-based costing is concerned, so far questionnaire research examining both the degree of diffusion as well as the usage of ABC in Polish companies has been carried out. The case study method (including surveys and interviews and action research), which is also used in Poland, enables a more detailed analysis of the problem. Bearing in mind all the research, it can be concluded that the number of companies using or implementing ABC or considering its implementation in the future is still growing.

Hitherto research on activity-based costing in Poland was considerably limited; it mainly came down to the statement whether the analyzed companies implemented/are implementing ABC in full/classic form or whether they only use certain elements of ABC. So far, there has been no wide-spectrum research on the functioning of activity-based costing in Polish companies (apart from a few case studies) nor detailed research on the attitudes of companies to activity-based costing and factors influencing the attitudes. Additionally, there was no research on activity-based costing implementation success nor analysis of development of literature about ABC/ABM in Poland. The author's preoccupation with the issue of activity-based costing functioning in Polish companies mainly stems from the following:

1) despite the fact that activity-based costing is a concept which has been known and used in companies since the late eighties, it is not widespread and therefore it is still perceived as innovation. Presentation of the concept's development may seem interesting;

2) one of the most interesting issues connected with the degree of activity-based costing diffusion in Poland, which has not been discussed in previous research, is the analysis of ABC/ABM literature development, in particular analysis of such issues as volume, authorship, research method, focus, and content of the publications;

3) so far, questionnaire research which studied diffusion of activity-based costing in Poland has not presented in detail the notion of a problem and what companies considering implementation of ABC understand by a problem. It seems that sometimes companies use the term ABC inadequately i.e. they use the term in a situation when a new and better cost accounting system is implemented which has many cost centres and a bigger number of cost drivers than previously. In such a case, only thorough analysis may help to conclude what ABC really stands for, whether it is real activity-based costing or maybe just its elements, or whether it is a developed form of traditional cost accounting;

4) another issue which has not been studied in Poland in a more detailed form is the attitude of Polish companies towards activity-based costing and the identification of factors which positively influence the implementation of ABC, as well as the reasons underlying abandoning implementation or reasons behind not considering ABC implementation;

5) apart from sporadic case studies (including action research) so far there have been no research which would look into the way ABC is implemented, especially the issue of initiative behind implementation or responsibility for implementation and occurrence of problems during the implementation process;

6) ABC systems which function in Polish practice have a different structure than ABC systems in foreign companies. Therefore, it may seem interesting to analyze the functioning of activity-based costing systems in terms of e.g. their size (e.g. the number of objects, activities, resources, drivers) or information structures which function in the companies (e.g. division of costs into fixed and variable, identification of costs of unused capacity, identification of value-added and non-value added activities);

7) information obtained from activity-based costing may be and is used in companies in many different ways. Numerous people use it in many different decision-making processes – therefore, it seems interesting to determine the main addressee of this information and in what decision-making processes it is mainly used;

8) yet another interesting aspect of activity-based costing diffusion in Polish companies is the attempt to evaluate the implementation's successes and benefits resulting from the process, particularly an analysis of the quality of ABC information, its usefulness and its influence on the company.

In the light of the presented facts, filling the previously identified research gap i.e. analysis of the extent and how activity-based costing in Polish companies how seems important.

The main objective of this work is an analysis of the development and diffusion of activity-based costing, as well as an evaluation of the extent and how activity-based costing is used in Polish companies. Attaining the main objective will be possible by achieving the following partial objectives:

1) presentation of activity-based costing concept development as a point of reference for further and detailed research into the use of activity-based costing systems in Polish companies;

2) analysis of ABC/ABM literature in Polish journals in the dimension of: volume, authorship, research method, focus, and content of publications;

3) analysis of ABC implementation extent in Polish companies at the beginning of the 21st century in the light of ABC diffusion in the world;

4) presentation of factors conditioning the attitude of Polish companies towards activity-based costing (companies which implemented ABC, those which consider its implementation in the future and companies which do not consider implementation or quit the process after cost and benefit analysis);

5) examination of the activity-based costing implementation process in Polish companies, examination of ABC systems structure and way the information generated by the systems is used;

6) analysis of the satisfaction and benefits resulting from ABC implementation in Polish companies, particularly analysis of the attitudes of preparers and users of ABC information, and also the quality of ABC information, its usefulness and its influence on the company.

In order to attain the main objective of this work as well as its partial objectives, it has been attempted to prove the main thesis and the following specific theses. The main research thesis is: diffusion of activity-based costing in Polish companies, although the practice is delayed in comparison to highly-developed countries, is conditioned by the same factors and develops in the same direction as in those countries.

In order to prove the main thesis and, additionally, to prove specific theses as well as to verify specific hypotheses, the following research methods have been applied: a literature study, surveys, and case study (including action research).

1. In terms of the literature study, both Polish literature and foreign publications have been analyzed. Such extensive literature studies enabled the author to formulate his own findings and to compare the findings with other

research carried out in Poland and other countries. On the basis of the literature study, it has been attempted to prove the following specific theses of the work:

a) the concept of activity-based costing, since its emergence in the late 1980s, has evolved from the measurement system of resource costs, activity costs and cost of products into the activity-based management system;

b) the development of ABC/M literature in Poland is considerably delayed (by 6–8 years) in comparison with publications from the United States, Great Britain and other highly-developed countries;

c) there are more publications on the ABC/M concept in the journals for practitioners than in university publications, and the authors of those publications are mainly university researchers;

d) the percentage of ABC/M enthusiasts among consultants is close to the highest possible level, while the ratio among practitioners and university researchers is only slightly lower;

e) among research methods used in the publications, it is more common to encounter descriptive works, surveys and case studies than literature reviews and analytical papers;

f) the subject area of the publications evolved from the activity-based costing in production companies and only in the main area of activity, into ABM in production and service companies in the main and supporting processes with reference to other concepts and tools of management accounting.

2. In order to attain the main objective of this work, three surveys have been carried out. The first survey (survey A) examined the attitude of Polish companies towards the notion of activity-based costing. The surveys were distributed among representatives of 1,267 companies; 495 correct surveys were sent back which constitutes 39.1%. The second survey (survey B) analyzed the way activity-based costing operated in Polish companies. In general, 71 companies which used this type of cost accounting system have been identified; 33 correct surveys were sent back which constitutes 46.48%. The third survey (survey C) examined the satisfaction and benefits resulting from activity-based costing implementation. This survey was carried out among 28 respondents from 7 companies where activity-based costing was used. On the basis of the conducted surveys, the following specific hypotheses have been verified:

a) companies operating in Poland mostly use traditional systems of cost accounting; modern systems such as target costing or activity-based costing are used sporadically and their diffusion is significantly lower than in Western countries;

b) implementation of activity-based costing is influenced by various factors; the most important are: headquarters' demand (e.g. parent company), rise of competition and the drive to expand into new sales markets, dissatisfaction with the previous cost accounting, a change of organizational structure or strategy, implementation of new technologies, the desire to reduce costs and improve results, a change-oriented attitude of employees, and accessibility of financial and human resources;

c) among the most important problems relating to the process of activity-based costing which companies are afraid of, one could mention: the lack of management support, high implementation and maintenance costs, significant labour input during ABC implementation and maintenance, other priorities, insufficient knowledge of ABC, difficulties with system structuring, and lack of adequate resources;

d) a lack of interest in implementation of activity-based costing or giving up ABC implementation are conditioned by: satisfaction with the current cost accounting system, low indirect costs, lack of management support, high costs of ABC implementation and maintenance, high labour input during ABC implementation and maintenance, other priorities, insufficient knowledge of ABC among employees, difficulties with system modelling, and lack of adequate IT resources;

e) the most important factors which positively influence ABC implementation are: high direct costs, high competition, foreign capital share in the company and size of the company;

f) the structure of activity-based costing systems which function in Polish companies is consistent with the structure of systems used in foreign companies;

g) in companies which implemented activity-based costing, information obtained from the system is used in different ways by particular departments and it enables various decisions to be made;

h) companies in which activity-based costing operates simultaneously use other modern methods of management;

i) managers and employees are positively oriented towards ABC implementation;

j) managers and employees rank the information from ABC higher than from the traditional cost accounting system;

k) managers and employees evaluate positively the usefulness of the ABC information;

l) managers and employees are convinced that ABC implementation influenced their company in a positive way;

m) the opinions of preparers and users of ABC information on implementation benefits will differ considerably.

3. Research in the form of case studies (including action research) aimed to verify the same hypotheses which had been verified by means of survey B, however the case study research, in comparison to the questionnaire research, was extended and more detailed. Another reason underlying the application of this type of research method was the analysis and explanation of methodological and organizational changes which occurred after activity-based costing implementation in the analyzed companies. Representatives of three companies to which the case study method by means of surveys and interviews was applied, were asked to fill in surveys A and B. Subsequently,

numerous direct interviews with employees and managers were conducted. Then the author analyzed the gathered information and that enabled him to gain in-depth knowledge about the conditioning of the design and implementation of activity-based costing in Polish companies. By action research the author means his participation in the design, implementation and evaluation of activity-based costing in a production and trading company. This kind of research enabled (in comparison to case study by means of surveys and interviews) a more detailed analysis of activity-based costing operation in the company: (a) the author cooperated for a few months with the company's employees at the stage of implementation, and later he also cooperated at the stage of ABC evaluation, (b) the author co-developed the ABC system, therefore he had unlimited access to the system's documentation, (c) the author had access to all information generated by the cost accounting system and he could observe how the information was used by the company's management. Based on the case study, the following specific hypotheses have been verified:

a) the process of activity-based costing implementation is positively influenced by three groups of factors: motivators, catalysts and facilitators; during the implementation process, the factors work jointly and they promote the process of change;

b) among the obstructors, factors which negatively influence activity-based costing implementation, one should mention: attitude not favouring changes, substantial labour input needed for implementation and insufficient knowledge of activity-based costing;

c) implementation of activity-based costing in the companies caused many methodological changes, especially as improvement in the accuracy of calculating indirect costs and as improvement in accuracy of profitability analyzes is concerned;

d) implementation of activity-based costing triggered institutional/ organizational changes in the company, especially nearing the function of management accounting closer to operational functions and improvement in the significance of information from management accounting and its more frequent use especially in the decision-making process.

4. Additionally, apart from the above research methods, a comparative analysis of the author's own research in the form of surveys and case studies (including action research) with similar research conducted both in Poland and in the world has been carried out.

It needs to be highlighted that the author is aware of the fact that the findings of empirical research should be interpreted with great caution. Particularly, due to sample choice, they cannot be treated as research on activity-based costing in all the companies operating in Poland. Although in the questionnaire research the sample was large, it was not representative; in these case studies, the choice of companies was deliberate. According to the author, these limitations were partially reduced due to a triangulation of various research methods and comparison of his own findings with research conducted by other authors.

This work is an outcome of literature studies and empirical research carried out by means of questionnaires and case studies over the course of several years. It is also a product of the author's own cogitation resulting from cooperation with professor Alicja Jaruga, who was the author's doctoral thesis supervisor, and cooperation with professor Irena Sobańska, with whom the author collaborates both on a professional and academic level – therefore I would like to thank them and express my great gratitude for their support. Moreover, I would like to thank my all Colleagues from the Accounting Department of Łódź University and the hundreds of respondents who participated in the research.

I owe special thanks to Karolina Pel for her invaluable help with the translation of the book.

CHAPTER 1

THE ORIGIN AND DEVELOPMENT OF ACTIVITY-BASED COSTING

1.1. Precursors of activity-based costing

The earliest traces of an activity-based concept may be found in the works of Schmalenbach, who as far back as 1899 indicated the possibility of isolating the cost of processes and calculating them for products (Szychta, 2007a). Some pioneer studies on *activity accounting* appeared in the 1930s and in the works of Kohler, who worked out guidelines for *an activity accounting* concept and put them into practice in Tennessee Valley Authority (the United States). Kohler assumed that all costs, including depreciation costs, should be allocated to people responsible for the transactions (activities) taking place in the company. Each manager was in charge of an *activity account* where all incomes, costs and profits were allocated and which the person controlled.

Drury stresses that ABC is not an 'invention' of the 1980s and that its origins date back to the late forties in Goetz's works (1949, p. 142, [in:] Drury, 2000, p. 340), who introduced principles of accounting based on activities, "Each basic (indirect costs) class should be homogenous in terms of every significant dimension of a management problem related to planning and control. Some of those significant dimensions, along with which (overheads) may change, are number of production units, number of orders, number of operations, company's capacity, number of provided catalogue items".

Horngren sees the origins of the ABC concept in the 1950s. According to him ([in:] Robinson, 1990, p. 23), a form of activity-based costing called *functional cost accounting* may be already found in a work entitled *Practical Distributions Cost Analysis* by Longman and Schiff from 1955. In Kaplan's opinion, who referred to Horngren's viewpoint, "it is not important who wrote the articles a few dozen years ago. The articles must have been extremely unconvincing or our teaching must have been very ineffective, since the articles had little influence on the practice. Our works are not based on articles or books but on systems which function in practice" ([in:] Robinson, 1990, p. 29).

Johnson (1991) sees the origins of practice, similar to activity-based costing, in the cost accounting which functioned in the 1960s in General Electric. In this system, different indirect production activities were assigned to departments (technological, quality control etc.) and how the work of one department influenced the work of other departments was analysed. The number of units of performed activities, the costs of those activities and cost rates per unit of activity were also defined. In the course of time, cost accounting in General Electric was developed and improved; it included the creation of a list of standard activities (activity dictionary) or an improvement in gathering data about activities.

The drive to take the structure of processes into consideration was also evident in the cost accounting systems of German companies. Jaruga (2001) mentions Böhrs (1968) and his attitude to grouping indirect costs as one of the pioneers of activity-based costing. Böhrs perceived costs through the prism of a certain range of activities seen as elementary functions (Jaruga names the concept functional cost accounting). Böhrs's concept claims that in order to meet the company's objective it is necessary to use its potential in the most optimal way. To do that, it is essential to differentiate the company's functions and work out accounting procedures which would be in compliance with the activities performed within these activity functions. In the functional cost accounting system three groups of functions have been distinguished (each function has a particular range of activities):

• direct functions: a function coordinated with the degree of used capacity, material supply, servicing of production orders, development, expanding sales market, servicing of consumers, and company management;

• indirect functions necessary to perform direct functions: management and administration of personnel, preparation of new workplaces, and supply with energy sources;

• indirect functions – services: improvement of the work process, maintaining technical equipment on stand-by, information services, legal advice, administration services, transport and storing.

In Böhrs's concept, in order to calculate the costs of a product, first the costs of indirect functions to the benefit of direct functions should be calculated and then one should calculate the costs of direct functions for products[1]. According to Jaruga (2001, p.108), "Böhrs's concept dating back to the late sixties constitutes

---

[1] In Böhrs's concept eight blocks of costs of direct functions have been distinguished: "(a) costs of raw materials, (b) production costs for particular level of production capacity time use, (c) company's stand-by costs, (d) costs of product research and product development, (e) costs of raised production volume (additional orders), (f) costs of advertising and marketing, (g) costs of customer service, (h) costs of management" (Jaruga, 2001, p. 108).

a pioneer solution with relation to later variations and modifications called concepts based on activities. It is evident that it helps to control the costs of used capacity of particular functions (activities), and it takes into account the significance of cost measurement of different orders (the size of order) which employ only some of the functions. Therefore, it fosters accommodation of information to decisions taking place in the changing conditions of the environment (market)".

Johnson sees the origins of an activity-based costing system in Staubus's (1971) works, who emphasized the significance of activities in cost accounting[2]. It was Staubus's idea to have accounts for each function, operation, task or process, which provided information required by the management of the company. In Staubus's *activity costing*, it is activities and not products which constitute cost accounting objects (production process constitutes a cost object and not a product itself). According to Johnson (1992, p. 27), the concept of activities advocated by Staubus and Shilinglaw "has not had any influence on academic thought (until recently) and it seems that it also did not influence the development of activity-based costing in practice".

Johnson (1992) looks for some pioneering solutions in terms of activity-based costing in the achievements of two consulting companies Bain & Co. and the Boston Consulting Group (BCG) in the 1970s and 1980s. This opinion is also shared by Kaplan, who thinks that Bain & Co. and BCG have in-depth knowledge about cost accounting.

In the Polish literature the concept of costs of production factors worked out by Skowroński (Jarugowa, Skowroński, 1982) is also known; the concept heads in the same direction as the later concept of activity-based costing. Skowroński's concept aims to rationalize the administration of limited resources and it takes elimination of constraints characteristic of full costing and disadvantages of variable costing as a starting point. Instead of dividing costs into direct and indirect ones and treating fixed costs as a time function, the concept of production factor costs assumes that common product costs may be individual unit costs of reference, which are, for the process of planning and control, expression of important, production factors in three stages: acquisition and possession, maintenance on stand-by, and exploitation with different intensity. As a production factor, a set of activities related to securing possession, maintenance on stand-by and exploitation of a certain group of resources which determine production (e.g. management of work resources, management of work tools, management of materials, management of energy, sales) is meant here. In Skowroński's concept (Jarugowa, Skowroński, 1982) the emphasis was put onto the effective use of resources whereas relation to the environment (market) was ignored. This concept enables managers to acquire information which is significant in making decisions about the change of production scale, expansion of resources or their more intensive use, and influence on the readiness of capacity or efficiency of resources.

---

[2] The idea of *activity accounting* was also analyzed, in terms of standard cost accounting system, by Solomons (1968, [in:] Innes, Mitchell, 1998, p. 1).

Different works which included elements of *an activity accounting* concept had been published a few decades before the publications by Cooper, Kaplan, Johnson or CAM-I (Consortium for Advanced Management – International)[3] reports, however, they did not come into practice. Attempt to find the reasons seem extremely interesting. In the first decades of the 20th century, accounting systems of organizations concentrated on issues of financial accounting and taxes, and cost accounting became a separate and less significant system (Johnson, Kaplan, 1987). The focus on tax issues and financial accounting stemmed from the fact that the two areas were obligatory. In many companies the function of cost accounting was limited to providing data for the needs of financial and tax accounting[4]. It seems that there were three reasons for such a status quo (Hicks, 1999, p. 3):

• firstly, many experts on cost accounting were previously related to financial and tax accounting. They were oriented towards the needs of external users and not the needs of managers; most of the time they were not aware of the fact that using financial accounting information in making managerial decisions was inappropriate;

• secondly, the overwhelming majority of managers were convinced that the maintenance of two separate cost accounting systems (one for external needs and the other for internal needs) was extremely expensive and unjustified in terms of cost and profit. This conviction, and the necessity to use financial and tax accounting systems led to a situation in which systems oriented towards external needs were used in terms of management needs;

• thirdly, managers were aware that the implementation of IT systems which supported management was difficult, and that cost accounting in the systems was very simplified. Therefore, if implementation, in the case of simplified cost accounting, was difficult, then would it be possible to implement it in the case of a more complex system, and how difficult would it be?

Emergence and diffusion of activity-based costing in the 1980s was possible thanks to the inaccuracy of cost accounting systems and, on the other hand, thanks to the decrease of costs related to maintenance of more sophisticated systems.

1.2. Development of activity-based costing in 1984–1989

At the beginning of the 1980s, criticism of management accounting was accompanied by a search for innovative practices in cost accounting in American companies. The most eminent representatives of this research stream were Kaplan,

---

[3] CAM-I, originally, it was Computer Aided Manufacturing – International, then it changed to Consortium for Advanced Manufacturing – International and recently to Consortium for Advanced Management – International.

[4] In the 1930s, representatives of the London School of Economics pointed out that an "arbitrary system used by accountants to allocate costs to products made product costs literally useless in terms of decision making" (Johnson, Kaplan, 1987, p. 156).

Cooper and Johnson – Johnson worked at Portland State University and Kaplan and Cooper worked at Harvard University.

In the mid-eighties Kaplan (1985), began his research on the practice of management accounting in American companies. He selected a group of innovative firms. He assumed that companies which used advanced production technologies and innovative methods of management such as JIT and TQM would probably use innovative methods of management accounting. He hoped to find innovations in the fields of quality measurement, supply reduction, flexibility of manufacture, employee morale, and productivity etc.; instead he identified a gap (delay) in diffusion of management accounting innovative methods. Kaplan (1985, p. 78) claimed that "the key to explaining of the delay in the diffusion of accounting methods is that top management did not emphasize the need to improve the significance of management accounting systems". In the course of his research, Kaplan found no use of 'first versions' of activity-based costing but he also failed to identify any innovative methods of management accounting.

The first example of an innovative approach to cost accounting in practice was the case study of Schrader Bellows studied by Cooper (Cooper, Montgomery, 1985a, b; Cooper, Weiss, 1985). The company offered a wide range of products in many versions which led to the manufacturing of more than 2,700 products. In the beginning, product costs were calculated as a sum of material costs and direct remuneration costs and indirect costs. Costs of auxiliary departments (setups, quality control etc.) were calculated for primary departments, and indirect costs for each department were calculated as a quotient of indirect costs and the number of man-hours. In 1983 a product profitability analysis was carried out in the company. The analysis was conducted by means of a new method of indirect cost allocation. Changes appeared in auxiliary departments' costs calculation, calculation of sale costs and administration costs – in the new system they were directly accountable for products by means of different rates. The case study proved to be important because all the indirect costs were calculated for products, not only indirect the costs of manufacture, but also costs of sales, administration and overheads were calculated in the way.

Two years after the case study of Schrader Bellows was worked out by Cooper (1985), Kaplan (1987a) found an innovative example of cost accounting use in the John Deere Component Works. Initially, the company used a similar standard cost accounting to the one used in Schrader Bellows (indirect costs were accountable for products proportionally to man-hours, subsequently, proportionally to machine hours, the company used two cost pools). In 1985 a new system of cost accounting, called ABC[5], emerged in the company; within the system, seven

---

[5] A new form of cost accounting based on activities began to appear in the literature in the late 1980s. In Johnson and Kaplan's work (1987) the method still was not named; the authors only talked about a new system of cost accounting. One of the first publications, which implied the abbreviation

activities have been distinguished: employee support, production on machines, setups, production management, material management, administration of components and management. From the two initial cost pools (employee support and production on machines) 40% of costs were allocated to five new pools (setups, production management, material management, administration of components and management). In the first stage, general ledger costs were allocated to relevant activities and then the activity costs were accounted for products. The new cost accounting in the John Deere Component Works was used in product pricing, the profitability evaluation of long-series production, making decisions about choosing products to be manufactured on automatic machines, and it also aided the process of decision-making in terms of production departments. Similar to the new cost accounting system in Schrader Bellows, in the John Deere Component Works it was mainly used to account indirect costs for products and to make business decisions.

In parallel to Cooper and Kaplan's works, yet another case study was researched by Johnson and Loewe; the case study of Weyerhouser (1987) turned out to be crucial for the formulation of ABC method. In the company, a new system of accounting costs of auxiliary departments for customers had been created. It not only embraced traditional auxiliary departments, but it additionally related to other departments previously treated as general e.g. the Financial Department. However, the most interesting practice observed by Johnson was the fact that the managers of the departments, which were recipients of services, could question the rate for services of auxiliary departments, they could even purchase similar services outside the company if the cost was lower (auxiliary departments could also sell their services outside). The system of internal settlements operating in Weyerhouser, outsourcing of certain services, lowering rates for other services, staff reduction in auxiliary departments and sales of those departments' services outside the company made the employees aware of who the customer is, what kind of services are provided to that customer and what sort of costs are associated with those services. The new system made the managers of the operational departments realize how their departments generated demand for work in auxiliary departments and that forced them to manage activities instead of costs. The case of Weyerhouser is simultaneously similar and different to the cases of Schrader Bellows and John Deere. As far as similarities are concerned, the procedure of cost calculation i.e. costs were first allocated to internal recipients or products, was comparable.

---

of ABC was Cooper's article (1988a), where he related to his earlier work where the term of *activity-based costing* was used (Cooper, Kaplan, 1988a). However, this article related to an even earlier work (Cooper, Kaplan, 1988b), in which the term of *transaction accounting* was used. Some researchers (Jones, Dugdale, 2002) think that the term ABC/activity-based costing was not coined by Cooper or Kaplan, but they claim that it was the name for the cost accounting system functioning in one of the companies visited by Kaplan (John Deere Component Works).

In terms of differences, Johnson paid less attention to improvement of accuracy of indirect costs calculation for products, whereas he emphasized the necessity to manage the activities.

The cost accounting systems researched in practice by Cooper, Kaplan and Johnson were very similar even identical, as Kaplan (1994b, p. 248) claimed, "After prefatory observations of the new transaction accounting, Robin Cooper and I saw, in fact, identical systems, which were used in other manufacturing companies: John Deere, Hewlett-Packard and Tektronix in the USA, Siemens in Germany or Ericsson and Kanthal in Sweden". Interestingly, in the meantime, manufacturing companies in many other countries in the world began to use innovative systems of cost accounting and the systems turned out to be extremely similar, even identical. The implementations were undertaken not only by manufacturing companies, but also service companies operating in such sectors as banking, insurance, transport, health service and public sector started to be interested in the method of cost accounting based on activities. Examples of ABC implementation case studies published in the late 1980s are presented in Table 1.1.

Table 1.1. Case studies of ABC implementations published in the late 1980s

Company	Type of business	Author
Schrader-Bellows	Pneumatic control systems	Cooper (1985)
Mueller-Lehmkuhl GmbH	Clothing	Cooper (1986)
John Deere	Mechanics	Kaplan (1987a)
American Bank	Retail banking	Kaplan (1987b)
Weyerhouser	Woodworking industry	Johnson, Loewe (1987)
Winchell Lighting Inc.	Lighting distribution	Cooper, Kaplan (1987a, 1987b)
Monarch Paper	Paper manufacture	Shank, Govindarajan (1988)
Tektronix	Measurement and control electronics	Cooper, Turney (1988)
Siemens Electric Motor Works	Electric motor manufacture	Cooper (1988b)
The Rossford Plant	Glass manufacture	Colson, MacGuidwin (1989)

At the same time as Cooper, Kaplan and Johnson became interested in the new methods of management accounting, CAM-I (Berliner, Brimson, 1988) followed in their footsteps. CAM-I is a research organization sponsored by a group of several large companies, government agencies, consulting companies and professional associations. The organization constituted employees of the above companies, as well as researchers from leading universities.

CAM-I's main aim was to promote IT use in production companies and becoming interested in cost accounting was a *by-product* of their operation. Within the organization, a Cost Management System group (CMS) operated, which was formed in 1986, and it dealt with cost management systems. CMS's preoccupation with cost accounting stemmed from problems with procedures of investment evaluation in numerical control machines and devices. The problems were related to the means of indirect costs calculation because benefits resulting from the use of computerized control machines meant savings in those costs. CMS's task was to create, on the basis of CAM-I member companies' experience, a unified system of cost management, which would be accessible to all the associates of the organization. The creation of *an activity accounting* concept was a result of CMS's operation. The concept aimed to "measure costs of resources used in crucial activities of the company" (Berliner, Brimson, 1988, p. 85). *Activity accounting* focused on the provision of information for the calculation of costs of products, measurement of costs in the dimension of a product life cycle, and non-value activities. The information was taken into consideration during pricing, product life cycle management, evaluation of performance and investment decision-making. One of the most important conclusions stemming from CMS's work, was the fact that products did not directly cause cost formulation but costs were generated by activities, which are used by products. Despite the fact that CAM-I, in terms of the new cost accounting, used the term of *activity accounting*, the concept is concurrent with ABC and even members of CAM-I used expressions of *activity accounting* and *activity-based costing* interchangeably (Jones, Dugdale, 2002).

It seems almost impossible to provide an answer to the following question: who 'invented' *activity accounting/activity-based costing*? The concept itself mainly developed due to practices implemented by the member companies of CAM-I. However, undeniably, researchers such as Cooper, Kaplan and Johnson, but also Foster or Brimson, contributed hugely to the development of the concept. These researchers spent a lot of time working in CMS (Cooper, Kaplan, Foster), leading project works (Brimson) or developing ABC outside the structures of CAM-I (Johnson). Although, the terms *activity accounting* and *activity-based costing* vary, they are both used to describe concepts which are technically concurrent. It needs to be mentioned that Cooper and Kaplan on the one hand created the term *activity-based costing*, and on the other hand, they participated in the works of the CMS group, which worked out the concept of *activity accounting*. Yet, it seems that objectives which made these concepts emerge were slightly different. *Activity accounting* was devised to manage activities and the concept of *activity accounting* was perceived as a method of performance measurement. *Activity-based costing*, on the other hand, was mainly a tool used in strategic management and was meant to facilitate making decisions in fields such as pricing or resource management. A simplified diagram presenting development of the first generation of activity-based costing is shown in Figure 1.1.

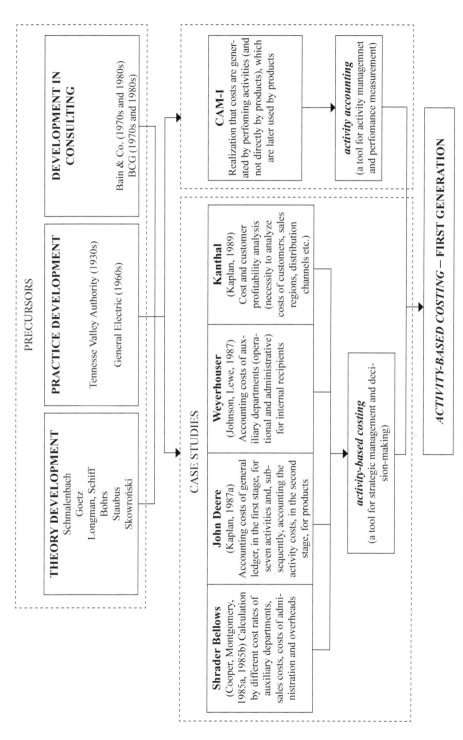

Figure 1.1. The development process of first generation ABC

The principles of the new cost accounting based on activities, created in the late 1980s, had to be diffused. Interestingly enough, publications about ABC did not appear in university periodicals at that time, but rather in publications oriented towards practitioners. The majority of works on activity-based costing were published in three American journals: *Harvard Business Review*, *Management Accounting* and *Journal of Cost Management*. These periodicals, between 1988 and 1999, published numerous articles, which presented the first generation of activity-based costing: Cooper (1987a, b, 1988a, b, 1989a, b), Kaplan (1988), Cooper, Kaplan (1988a, b), Johnson (1988).

The new method of cost accounting used some common terms (CAM-I, 1992): resource, activity, cost object, resource driver, activity driver, and cost driver. An attempt to formulate a general structure of activity-based costing, which can explain the concept of ABC, was undertaken by CAM-I (see Figure 1.2).

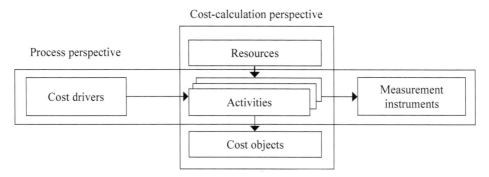

Figure 1.2. Basic model of activity-based costing
Source: CAM-I (1992), p. 22

The model should not be treated as a full illustration of cost flow in activity-based costing, but rather as a general pattern which may be adapted to the needs of an individual company. As is shown in Figures 1.2 and 1.3 which illustrate an extended version of activity-based costing, the model has two axes – the vertical one represents the cost-calculation perspective and the horizontal represents process perspective[6]. In the cost-calculation perspective, resources, and activities and cost objects should be identified consecutively. In the first turn, the costs of resources, identified in the company are calculated for activities isolated within the company with the use of resource cost drivers. Subsequently, such activities are calculated for cost objects isolated in the company i.e. products, customers etc.

---

[6] In the general model of activity-based costing structured by CAM-I, the cost-calculation perspective from the early works by Cooper and Kaplan, was accompanied by the perspective (dimension) of processes. The CAM-I model, therefore, constituted a developed model of the one by Cooper and Kaplan.

with the use of activity cost drivers. The cost perspective, in other words, is a set of rules which help to calculate costs within the company. The horizontal axis i.e. the process perspective illustrates what happens in the company and it initiates with an incident which is called a cost driver. The cost driver causes an activity to use resources necessary to achieve a certain result (the activity provides a certain result). The effectiveness of activities, from the process perspective, is measured both before and after performing an activity, and measurement instruments are such criteria which enable the company to define performance and activity effectiveness. Control and analysis of activities facilitate improvement of the realized processes e.g. designing products which are easy to manufacture or easy to service and repair.

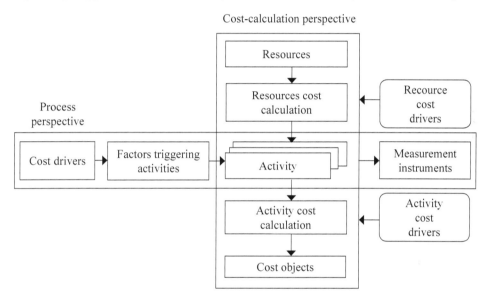

Figure 1.3. Developed model of activity-based costing
Source: CAM-I (1992), p. 24.

In the developed model of activity-based costing, which is presented in Figure 1.3, all the elements from the basic model have been enclosed (Figure 1.2) and there are additionally:
- databases of resource cost drivers and activity drivers (they collect information from different systems in the company; the information is used for resource costs calculation for activities and calculation of activities for cost objects);
- a factor triggering an activity (it sometimes links the emergence of a cost driver to the beginning of a certain activity e.g. in the case when quality control identifies a faulty finished product, it does not automatically mean that the product must be mended – it is the manager who makes such a decision about repair or disposal);

• in the developed model, the moment of resource costs calculation and the moment of activity costs calculation has been directly identified.

The developed model of activity-based costing devised by CAM-I is presented in figure 1.3.

According to Kaplan, practically all activities within a company are performed to support operational activities and provide products and services, and, therefore, these activities costs may be treated as product costs. Activity-based costing relates to all the costs of a company, not only to production costs, and thus practically all costs should be accounted for regarding products. In the first generation of activity-based costing only two categories of costs, which should be accounted for regarding products, have been distinguished:

• excess capacity costs should not be accounted for regarding products – the costs constitute period costs and should be separately accounted for in the profit and loss account (despite the fact that even the first generation of ABC stressed the necessity to isolate and account for the result of excess capacity costs, the problem was solved in the second generation of ABC systems);

• research and development costs, related to working out entirely new products, also should not be calculated for products.

In accordance with the first generation of activity-based costing, all costs in a company (excluding costs of unused capacity and research and development costs) constituted product costs, thus it was possible, even necessary, to calculate them for products. A simplified diagram of cost calculation in the first generation of activity-based costing is presented in Figure 1.4. The figure does not take into consideration the isolation of excess capacity costs because, although some publications emphasized such necessity, the first-generation ABC systems operating in practice ignored the problem. The figure additionally does not present the calculation of costs for such objects as customers, sales regions or distribution channels – despite the fact that the first generation of ABC systems allowed cost calculation for such objects (e.g. Kaplan, 1989), yet in most of practical implementations, the objects were not isolated.

The first generation of activity-based costing was supposed to be a more suitable tool for managers than the traditional standard cost accounting. ABC was more suitable not only because it was more precise and objective, but additionally it linked cost objects with the activities they use and activities with used resources in a more realistic way. According to Kaplan (1988), the first generation of activity-based costing was not supposed to replace the traditional cost accounting systems, but the systems were supposed to exist and function in parallel – traditional cost accounting was meant to satisfy external needs, whereas activity-based costing was to satisfy the internal ones. Yet it needs to be stressed that not everyone agreed with Kaplan e.g. managers of the John Deere Component Works, a company researched by Kaplan, rejected the idea of two cost accounting systems' coexistence.

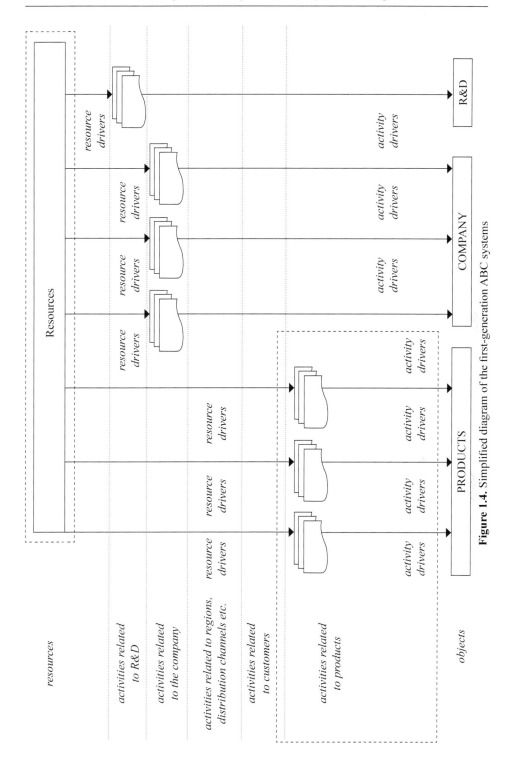

Figure 1.4. Simplified diagram of the first-generation ABC systems

They claimed that maintaining of two systems would be too expensive, and they wanted their previous standard cost accounting to be replaced by the new ABC system (Kaplan, 1988).

Unlike traditional standard cost accounting system, activity-based costing used more bases of allocation in accounting indirect costs for products, which led to substantial changes in product costs. In the analyzed company Schrader Bellows (Cooper, Montgomery, 1985a, b; Cooper, Weiss, 1985), changes in cost of products ranged from minus 10% to plus 1.000%. Cooper and Kaplan (1988a, p. 25) interpreted the changes as "serious, systematic and (generally) impossible to avoid without using bases for indirect costs calculation based on the number of conducted transactions and not the number of products". Differences in product costs, both in the case of Schrader Bellows and other companies, were to prove the superiority of the first-generation of activity-based costing over the traditional cost accounting system – interpretation was straightforward – ABC provides a more accurate product calculation. The cost of products, evaluated on the basis of activity-based costing, should be taken into consideration when making decisions about abandoning products, raising prices of products, and redesigning production and distribution processes etc.

According to Cooper (1989c, p. 1), "activity-based costing systems are more accurate than the traditional systems of cost accounting [...] they are based on a two-stage cost allocation procedure, which enables accounting indirect costs of resources used in the production process for finished products". In the late 1980s cost objects, other than products, for which calculation and analysis were prepared, were noticed. In the case of Swedish company Kanthal (Kapalan, 1989), ABC enabled ranking of customers in terms of their profitability. It became evident that, apart from employing ABC for analysis of manufacturing indirect cost for redesigning production processes, the system could also be used as a tool for marketing costs analysis, sales and distribution cost in a customer cross-section analysis, sales region cost analysis or distribution channels cost analysis.

In the late 1980s, the first generation of activity-based costing was supposed to improve the accuracy of cost accounting and provide information necessary for making decisions. According to Cooper and Kaplan, ABC was supposed to be a parallel system which simultaneously functioned with traditional cost accounting systems and ABC was to provide managers with key information needed for strategic cost management[7].

---

[7] Cooper's and Kaplan's views on the issue of management accounting in the late 1980s and early 1990s were concurrent. Kaplan appreciated Cooper's dedication in creation of the technical aspect of activity-based costing; Cooper also participated in preparation of ABC software (Kaplan was also deeply involved in marketing of the software). Later, when Cooper (1996a, b) anticipated

Johnson had a slightly different approach to activity-based costing than Cooper and Kaplan. In his article written in 1988 (p. 23), he stated that, "companies, in order to be competitive, must manage activities – not costs". Johnson was aware of the usefulness of information generated by the system of activity-based costing in terms of long-term product management, however, he concentrated more on activity management, which he perceived as a key factor to achieving competitive advantage. Unlike Cooper and Kaplan, who stressed the meaning of accurate cost calculation, Johnson focused on the activities which generate these costs. He identified four steps in managing waste in operating activities (Johnson, 1988, pp. 28–29): "chart the flow of activities throughout the organization, identify the sources of customer value in every activity and eliminate any activities that contribute no value, identify the causes of delay or other unevenness in all activities". Johnson thought that managers for proper management need information which enables the identification and elimination of non-value activities. He argued that information about activity costs would not be necessary for that, and managers should rather use non-financial information e.g. elapsed time, distances moved, space occupied, number of parts etc. For Johnson activity-based information was purposeful when it could be used for the elimination of non-value activities because that enabled companies to gain a competitive advantage.

To sum up the development of activity-based costing at the end of 1980s, it should be concluded that the system consisted of several related components: joint analysis of activities with department managers, identification of resource costs and activity drivers, and allocation of resource costs to activities and activity costs to objects (products, customers etc.). It was assumed that the system of activity-based costing would provide data on full product costs or customers, various data needed in decision-making (e.g. in terms of products and customers), and that it would attract managers' attention to customer non-value activities. The system's terminology, structure and objectives were influenced by CAM-I, in particular by three authors – Cooper, Kaplan and Johnson. The first generation of activity-based costing emerged due to the cooperation of researchers and practitioners, who were involved in the work of CMS, and due to the case studies of Schrader Bellows, the John Deere Component Works, Weyerhouser, and Kanthal. The companies, which use activity-based costing developed in the late 1980s concentrate on:

• accuracy improvement of product cost calculation by means of higher accuracy in indirect costs calculation – this objective was mainly emphasized by Cooper and Kaplan, who perceived ABC as a system which could be used in management in parallel with traditional cost accounting systems;

---

changes in the profession of management accounting specialists, his point of view was not supported by Kaplan.

- cost reduction by means of waste elimination – this objective was highlighted in Johnson's works, who thought that activity-based costing was mainly to eliminate non-value activities;
- improvement of operational management by means of a better performance measurement – this ABC objective was emphasized by CAM-I.

1.3. Development of activity-based costing in 1989–1992

In the very late 1980s and early 1990s of the 20th century, the concept of activity-based costing underwent two crucial changes – firstly, provided resources and resources used were differentiated, secondly the concept of cost hierarchy was introduced. The changes had substantial influence on the shape of activity-based costing, thus they will be discussed in more detail.

As mentioned in the previous section, the publications on ABC which appeared in the late 1980s, were mainly published in journals for practitioners (e.g. *Management Accounting* (United States), *Harvard Business Review* and *Journal of Cost Management*). University researchers became interested in the concept of activity-based costing later on. Once ABC became a point of their interest, it provoked strong criticism. The most severe critical standpoint was expressed by Goldratt, who was the author of *theory of constraints* – TOC a concept which competed with activity-based costing. Goldratt (1990) questioned the precise product cost calculation, he called activity-based costing a mistake and, in general, questioned its adequacy. The introduction of provided resources and resources used was, to some measure, Cooper's and Kaplan's answer to Goldratt's criticism. Cooper and Kaplan claimed that there was some discrepancy in the definition of resource costs within activity-based costing and theory of constraints – in TOC, a cost represents costs of provided resources, whereas in ABC it represents the cost of resources used. Earlier, Cooper and Kaplan (1992) used the term of *excess capacity*, which was replaced by *unused capacity*. It was not just a minor change in nomenclature, the concept of unused capacity was the key to distinguishing between provided resources and resources used. According to Kaplan (1992, p. 1), "activity-based costing systems estimate costs of resources used by processes performed in an organization to manufacture products [...] costs of provided resources or available ones are revealed in periodic financial reports of the organization".

Apart from differentiation between provided resources and used resources, there was another change in the second generation of activity-based costing systems i.e. introduction of cost hierarchy. Cooper and Kaplan (1991) distinguished four levels of activities:

- unit-level activities, which are a function of production volume for every unit that is being produced. Unit-level activities are, for example, production on a press and manual assembly;

• batch-level activities, which are not directly dependent on the production volume but rather on the number of batches in which the product is being produced (the costs of those activities change when the number of batches alternates, but they remain unchanged regardless of the number of units in a given batch). Examples of batch-level activities are machine setups or batch quality control;

• product-level activities, which are not directly dependent on the volume of production nor the number of batches in which the product is produced, but they depend on the number of types of manufactured products (these activity costs change when the number of types of manufactured products changes, yet they remain unchanged regardless of the number of units in a given batch or the number of batches manufactured). Product-level activities are e.g. technical specification of products or construction of prototypes;

• facility-level activities, which are not directly dependent on the volume of production nor the number of types of products being produced – these activities are common for all products manufactured in the facility. Examples of facility-level activities are e.g. company management or safety management.

The distinction of activities at the level of product series, type of product and facility made the list of costs, which should not be counted among costs of unit, expand. Apart from costs of excess capacity or costs of research and development, which, with reference to the first generation of ABC, should not be calculated for products (units), in the second generation of activity-based costing these costs were accompanied by costs at the level of batches, type of product and costs on the level of a facility. Cooper and Kaplan (1991, p. 132) claim that, "calculation of costs on units may convey signals which will be wrongly interpreted by managers. If costs of batch-level activities or product type costs are divided by the amount of products, you may be left with a bad impression that those are the costs which change along with the of number of products". In the second generation of activity-based costing, costs of products manufactured in a particular period of time are a total of direct costs and indirect activity costs at the level of a unit, series and type of product. However, facility-level activity costs will not be included in the costs of products perceived in that manner. These costs should be seen as the fixed costs of a company because none of the activities related to products has an influence on their level.

The distinction of activities at the level of unit, batch and type of product, as well as activities on the level of the entire company constitutes a crucial change in the second generation of ABC. The systems of activity-based costing from the first generation, in contrast to traditional cost accounting, were advertised as a tool, which enabled accurate calculation of all cost for products. However, precise calculation of product costs was not the main objective of ABC systems from the second generation (in general, Cooper and Kaplan stopped discussing the issue of accurate product costing as an objective of ABC). In the early 1990s, understanding of cost

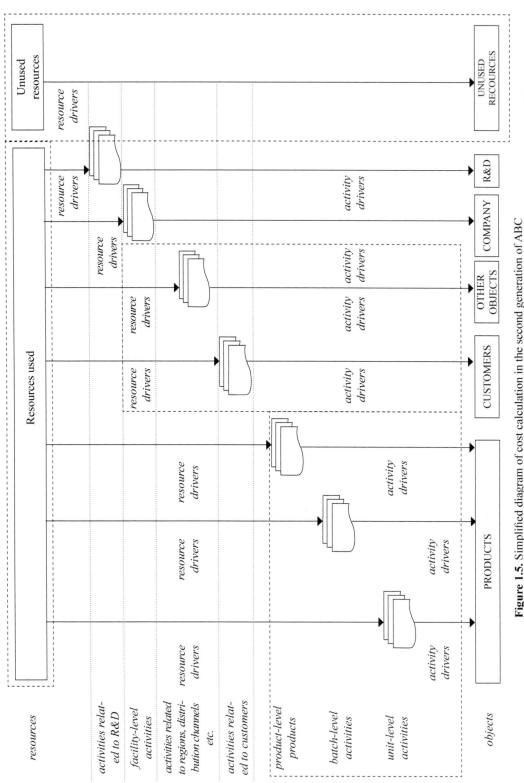

Figure 1.5. Simplified diagram of cost calculation in the second generation of ABC

hierarchy in the company and the identification of important incomes and costs, as well as the provision of information needed for the process of decision-making became the main focal point of activity-based costing[8]. A simplified diagram of cost calculation in the second generation of activity-based costing is presented in Figure 1.5.

Replacement of the first-generation activity-based costing with its second generation meant changes of two extremely important concepts – the first one was the concept of cost allocation and the second one was an approach to variable costs. In terms of the first issue, Kaplan (1992) claimed that instead of *cost allocation*, it is more proper to use the term of *cost estimates*. Yet it needs to be stressed that the change had far more serious consequences than it might seem at first glance. Along with the change of nomenclature from *allocation* to *estimate*, a shift of emphasis in the whole concept of activity-based costing occurred; the objective of ABC from the second generation was no longer identification of the more precise full costs of products, but provision of data *accurate enough* for managers to use them in the decision-making process[9]. It is also worth noting that the second generation of activity-based costing was supposed to provide information which was *accurate enough* and not "more precise than traditional systems of cost accounting" (this type of information was required from the first generation of ABC). The change is significant due to the fact that the first generation of activity-based costing was built around the system's ability to calculate product costs in a more accurate manner, in comparison to the traditional cost accounting.

Besides the concept of *cost allocation*, the approach to the issue of variable costs also changed in the second generation of ABC. The first generation of activity-based costing perceived almost all costs as variable at the level of a product (Johnson, Kaplan, 1987; Cooper, Kaplan, 1988a). The approach changed in the second generation of ABC. Costs are not treated in that concept as variable or fixed, but instead the concept helps managers to understand the causes of cost variability. Attention is focused on the idea that, in order to reduce costs, it is not enough to reduce demand for resources available within the company. Reduction of resource demand itself will cause emergence of unused capacity resources, and, subsequently, only a reduction of that capacity, or its alternative use, will cause a cost decrease or profit increase. The change in approach to variable costs was accompanied by changes in the approach to variable costing. In the late 1980s (the first stage of ABC), the authors of activity-based costing criticized traditional full costing along with the usefulness of variable costing (Cooper, Kaplan 1988b). They claimed that variable costing system, although correctly implemented, will

---

[8] Interestingly, in 1990, Kaplan stated for the first time that neither he nor Cooper coined the term of ABC; he claimed, "we did not invent the name: it was already used in John Deere company" (Robinson, 1990, p. 5).

[9] Costs, which were *accurate enough*, were calculated on the basis of estimations that used interviews with managers, employees' evaluations and other accessible operational data (Kaplan, 1992).

not be useful in terms of pricing products in the current market and technological environment. After a few years, in the early 1990s (the second generation of ABC), Kaplan's attitude to variable costing underwent changes. He stated that after the introduction of an activity cost hierarchy to the concept of ABC "we understood that ABC was a concept based on gross margin, and not a concept which attempted to calculate full unit costs in a more accurate manner" (Kaplan, 1992, p. 59).

To sum up, it needs to be emphasized that by 1992 the formulation of the second generation of activity-based costing had finished, and it turned out that the second generation varied considerably from the first one. Instead of a concept based on full costing and concentration on the calculation of more accurate unit costs, another concept emerged, which was based on gross margin with two types of resources (provided and used) with a hierarchy of activities, in which the calculation of unit cost was disparaged[10]. It is worth noting that the changes which appeared in the second generation of the ABC system, in comparison to the first generation, were authored by Cooper and Kaplan; Johnson did not take part in the construction of the second generation of activity-based costing. In the late 1980s, when the foundations of activity-based costing were established, Johnson had extremely high expectations towards the system of ABC, however, in the early 1990s his views changed. At first Johnson (1991) doubted if activity-based costing could provide operational managers with information which would be useful in terms of cost reduction and profitability improvement. Later, his point of view became even more radical, he claimed that (Johnson, 1992, p. 26), "as the one who contributed to activity-based costing diffusion, I feel obliged to warn you that in my opinion, it went too far. I am convinced that the concept should be changed and its diffusion slowed down, if not ceased." He justified his criticism by claiming that information generated by accounting systems, in terms of the current global business environment, is unable to facilitate, in the long run, the competitiveness and profitability of companies.

1.4. Development of activity-based costing after 1992

Activity-based costing which was shaped between 1984–1989 became the first generation of ABC, and the crucial changes in the concept, which occurred between 1989–1992 are called the second generation of ABC. Modifications in the system of activity-based costing, which took place after 1992 are called the third, and even the fourth generation of ABC. As far as the structure of ABC

[10] The key differences between the two generations of activity-based costing brought about the emergence of at least two attitudes. One group of researchers and practitioners ignored the changes and still perceived the ABC system as a tool which enabled the accurate calculation of full unit cost. The other group of academics and practitioners recognized the second generation of ABC as a better and developed version of the first generation systems. It is still quite common to encounter, both in university textbooks and in practice, ABC systems from the two generations.

systems is concerned, Mecimore and Bell (1995) distinguished three generations of activity-based costing. They additionally claimed that the emergence of the fourth generation was possible in the future. Consecutive generations of ABC, differentiated by the two authors, accentuate different areas:

- the first generation of ABC accentuates activities and the cost of product calculation;
- the second generation stresses the importance of processes and activities related to them;
- the third generation focuses on the value chain within a company (department);
- the fourth generation accentuates the relation between activities and processes among the different departments of a given company.

Table 1.2. Comparison of three generations of activity-based costing

Items compared	Generations		
	first	second	third
Structure	Cost center	Cost center	Business unit
Activities	Product orientation	Process orientation	Firm orientation
Costs	Manufacturing	Process – both manufacturing, administration and selling	Internal and external
Focus	Product costing	Process costing	Value chain costing
Relationship between activities	No linkage	Linkage	Linkage
Cost drivers	Internal	Internal	Internal and external
Planning	Cost center	Cost center	Business unit
Controlling	Cost center	Cost center	Business unit
Cost analysis	Tactical	Tactical	Strategic
Hierarchy	Product	Process	Firm

Source: Mecimore, Bell (1995), in: Szychta (2007b), p. 283.

The first two generations distinguished by Mecimor and Bell correspond to the development of ABC presented in the previous sections respectively between 1984–1989 and 1989–1992. The foundations of activity-based costing which had been laid by 1992 constitute a model of ABC that is well-known and wide-spread in practice to date. After 1992, the concept, however, underwent further changes, and that enables the formulation of other generations of ABC. The third generation (Mecimore, Bell, 1995) concentrates on linking activities to processes and then linking those processes to the complete business unit. The focus is on the way a company adds value to manufactured products or offered services. In the third generation of ABC, the values which influence the level of activities are used to gain a competitive advantage by means of value chain analysis. According to Mecimore and Bell (1995), in order to gain a competitive advantage, it is necessary to analyze all the internal activities within a company and also the external ones which have an influence on the business unit. While constructing the third-generation activity-based costing system, it is important to design such a process structure so that it complies with the value chain in the company. In order for the implemented system of ABC to support the formulation and realization of a strategy, it is crucial to include measuring instruments in the system, which enable the achievement level to be measured. Apart from the focus on adding value to products and stressing the significance of the value chain concept, in terms of formulation and realization of competitive strategy, the third generation of ABC characterized a special category of activities i.e. support activities. Support activities are often very expensive and important for a business unit; the third generation of ABC emphasized the need to improve them and that, in the long run, they could have an influence on the improvement of the company's competitiveness. A comparison of the most important features of those three generations of activity-based costing systems is presented in Table 1.2.

Summarizing the three consecutive generations of activity-based costing, which are presented in Table 1.2, it may be concluded that the first one concentrates on improving of product cost calculation, the second one focuses on providing information needed to improve effectiveness and measure achievements, and the third one stresses the importance of the value chain concept in the formulation and evaluation of a competitive strategy. According to Mecimore and Bell (1995), in the future, the fourth-generation ABC may emerge which would integrate cost the accounting system of multiple branches or plants of one company or even multiple companies belonging to one corporation. The creation of such cost accounting systems, which will be integrated in terms of one, big international corporations is possible, especially in the era of globalization, yet the implementation of such systems may be extremely difficult.

Development of activity-based costing which took place at the turn of the 20th and 21st centuries led to a differentiation of the basic model of ABC that was known at the turn of 1980s and 1990s. This model contained a simple two-stage procedure of cost calculation i.e. first, resource costs were allocated to activities, and later activity costs were allocated to products, customers etc. However, this simple procedure did not take into consideration the complexity of all the problems which occur during construction and implementation of ABC systems in companies operating in various lines of business. Besides such previously analyzed modifications as the distinction of an activity hierarchy and the recognition of a concept of provided and used resources, the first-generation activity-based costing also has other extensions to the basic model of cost calculation e.g.:

- identification of unusual cost objects – the cost accounting systems of some companies have objects to which costs are assigned other than the usual ones. In one of the biggest telecommunication companies in Poland, apart from resources, activities and cost objects, to which activity costs are allocated (e.g. motion fractions, products, customers), there are objects such as telecommunication network elements or technical network layers (it should be noted that in the ABC of that company, these objects are defined differently than resources);
- cost classification rules – it sometimes happens that in activity-based costing systems functioning in practice, costs are directly allocated not only to resources or products, customers etc., but occasionally they are directly assigned to activities, omitting resources. In the ABC system functioning in an average-size manufacturing and trading company costs are allocated to objects, however the following rules must be taken into account: (a) costs (identified in the accounting system according to type of costs and cost centres) are first directly traced to a certain product, customer etc. (b) if the cost cannot be directly traced to a given product, customer etc., then, secondly, it should be attempted to directly trace it to a certain activity, (c) however, if such an allocation is impossible, then the cost should be allocated to a given resource;
- calculation of support activities for other activities or resources – apart from basic activities (at the level of a unit, batch or type of product), which may be calculated for products, customers etc., and general activities (activities related to the whole business unit), which cannot be calculated for products, customers etc., support activities have been distinguished. Support activities are defined as those which either support the performance of other activities (basic, support or general) or are performed in relation to resources. Thus, in cost accounting systems of some companies, one may find activities (support) whose costs are calculated: (a) for resources, and later from those resources, for example, for basic activities, (b) for basic activities, and later for products, customers etc.;
- calculation of the same activities for different cost objects – it sometimes happens that in activity-based costing systems functioning in practice, calculation of the same activity for different types of cost objects, depending on the needs, occurs. It means that e.g. costs of *considering a complaint* activity will be calculated for products for the purpose of product profitability analysis (depending on the number of complaints related to a product), and for the purpose of customer profitability analysis, these activity costs may be calculated for customers (depending on the number of complaints filed by a certain group of customers);
- calculation or non-calculation of unused capacity costs – ABC systems which operate in practice may sometimes treat costs of unused capacity in a different manner. These costs, for the purpose of different needs, could be, for instance, demonstrated as a separate item in the profit and loss account (it does not charge products), which is in compliance with the second generation of activity-

based costing, or they could be calculated for products, which is in agreement with the first generation of ABC.

The above examples of the classic activity-based costing modification illustrate but do not exhaust the problem of the system's complex use (and accommodation). The examples also highlight that the concept of classic activity-based costing may be developed and adapted for the purpose of different company needs. Although, probably in all the systems of activity-based costing functioning in practice (at least those in the Polish companies which were analysed by the author of this work) there is this two-stage cost calculation from resources to activities and from activities to products, customers etc., details of the structure and functioning of those systems differ considerably. The issue will be further analysed in chapters 4 and 5.

1.5. Activity-based management

The foundations of activity-based costing were laid between 1984 and 1992, however, it may seem interesting to investigate what happened to the concept in the following years. In the 1990s, Cooper and Kaplan continued their research on activity-based costing implementation in different companies all over the world (Kaplan, Cooper, 1998). They also got involved in cooperation with a supplier of IT management support systems and participated in the creation of an activity-based costing module functioning in terms of ERP system[11]. Johnson, in turn, focused on the management concept based on activities, stressing the fact that activity management, instead of cost management, is the key to a company's success. Many people and companies involved in CMS operation limited or abandoned collaboration with CAM-I and took up consulting activity. Also Cooper and Kaplan, along with global service companies such as KPMG Peat Marwick or Ernst & Young began their consulting activity[12].

In the process of activity-based costing evolution from cost calculation to management philosophy, consulting companies emphasized the connection between ABC and ABM (without distinguishing the concept as suggested by Johnson). In the practice of consulting companies and organizations implementing ABC/ABM, ABC/M (activity-based cost management) is used as a synonym for ABM. The relation between ABC – ABM is quite often perceived as follows: ABC, as a cost accounting system, provides information which is further used by ABM, a management concept, for the continual improvement of processes

---

[11] Activity-based costing was recognized as a module in ERP systems, just as standard costing was previously incorporated into modules of MRP II integrated systems. Apart from being a separate module in ERP systems, activity-based costing is very often implemented on the basis of systems exclusively dedicated to ABC.

[12] Ernst & Young even created its 'own version' of *activity-based costing*, which is called *total cost management* – TCM. In practice, the model did not vary from the well-known concept of ABC (Ostrenga, 1990).

in the company (Turney, 1992). When analyzing ABC/ABM publications in English-speaking journals on business and management, Jones and Dugdale (2002) noticed that ABM was more frequently discussed irrespective of ABC. Until 1995, excluding a few exceptions, there had been no publications on ABM without reference to ABC, however, in 1998 the number of such publications was similar to the number of works about ABM itself[13]. Information received from the systems of activity-based costing led to the emergence of the next concepts i.e.:

• activity-based cost management – ABCM – it is a concept in which activity-based costing is a source of information necessary in the decision-making process (it means that, in order to use ABCM in the company, activity-based costing must be implemented first);

• activity-based management – ABM – it is a concept in which decision-making about efficiency improvement and the effectiveness of performed activities is fed on information about activities and their costs (it means that, in order to use activity-based management, first activities and their costs must be identified, however, the calculation of product costs, customer costs etc. is not essential).

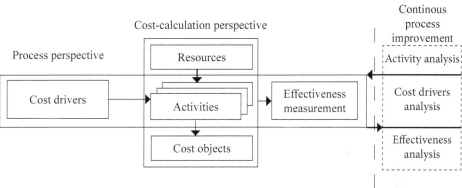

Figure 1.6. Activity-based management model
Source: CAM-I (1992), p. 20.

---

[13] In the light of the publications which appeared in the leading journals for practitioners, in the late 1990s, ABM emerges as a method that accentuates the identification and elimination of non-value adding activities. Interestingly, numerous publications associate non-value adding activities with support processes instead of operational processes (e.g. production process) and identification, as well as elimination of waste in those processes. The association of non-value adding activities with support processes (e.g. administration, management) stems from the views of operational managers, who perceive many activities performed within those processes as non-value adding; in their opinion, the activities only increase a company's indirect costs. According to the ABM concept, all activities may be analyzed in terms of their value adding or non-value adding properties. Gradually, ABM became a tool for management control, which was supposed to help managers limit and eliminate non-value adding activities, mainly within the bureaucratic structures of a company (Armstrong, 2002).

According to Szychta (2007a, p. 266), "the development of management accounting, which takes activities into account, started with ABC, evolved into ABCM and then into ABM, and that means the evolution of the ABC system uses – from focussing on the unit product cost calculation to process and activity management". Activity-based management concentrates on improvement of value for the customer (external or internal), as well as profits for the organization which are generated after value increase for a customer (CAM-I, 1992). Activity-based management incorporates: activity analysis, activity cost drivers analysis, activity capacity analysis, effectiveness measurement tools analysis, and cost drivers analysis. ABM focuses on: (a) analysis of activity costs causes and factors, (b) analysis of crucial strategic, organizational and operational implications, (c) identification of improvements in organizational, operational and strategic functions, (d) creation of solutions which generate profit. Activity-based management model is presented in Figure 1.6.

Figure 1.6 shows the elementary relations between activity-based costing, presented on the left, and analytical instruments on the right, which are necessary for a company implementing activity-based costing to fully benefit from the implementation. Activity-based costing functioning within a company generates a lot of important management data e.g. information about cost drivers, activities, resources and effectiveness measurement instruments, however, activity-based management is a tool which focuses on the value improvement of manufactured products and provided services (CAM-I, 1992). Within the activity-based management system (ABC) a whole range of methods and tools can be distinguished: costs of products, customers etc. analysis, profitability analysis by products, customers etc., activity-based budgeting (ABB), activity analysis, continuous process improvement, benchmarking, and business process reengineering.

With time, the systems of activity-based costing and activity-based management, which are used by experienced users, become a part of the key information systems within the organization. There are a few tendencies evident in the phenomenon (Cookins, 2001):

• integration of ABC/ABM output information with decision support systems such as a future cost estimating system, activity-based budgeting, customer relationship management (CRM) or balanced scorecard;

• learning how to make the structure of ABC/ABM systems more detailed, general and, on the whole, modify it when problems within or outside the company occur;

• automatization of financial and non-financial data collection from different information systems to feed activity-based costing and activity-based management;

• automatization of ABC/ABM information export to users from different levels of an organization.

It is assumed that, in the years to come, the tendency to integrate information systems of a company into a set of tools indispensable for every manager and analyst will become even more evident. The use of ABC/ABM also changes – instead of just being an accounting tool, ABC/ABM becomes an instrument which supports operational and strategic decisions. Thus, the nature of information used by the systems changes; apart from information about costs, the systems are fed on non-financial information, as well as information needed for performance evaluation.

1.6. Summary and conclusions

On the basis of the investigation presented in chapter one, it is possible to formulate the following, general conclusions, which support the main research thesis and specific theses:

1. The concept of ABC emerged in the late 1980s as an answer to Johnson and Kaplan's criticism of traditional management accounting. Activity-based costing became one of the key concepts in theory and practice of management accounting relatively fast. Undoubtedly, the creation and diffusion of ABC triggered an improvement of management accounting significance in practice in companies all over the world. Although it is probably the most important general consequence of ABC's development and diffusion, the influence of activity-based costing, and the concept of management accounting based on activities in general, was multifaceted:

a) the implementation of activity-based costing in many companies all over the world, numerous publications on ABC and ABM and the incorporation of that concept into university and vocational curriculums, as well as textbooks about management accounting, greatly influenced the process of the creation of cost accounting new logics. Cost objects, activities and cost drivers are the key terms of this new cost accounting logics;

b) before the concept of ABC was created, estimation of product costs was the main objective of cost accounting in manufacturing companies (it was done for the purpose of inventory pricing for financial accounting). When the concept of activity-based costing emerged and developed, manufacturing companies, on a larger scale, started to calculate the costs of objects other than products e.g. customers and groups of customers, distribution channels, sales regions, projects, internal services, activities and processes. A wider understanding of the cost object notion would probably have happened anyway even if the activity-based costing concept had never emerged. However, the creation of the concept definitely accelerated the process;

c) development of activity-based costing changed the way costs of a company were perceived – prior to ABC's emergence, costs within a system of cost accounting in an average company were classified according to their types (economic categories) and cost centers (department, section). Thanks to ABC, costs were seen from the perspective of processes and activities, thus not from the perspective of what cost it was and where it was generated, but it was rather more important which process generated it and why;

d) the concept of cost drivers and activity drivers, which diffused thanks to ABC diffusion, turned out to be extremely useful in cost management because it drew the attention of management accounting specialists to the significance of other drivers than those based on production volume or sales. The concept of activity hierarchy was especially important; it drew attention to the significance of activities and activity cost drivers not only at the level of a product unit, but also on the level of a batch or a type of products and company as a whole;

e) development of the ABC concept resulted in its wider range of use, outside manufacturing companies. ABC methods entered other organizations, especially service companies (e.g. financial firms and telecommunications companies), trading companies and non-profit organizations (e.g. healthcare, administration, education);

f) development of activity-based costing and management accounting based on activities fostered the emergence and development of such methods as cost analysis and customer profitability analysis, distribution channel analysis or sales regions analysis. Development of activity-based costing made the focus move from cost calculation onto cost management;

g) despite the fact that the emergence and development of activity-based costing concept require a change of the paradigm in terms of such crucial issues as cost classification, cost behaviour analysis, activity definition, cost object definition and cost driver definition, activity-based costing should be seen as an extension of traditional full-costing system;

h) the emergence and development of activity-based costing also influenced the way management accounting specialists were perceived by management and personnel. Traditionally, management accounting specialists were perceived through the techniques and procedures they used. Numerous implementations of activity-based costing, as well as publications on ABC and ABM, made people come to realize that management accounting specialists, in order to implement ABC effectively, should also be interested in resources and their drivers, and performed processes and activities and their drivers. The specialists became aware of the fact that cooperation with other managers in multifunctional teams is necessary for the successful implementation of activity-based costing. ABC implementation is only possible when people with extensive knowledge of logistics, marketing or operational activity take part in the implementation process. The necessity of cooperation between management accounting specialists and management fosters changes in the image of specialists, and, additionally, improves their position within the organization;

i) development and diffusion of ABC and ABM required that management accounting specialists, as well as other managers, deepen their knowledge of cost accounting and management accounting. For an effective ABC implementation in an organization, a better understanding of processes, activities, resources, drivers and objects within the company is necessary. The process of understanding different aspects of a company's operation is difficult and time-consuming, yet it is a prerequisite for successful activity-based costing implementation.

Although activity-based costing has not diffused to the degree expected in the late 1990s, the majority of both practitioners and theoreticians agree that the emergence and development of this concept improved significance of management accounting and, thanks to it, management accounting specialists improved their image and position within organizations.

2. The concept of activity-based costing, since its creation in the late 1980s, evolved from a cost measurement system of resources, activities and products into a management system based on activities. The stages of its evolution are as follows:

a) the concept's development between 1984 and 1989 was a result of a collaboration between university researchers and practitioners, who worked in the CMS group; the scientific description of case studies such as Schrader Bellows, the John Deere Component Works, Weyerhouser and Kanthal also contributed to its development. The first-generation ABC system, which was shaped at that time, focused on the improvement of product costing accuracy by means of greater accuracy of indirect costs calculation. Additionally, the system emphasized cost reduction by means of waste elimination and operational activity management by means of better performance measurement;

b) the second generation of ABC, which significantly differed from the first, was formed between 1989 and 1992. Instead of a concept which focused on the accurate calculation of full product costs, the second generation of ABC offered two types of resources (provided and used) and activity hierarchy structure where the significance of unit product cost calculation was lesser. Substantial differences between the two generations of ABC systems made some of the researchers and practitioners ignore these changes; they still perceived ABC systems as a tool which enabled accurate full unit product costing. Another group of researchers and practitioners regarded the second generation of ABC as a more developed version of the previous concept;

c) after 1992, the ABC concept underwent further changes and that enabled the distinction of the subsequent generations of ABC. In the third-generation ABC, values influencing the level of activities are used for the purpose of competitive strategy by means of value chain analysis. Apart from being focused on adding value to products and accentuating the importance of the value chain for making and implementing competitive strategy, the third generation of ABC characterizes a special type of activity i.e. support activities;

d) various uses of information received from activity-based costing led to the creation of activity-based management, in which data about activities and their costs provide information for making decisions in such areas as improvement of efficiency and the effectiveness of activities performed in the company. It meant an evolution of activity-based costing, which evolved from a product costing system into an activity management system.

CHAPTER 2

MODIFIED VERSIONS OF ACTIVITY-BASED COSTING

2.1. Time-driven activity-based costing and resource consumption accounting

2.1.1. Time-driven activity-based costing

In the late 1990s and at the beginning of the 21st century, practitioners along with consultants and university researchers began to embrace the idea that the implementation of activity-based costing in its current form was troublesome. Among the main problems, they enumerated the high costs incurred and the fact that implementation of the method was time-consuming, which was manifested at the stage of management interviews and surveys, as well as at the stage of gathering, processing and presenting data. Activity-based costing is difficult in terms of updating and modification, and the input data is subjective and hard to verify[1]. In most of its practical uses, ABC systems are relatively constrained, which means that their use makes it impossible to get a real and full picture of the company's profitability (only such a picture enables effective profitability management and improvement). Yet another important, but a separate problem related to the activity-based costing system, is the inadequate solution to the problem of resource unused capacity.

As a reaction to the above problems, Kaplan and Anderson (2004) came up with a new form of activity based costing which is called *time-driven activity-based costing* – TD ABC. Although the first traces of the new concept are to be found in 1998 (Kaplan, Cooper, 1998, 2000), the full version and its name was created in

---

[1] It is quite uncommon in companies which use activity-based costing that e.g. employees show that idle time constitutes a part of their worktime. If the idle time is not identified, then the rates for a unit of activity cost driver will be calculated for the assumption that the capacity has been fully used, and that level is definitely too high (Szychta, 2007a, p. 369).

2004[2] (Kaplan, Anderson, 2004). In 2007 Kaplan and Anderson published a book in which they presented the new method along with a description of six case studies illustrating various aspects of TD ABC, as well as its use in companies from different business lines (a Polish translation of the book appeared in 2008). The authors see the concept as an independent structure and not an extension of ABC, and they call the previously known activity-based costing *rate base ABC*, *traditional ABC*, or *conventional ABC*. One of the paragraphs in Kaplan and Anderson's book (2008) entitled "Time-driven ABC: old wine in new bottles?" even questions all relationships between duration drivers in ABC and TD ABC.

Time-driven activity-based costing is not frequently used in practice. Most of its implementations were conducted by the consulting company Acron, which was founded by Anderson, while Kaplan has been a member of Acron's board since 2001. From that year on, Kaplan and Anderson worked on improving effectiveness of ABC. The cooperation led to integration of capacity costs calculation, which was suggested by Cooper and Kaplan (1998), with time equation algorithms modelling complex transactions, which were authored by Anderson. This shaped TD ABC into its current form (Kaplan, Anderson, 2008). Acron, run by Anderson and Kaplan, is said to have implemented more than 200 TD ABC systems (Kaplan, Anderson, 2008, p. 10), both in its initial form with the time equations used, but without taking into account the degree of capacity use (1997–2001), as well as in its later variation when implementation of time equations was extended by the problem of capacity use degree (after 2001).

According to the authors of TD ABC, their method's basic advantage is the lack of necessity to interview and survey people, which was crucial in the initial form of ABC to allocate resource costs to activities. Resource costs in TD ABC, by means of time equations, are directly allocated to cost objects (products, customers etc.) using two types of data: cost rate per unit of resource capacity (stage one) and resource capacity use consumed by each activity performed in an internal unit (stage two).

In the first stage of the procedure, the costs of all resources in a given internal unit (or a process) are calculated – for example the costs of an internal unit (process) such as management, employees, space, IT resources, and vehicles etc. must be calculated. Then, the practical resource capacity of a given unit is estimated[3]. There are two methods of practical resource capacity calculation – simplified and analytical.

---

[2] Kaplan and Anderson (2008, p. 10) claim that the term *time-driven activity-based costing* was used for the first time in 2001. Before, Anderson and the consulting company Acron, which had been using the new concept since 1997, applied the term *transaction-based ABC*.

[3] Although in most of cases resource capacity of a given internal unit is expressed by means of workers' time, this is not permanent. Capacity can be expressed by means of e.g. number of machine hours (in a production department), number of pallets (in a warehouse), mileage (in a transport department) etc. Kaplan and Anderson (2008, p. 59) suggest that capacity-driven activity-based costing would be a more appropriate term for time-driven activity-based costing.

When calculating the practical resource capacity by means of the simplified method, it should be assumed that practical capacity constitutes 80% of theoretical capacity (Kaplan, Anderson, 2008). Knowing the theoretical capacity, it should be multiplied by 80% to get the practical capacity. In the analytical method, it must be taken into account that not the entire time for which an employee is paid, is actual work performance, since personnel allow for breaks, training sessions, education, repairs, maintenance, startups and downtime. Thus, this time should be subtracted from the time for which personnel receives remuneration e.g.:

   worktime for which personnel is paid
   – time for break, training, education etc.
   = practical resource capacity of a given internal unit.

The estimated practical resource capacity of a given internal unit does not have to be precise (Kaplan, Anderson, 2008, p. 24) and a few percent mistake is not important (major mistakes can be detected and corrected when unexpected shortages or surpluses of resource capacity of a given internal unit come up). Estimates of resource costs in a particular internal unit and estimates of practical resource capacity of a given internal unit enable the calculation of cost rate per resource capacity unit:

cost rate per resource capacity unit =
= resource costs / practical resource capacity.

In the second stage of cost calculation according to the concept of TD ABC, cost rates per unit of resource capacity are used to assign resource costs of an internal unit to cost objects (products, customers etc.). This procedure starts with an estimation of how much time from the practical resource capacity of a particular internal unit is needed to perform each activity within the unit. These estimates may be done by means of interviewing and surveying managers and employees or by means of direct observation and measurement. Similarly estimates of the total resource capacity of a given internal unit do not have to be extremely precise, in most of uses approximate calculations are enough. Kaplan and Anderson (2008) claim that, in contrast to the time structure subjectively estimated by employees for the purpose of classic ABC, in TD ABC the degree of use of total resource capacity of a particular internal unit is easy to evaluate and verify. Once the time needed to perform each activity in a given internal unit is estimated, the cost drivers rates of all types of activities performed in the given unit are calculated. To do that, the cost rate per resource capacity unit of a given internal unit is multiplied by the time estimates necessary to perform each activity. Alternatively, multiple activities performed within a particular internal unit in the conventional activity-based costing may be replaced by a single time equation for a given department:

time related to products =
  time of performing activity 1 * number of performed activities 1
+ time of performing activity 2 * number of performed activities 2
  …
+ time of performing activity n * number of performed activities n.

It is worth noting that cost drivers rates in TD ABC are slightly lower than similar rates estimated in the classic ABC. It stems from the fact that classic activity-based costing overestimates the costs of performed activities because it takes into account the costs of both used and unused resources. Through estimation of the time needed to perform each activity within the TD ABC system, the company receives information about the costs and efficiency of activity performance, as well as about time and costs of unused resource capacity. Unused capacity costs constitute period costs (they should not be calculated for products, customers etc. but they should be allocated to a profit and loss account of a given period).

According to the creators of time-driven activity-based costing, the system overcomes difficulties in the implementation process of classic ABC and has the following advantages (Kaplan, Anderson, 2008, pp. 31–32):
- it can be easily and inexpensively constructed, maintained and updated (the system does not require interviewing and surveying and integrates well with existing IT systems);
- it enables identification of unused resource capacity (both in terms of quantity – minutes, and in terms of value – money);
- it exploits time equations which enable incorporation of a certain type of activity, different from the standard activity, into the cost calculation;
- it can be implemented more easily than the classic ABC in an entire, large and complex organization (trading, service or production company);
- TD ABC can be used for forecasting future resource demands, which facilitates resource capacity budgeting on the basis of quantity projections and the degree of activity complexity.

Time-driven activity-based costing may be regarded as a step forward in the development of cost accounting methods based on activities (i.e. the classic ABC). However, the system does not provide solutions for all the problems characteristic of the classic activity-based costing; among the most important problems one could enumerate are:
- problem with actual costs use. Despite the fact that Kaplan and Anderson (2008) postulate the use of standard resource costs, in most practical uses actual costs are used. There are a few reasons for that (Gervais et al., 2009, p. 6).

Firstly, actual costs are perceived as more credible by managers using cost accounting. Secondly, the use of actual costs, instead of standard costs, makes the connection between financial accounting and management accounting clearer. Thirdly, some companies cannot use information about standard costs because they do not draw up budgets. The replacement of standard costs with actual costs causes well known problems and it may distort the results of the calculations. The common use of actual costs in the TD ABC system is not a fault of the method itself, but a fault of people implementing it, however, to reduce the problem, cost estimates should not refer to periods which are too short, longer periods should improve accuracy;

• the problem with the definition of a normal level of capacity use. Isolating unused capacity costs in TD ABC is not something new[4], however, defining a normal level of capacity use is not simple. Kaplan and Anderson (2004, 2008) claim that practical capacity is appropriate when it constitutes 80% of theoretical capacity[5]. The authors also ensure that little errors in its estimates are permissible, yet they will not have practical significance. Probably, in most cases, Kaplan and Anderson will not be mistaken. However, it must be taken into consideration that 'in most of cases' does not mean 'in all cases' and that the percentage of 80% is simply intuitive;

• the problem with activity homogeneity. Kaplan and Anderson (2008) emphasize that activities performed within a single unit should consume resources proportionally (homogeneity assumption). An example of a car garage which specializes in trucks and owns specialist equipment that suits repairs of only one make of vehicles illustrates and explains the problem. In that case, this specialist equipment must be taken into account separately from other garage resources because it being used for a completely different purpose than the remaining resources. Despite the fact that Kaplan and Anderson know how to tackle the problem, other consultants and managers implementing TD ABC may not know how to do it. If the activities are not homogenous, it might lead to essential inaccuracies in calculations;

• the problem with time measurement. TD ABC is mostly based on management's estimates (the time of individual activity performance is estimated in that way). It may be claimed that the estimate's inaccuracy of labor time spent on individual activities in the traditional ABC has been replaced by the estimate's inaccuracy of unit time spent on the performance of individual activities

---

[4] According to Garner (1954, p. 235), Gantt, who dealt with the issue of unused capacity at the beginning of the 20th century, stated in 1915 that he was preoccupied with that problem not because it was new but rather because it had great significance in practice and, on the other hand, it was little understood by practitioners.

[5] As previously mentioned, Kaplan and Anderson allow for practical capacity estimates as a disparity between theoretical capacity and idle time.

performance within TD ABC[6]. Additionally, the use of hours to measure resource capacity is not appropriate in every case; sometimes the use of e.g. machine hours, space or mileage would seem more suitable[7]. On the one hand, this may be questioned because Kaplan and Anderson condition the choice of capacity measurement on the type of activities performed within the unit. On the other hand, it should be taken into account that the majority of companies where the concept of TD ABC is used, use hours. Using time as an activity measurement was also possible in the classic ABC system, yet Kaplan and Anderson (2008) suggest that in TD ABC its use is different (in the classic ABC it is used at the first stage of calculation i.e. to calculate resource costs for activities, whereas in TD ABC time is used to calculate resource costs directly for products or customers[8]).

Figure 2.1 illustrates the development of the three basic generations of activity-based costing, which are used in practice: first-generation ABC, second-generation ABC and TD ABC. The third and fourth-generation ABC (see chapter 1.4) systems have been deliberately omitted, since they bear little significance in terms of practice.

As is shown in Figure 2.1, the first generation of activity-based costing (1984–1989) created a basic pattern of cost calculation including calculation of resource costs for activities and activities for objects (products, customers etc.). The second-generation of ABC (1989–1992) isolated activity hierarchy, which changed the rules of product costs calculation. It also differentiated provided and used resources, which enabled calculation of unused resource capacity costs. The origins of time-driven activity-based costing may be found in the Anderson's works who in 1997 used time equations in his work for the consulting company Acron. The TD ABC method was later supplemented by capacity costs calculation (Kaplan, Anderson, 2004).

---

[6] Kaplan and Anderson (2008) criticize a popular practice during ABC implementation when employees estimate the time percentage they spend on performing individual activities. The percentage often equals 100%, or even exceeds 100%, which is of course impossible due to unused capacity. Instead of such an approach, Kaplan and Anderson suggest a different one which is based on standard unit time estimates needed to perform a given activity. This type of approach creates two problems – firstly, the assignment of such time is very difficult and, secondly, unit times, which have been already assigned, may be very unstable in longer periods, and their frequent updates will be necessary (especially in area of support and general activities). Research by Cardinaels and Labro (2008) showed that activity time estimates in minutes are inflated, and estimates expressed by means of percentage give better results; it contradicted the theory by Kaplan and Anderson (2004). The research by Cardinaels and Labro revealed that activity time overestimates reached up to 35%. Research of a small distribution company using TD ABC, conducted by Gervais et al. (2009), proved that the differences between declared standard times and the real times were as high as 20%, thus they were definitely not insignificant.

[7] Due to the fact that almost all TD ABC systems use in practice, hours as the cost driver, it may be concluded that worktime is a category which is controlled thanks to the system.

[8] In time-driven activity-based costing there is no stage of calculating resource costs for activities, which is possible thanks to the use of standard time rates for performing individual activities.

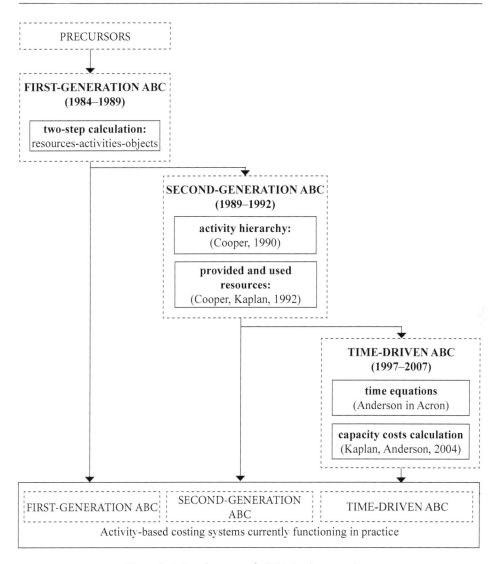

Figure 2.1. Development of ABC's basic generations

2.1.2. Resource consumption accounting

Resource consumption accounting (RCA) emerged at the turn of the 20th and 21st centuries (around the year 2000). At the end of 2001 CAM-I established a group interested in and devoted to the development of RCA (the group was a part of the CAM-I Cost Management Section). From then on the career of new management accounting technique began, the idea developed, it was validated and then popularized through articles and case studies of its use in professional journals (at the beginning) and also research papers in academic publications (later). The development of the resource consumption accounting method and its growing popularity resulted in the establishment of the RCA Institute (2008) which became a platform for refinement of the technique and also its popularization by educational and consulting activities. One year later (2009) the International Federation of Accountants recognized RCA as a costing method which attains a higher level of accuracy than traditional activity-based costing method and supported RCA as a method with a positive cost/benefit ratio. According to IFAC's Professional Accountants in Business Committee the incremental value of information provided by resource consumption accounting outweighs the additional costs of establishing and maintaining the system. In the view of the International Federation of Accountants, RCA can help organizations to improve understanding of costs in their costing systems and can also support better decision making in the companies (IFAC, 2009a). IFAC stresses that RCA offers companies the possibility to build proper cost allocation directly into their costing system and it allows an improvement of their performance.

Resource consumption accounting is a costing system (management accounting tool) based on two concepts – activity-based costing used from the late 1980s in many countries all over the world and *Grenzplankostenrechnung* (GPK which means 'flexible cost planning and control') used for decades primarily by German companies but to some extent by companies in other European countries (especially but not only companies in German speaking countries). The RCA combines (at the resource level) information on resource capacities and influence of input/output relationships on cost behavior with ABC. Resource consumption accounting just like activity-based costing and time-driven activity-based costing, has its supporters both in practice and in academia, and has sound theory which supports the method.

Resource consumption accounting as stated by IFAC (2009b, p. 17) is "a sophisticated approach at the upper levels of the continuum of costing techniques (which) provides the ability to derive costs directly from operational resource data, or to isolate and measure unused capacity costs. For example, in the resource consumption accounting approach, resources and their costs are considered as foundational to robust cost modelling and managerial decision support, because an organization's costs and revenues are all a function of the resources and the individual capacities that produce them".

Resource consumption accounting has three building blocks – it takes a comprehensive view of resources, an unambiguous view of cost behaviour and is a quantity-based cost model.

The first core element of RCA, the foundation of RCA, is company resources such as materials, employees, machinery, buildings. Resources are the source of company costs and revenues and information on resource capacity, utilization and efficiency is crucial for cost allocation and managerial decision making. Resource consumption accounting recognizes reciprocal allocation of resources and drivers of the resources pools. For all resources, capacity[9] is defined with respect to the manner in which the resource is consumed – the utilization of fixed costs for cost assignment is determined based on theoretical output, and proportional costs are assigned based on budgeted output. In resource consumption accounting, costs can be assigned through cost centres (vertically) like in traditional costing, and also through activities (horizontally), like in activity-based costing. For all resources idle/excess capacity is separated and is not allocated to cost objects (products, clients etc.) but is separately shown in profit reports. In resource consumption accounting, capacity is defined not in relation to activities but in relation to resources (the main idea of such a treatment of idle/excess capacity in RCA is to show it to managers responsible for the utilization of resource capacity and resource acquisition and to help them with decisions concerning resources).

The second element of RCA, quantity-based modelling, means that the whole model is built with the use of operational quantities (values follow quantities). In each resource pool quantifiable output is measured allowing for decoupling of monetary and output valuation which facilitate variance as well as capacity analysis (by providing a distinction between cost assignment and resource consumption). In resource consumption accounting valuation occurs only when the quantities consumed are multiplied by the output rates, which allows managers to analyze improvements in efficiency (quantity used) separately from output rates (prices). The resource consumption accounting model is quite detailed and sophisticated even in comparison to ABC or TD ABC. There are hundreds and in some cases thousands of cost drivers rates for resource pools in the model of cost assignment. Companies considering implementation should take into account the high degree of complexity in RCA models together with the high potential of the method in precise cost allocation (this means that the rate of RCA diffusion could be slow).

The third building block of RCA, the unambiguous view of cost behavior is the answer to the debate about variable and fixed cost and their suitability in decision making (cost behaviour in RCA is determined by changes in quantities of resources as they are applied to organizations operations). RCA makes a distinction between fixed and proportional costs in terms of resource consumption allowing for situations when proportional costs change to fixed costs. The idea of *different costs for different purposes* recognized in resource consumption accounting means that the method

---

[9] In resource consumption accounting, capacity is broken into three elements: (a) productive capacity – the resource is producing goods or providing a service, (b) non-productive capacity – the resource is engaged in maintenance, set-up, standby, waste, (c) idle/excess capacity – the resource is not working because there is no work to do (idle/excess capacity includes time that management or law require that no work be done).

uses various cost concepts to support decisions in different situations. RCA delivers information on throughput, contribution and gross margin for products, customers, market segments and other objects of the manager's interest. It is necessary to stress that costs that originate in the resource cost center (e.g. machinery) are primary costs of the resource and costs which are assigned to the resource cost centre from another resource (e.g. employees) are a secondary costs of the resource (allocated costs of employees are secondary cost of machinery). The total costs of the resource (primary and secondary costs) are then separated into proportional and fixed element depending on the correlation between the input quantities and output quantities from the resource. The often used notion of *proportional* costs is different from *variable* costs in RCA terminology as it stress the difference between costs that are *variable* with total production/sales volume and the costs that are *proportional* at the resource level. Separation of costs into proportional and fixed elements could be subjective and what is more resource costs that change proportionately to the output of a supplying resource may change classification and be named fixed if they are consumed in a fixed manner. To improve the decision usefulness of information from resource consumption accounting, some companies using the method employ replacement costs of the resources rather than historical costs.

In addition to the three building blocks of resource consumption accounting, the approach allows for better profitability reporting by tracing all direct costs to products and assigning indirect costs at causal and decision relevant levels to products and product groups, clients and client groups, market segments and so on (separation of proportional and fixed costs is maintained in profitability reports, and fixed costs include planned use of otherwise proportional resources in a fixed manner, e.g. use of labor for planned maintenance). Profitability reports in RCA present multiple contribution margins by deducting from revenues firstly the direct costs of products and secondly the various pools of indirect costs of different cost objects (product groups, clients etc.). An important element of RCA is activity based resource planning (ABRP). This planning and budgeting tool assesses the unit standards for each resource pool, determines the unit standards of resource consumption for consumers, estimates budgeted demand for resource output and converts budgeted resources output into dollar items.

Resource consumption accounting although based on the activity-based costing approach (and GPK), is considerably different both from ABC and its extended version, TD ABC – the main differences are shown in Figure 2.2. Panel A of the figure presents a simplified ABC model for a production department. Four resource pools were identified in the model (energy, depreciation, salaries and overtime wages) and linked to two activity pools: assembly (unit level activity) and setup (batch level activity). After allocating resource costs to activities and establishing activity cost pools, the costs of each activity are allocated to three final cost objects (products). Panel B presents the TD ABC model established for the same production department.

A. Activity-based costing

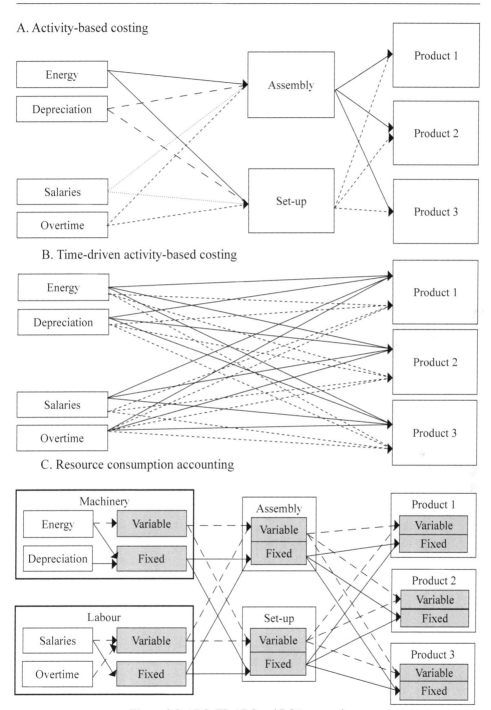

Figure 2.2. ABC, TD ABC and RCA comparison

Although the model looks similar to the ABC model in panel A (both models have the same resources and cost objects), it does not have activities. In TD ABC resources are directly linked to cost objects (products) through resource-activity cost drivers (Kaplan, Anderson 2004). Each driver represents a link between a resource and a cost object that consumes an activity. The number of activities that consume the same resource determines the number of resource-activity cost drivers between a resource pool and a cost object (it was assumed in the example that each resource is consumed by both activities – assembly and set-up). The value of a resource-activity cost driver is determined by multiplying the number of hours for an activity and the resource cost per hour. Resource consumption accounting model for a production department is presented in panel C. In this model two resource pools, machinery and labor, were established, each containing two resources (the machinery pool included energy and depreciation, and the labour pool included salaries and overtime). In comparison to ABC or TD ABC, proportional and fixed costs are separated in resource cost pools in RCA (salaries and energy were divided into proportional/variable and fixed element whereas depreciation was classified as fixed and overtime wages as proportional/variable). In RCA, similar to ABC, resource costs are allocated to cost objects under the two-stage procedure – at first resource costs are allocated to activities and then activity costs are allocated to cost objects, but it should be stressed that under RCA proportional and fixed cost are allocated separately and idle/excess capacity is eliminated from product costs. Treatment of idle/excess capacity costs in TD ABC and RCA is different. Whereas in the TD ABC model consumption of resources is driven by time spent on different activities only, in RCA there are different (multiple) drives which drive resource consumption. If the resources used in operations are homogeneous (and proportional to hours), the picture of unused capacity in TD ABC and RCA would be similar but if the resources used in operations are heterogeneous, RCA offers a better picture of unused capacity costs.

Keys and van der Merwe (2002) point out that resource consumption accounting could be a tool of control concentrating on comparisons of budgeted and actual results which may surpass ABC. The authors specify four control mechanisms within resource consumption accounting:

• management planning and control tiers – presenting an alternative to the CAM-I cross, the RCA cube recognizes strategic, tactical and operational levels of management (three levels) and also four tiers: (a) resource tier, (b) activity tier, (c) product tier and (d) market segment tier (Figure 2.3);

• authorized reporting – based on the flexible budgeting concept, RCA provides a much better basis for variance analysis than ABC does (authorized reporting compares actual results with standard costs for actual output whereas typical reporting in activity-based costing compares budgeted with actual results); authorized reporting when combined with resource, activity, product and market segment tiers provides various areas of the company with better information on performance measurement;

• a reflective view of operations – focusing on real-time measures of performance, RCA provides better information for operational control which enables managers to concentrate on present and not historical data (focusing on the costs and profitability of products or market segments in real-time allows for quick and effective actions);

• extensive variance analysis – presenting primary and secondary cost information for four tiers simultaneously (resource, activity, product and market segment tiers), RCA allows for very detailed variance analysis; what is more RCA enables variances such as controllable or uncontrollable to be classifield (it is necessary to stress that variance could be controllable in one tier e.g. resource tier and at the same time uncontrollable in another tier e.g. product or market segment); for variance analysis to be a tool for better company management, an accurate determination of responsibility for variances, especially with respect to excess capacity, is necessary (it is necessary, though, that the costing system in the company is well understood by managers); resource consumption accounting might not only be a method of variance calculation but also a means of variance analysis resulting in corrective actions taken by company managers.

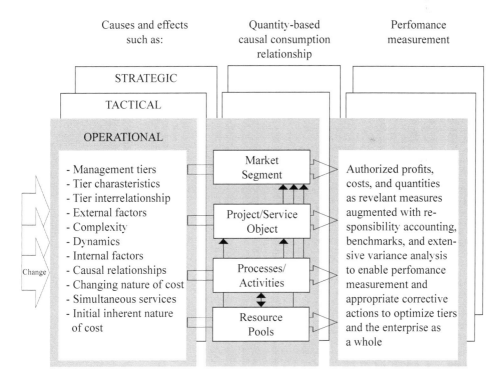

Figure 2.3. The RCA cube – basis for planning and control system
Source: Keys, van der Merwe (2004), p. 42.

The RCA approach, separating proportional costs from ones fixed seems to be suitable for planning and control decisions relying on reliable information about cost behaviour patterns (flexible budgeting). Flexible budgeting in the traditional format used a factory-wide or department-wide denominator volume and divided costs into variable and fixed elements based on production/sales volume (expressed usually in units or hours). The same concept (flexible budgeting) used in resource consumption accounting environment is much more detailed and precise as it allows for flexible budgeting application at the resources level. The use of flexible budgeting as a tool for planning and control at resource level (not factory or department level as in traditional methods) enable managers to isolate variances in the rate and quantity of resources used in the organization. Resource consumption accounting budget presents for each resource a difference between theoretical and budgeted capacity and also budgeted costs of idle/excess capacity (a higher or lower than budgeted demand for a resource directly influences the costs of unused capacity). Presenting unused capacity and its costs allows managers to take actions to utilize or eliminate excess capacity, or shows them possible shortages of resource capacity when future demand exceeds their supply.

Resource consumption accounting offers many benefits over traditional cost accounting systems – the most important are presented in Table 2.1.

Implementation of resource consumption accounting should be considered by companies who have problems with unplanned wasted resources and excess capacity costs which result in inadequate product decisions, shortage and undercosting of resources in cost budgeting and also distorted information for performance management. RCA can be implemented in different ways: (a) it can serve as a complete costing system (changing the current costing system), (b) it can be implemented in one area first with subsequent implementation in other areas, (c) it can be developed and used in parallel with existing systems and if it proves its validity it can switch with the current costing system, (d) it can be implemented in a general manner (not very detailed) and if provides enough benefits, modification to a more detailed version could be made.

Implementation of resource consumption accounting is possible in an ERP environment because these systems provide data for strategic, tactical and operational decisions (some ERP systems, e.g. SAP, provide RCA functionality). Implementation of resource consumption accounting in an ERP environment could enable the collection of more relevant information for decision making and could allow an organization to achieve its objectives.

Table 2.1. Benefits of resource consumption accounting over traditional costing systems

Resource consumption accounting	Traditional costing
Attributes the cost of excess/idle capacity to the person or level responsible for influencing the resource but does not allocate it to products	Excess/idle capacity is not identified and thus can not be associated with the appropriate person or level and is routinely allocated to products
Facilities capacity analysis by using theoretical volume for cost rates and making excess/idle capacity visible to managers	Obscures capacity analysis by using master-budget volume for cost rates and doesn't account for excess/idle capacity
Uses replacement cost depreciation to provide useful internal cost decision support information	Uses a depreciation prescribed by the external reporting system that often does not reflect economic reality
Pulls the cost of resources consumed to cost objects by using non-dollar, quantified output-consumption relationships based on causality	Pushes cost of resources supplied to cost objects by spreading all costs incurred over finished goods units produced
Identifies and assigns costs as innately fixed or variable (proportional) at the resource level, accurately specifying the nature of costs	Identifies and assigns costs as innately fixed or variable at the product level, obscuring true cost consumption patterns
Recognizes that innately proportional costs can be consumed in a fixed manner and provides required treatment	Provides no recognition of cost consumption patterns at the resource level
Provides decision makers with the ability to track and group cost information at virtually any level – from the resource level to the organization level	Groups costs at a department or product level with little or no provision for tracking or accessing costs at lower levels
Facilitates operations management with quantified actual nonfinancial information to compare it to planned or standard quantities	Nonfinancial information is often sparse or unavailable since costs are frequently allocated based on percentage relationships without tracking resource quantity consumption

Source: Clinton, Webber (2004), p. 21.

2.1.3. TD ABC and RCA compared

In reaction to the low level of activity-based costing adoption caused on the one hand by unsolved problems inherent in the ABC method and on the other by the complex nature of the ABC implementation process, two approaches emerged as the possible solution – time-driven activity-based costing and resource consumption accounting. Both systems were developed as a response to the shortcomings of activity-based costing but represent different philosophies on the development of cost allocation and management systems.

Cost management systems like TD ABC and RCA must meet one cost/benefit criterion meaning that benefits from the systems should be greater than the cost of operating the systems. Whereas the cost of costing system consists of costs of its implementation, modification and operation, benefits from the system can be measured by the quality of information provided by the system especially for decision making. It seems that both time-driven activity-based costing and resource consumption accounting offer three main benefits in the context of decision making:

• improvement of cost allocation which is achieved by not allocating unused capacity costs to cost objects;

• linkage between resource pools and cost pools which is done by applying activity-based costing paradigm in both models;

• separation of idle/excess resources which is achieved by providing information on unused resources and their costs which enable managers to address the problem of efficiency in the organization.

The purpose of TD ABC was to simplify the process of activity-based costing implementation and operation. It was achieved by use of a single measure of resource capacity (time) and quantity-based resource-activity cost drivers (activity pools were removed from the model). Kaplan and Anderson (2004) maintain that time-driven activity-based costing could provide more relevant cost calculations while making employee surveys to maintain the allocation model and enabling separation of unused capacity costs unnecessary. The TD ABC approach to cost management could be beneficial for organizations with standardized, homogenous operations especially for these with large proportion of employee costs in their cost structure (e.g. service organizations with a lot of human costs).

The second method which developed in response to the shortcomings of activity-based costing was resource consumption accounting. The method was based on the principles of traditional activity-based costing model and also the German *Grenzplankostenrechnung* (focusing on resource cost management and quantity-based modelling in the environment of enterprise resource planning systems, e.g. SAP). In comparison to TD ABC, the purpose of RCA was to recognize complex relationships between resources and cost objects by relying on its integration with enterprise resources planning models to capture organizations' complex processes. RCA is thus a more universal system suitable to use in organizations with heterogeneous resources driven by multiple drivers and not only by time e.g. by complex manufacturing organizations where time is only one of the resource drivers.

Although there are some differences between the models (TD ABC and RCA), there are also some similarities as they are built on activity-based costing foundation, but perhaps the most important difference is the separation of unused capacity costs. Both models do not allocate costs of unused capacity to cost objects (products, clients, market segments etc.) but separate them and present them in the profitability reports. The difference between TD ABC and RCA allocation of resources is that in the time-driven activity-based costing model, resource cost allocations are driven by activity levels which in turn are driven by output level. In resource consumption accounting, resource cost allocation is driven by the usage of each resource separately (usage of resources is not necessarily related to the level of output). RCA users can manage unused capacity at the level of individual resources. A comparison of time-driven activity-based costing and resource consumption accounting systems is presented in Table 2.2.

Table 2.2. Comparison of TD ABC and RCA

Feature	TD ABC	RCA
Relationship with other information systems	System independent	ERP-compliant
Organization of resource pools	Cost-based resource pools	Technology-based resource pools
Composition of resource pools	All resource costs are variable	Resource costs can be either fixed or variable
Cross-allocation of resource costs among resource pools	No cross allocation among resource pools	Cross allocation among resource pools is allowed
Allocation of resource costs to cost objects	Activity-based cost allocation	Both activity-based and volume-based cost allocation are allowed

Source: Tse, Gong (2009), p. 45.

As far as the time frame of the decisions is concerned TD ABC (just like traditional ABC) might provide useful information for long-term decisions, but may be not suitable for short-term decisions. In contrast for this kind of decision (short term) resource consumption accounting seems most appropriate, as it is suitable for all situations when a distinction between proportional and fixed cost could be made. RCA could also provide meaningful information further down the line. That kind of decisions rely on capacity requirements and resource consumption accounting is suitable in such situations as it provides insights into resource capacity.

Advanced cost management methods like TD ABC or RCA may not be suitable in a simple production environment e.g. in companies using lean management. In these organizations sophisticated cost accounting methods are not necessary but when complexity increases information from TD ABC or RCA may meet the cost/benefit criterion and may enhance companies' efficiency. When the organization makes decision to choose an appropriate cost management system, managers should understand what alternatives are available (see Figure 2.4), what the strengths and weaknesses of the alternatives are and what the conditions for successful implementation of the chosen system are. To choose correctly, an understanding of the concepts and mechanics of each system is necessary.

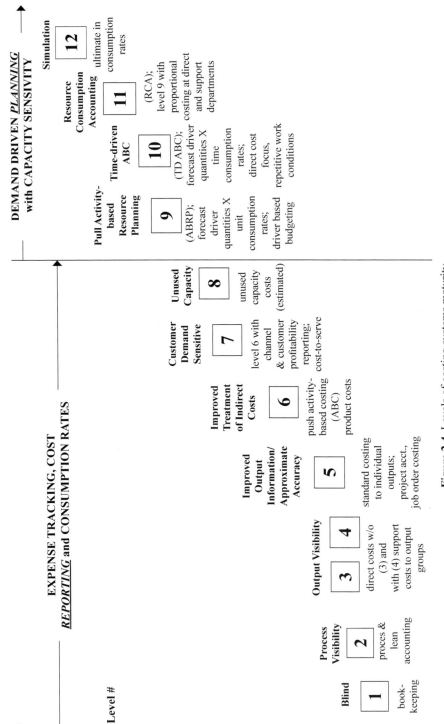

Figure 2.4. Levels of costing systems maturity
Source: IFAC (2009b), p. 19.

2.2. Comparison of ABC, TD ABC and RCA – a case study

A comparison of different costing techniques based on activities would be better understood if it were shown via a more practical example. Although examples of activity-based costing and, to a lesser extent, time-driven activity based costing are quite popular in articles and textbooks, resource consumption accounting examples are quite rare. There is number of articles addressing this method, but in rather a general manner, and the basic costing procedures required for its implementation are not, according to the author's knowledge, fully understood. There is especially a lack of comparison of technical aspects of RCA with TD ABC and ABC, suitable both for academics and managers to fully understand the potential of the methods and also some barriers for their implementation.

In order to address this issue the purpose of the case study below is to show the features of ABC, TD ABC and RCA and offer some guidance on the conditions in which each system could be appropriate. The example below is based on a hypothetical company called ProduCo and is intentionally kept simple to concentrate on basic theoretical differences between the methods and not to draw attention to their complex technical aspects. ProduCo is a production company which manufactures two consumer products: Standard Product and Luxury Product. Production is performed in two departments, the Machining Department (MD) and the Assembly Department (AD), which are located in one building (the Production building – PB). Sales, marketing, accounting and management board costs are posted to the single cost center called General Administration (GA).

2.2.1. Activity-based costing

In the first part of the example, let us suppose that ProduCo has implemented an activity-based costing system which separates the costs of the two cost centres – the Production building and General Administration, and also four production activities which are Machining (M), Assembly (A), Materials handling (MH) and Setups (SU). It should be mentioned that Materials handling and Setups are activities separated from the costs of the Machining and Assembly departments and Setups are a batch level activity, whereas Materials handling is a product level activity (together with Machining and Assembly). The primary costs of the production activities together with the costs of Production building and General Administration are shown in Table 2.3.

Table 2.3. Activity costs

Cost	Machining	Assembly	Materials handling	Setups	Production building	General administration
Depreciation	20,000	4,000	1,000	3,600	10,000	2,000
Salaries	8,000	5,000	3,000	6,000	3,000	5,000
Other	17,000	9,600	3,000	4,000	6,600	1,000
Primary costs total	45,000	18,600	7,000	13,600	19,600	8,000

Production building is used by the Machining activity (1,000 m²) and Assembly activity (800 m²). Basic information on total revenues, total direct material costs and the number of products manufactured is presented in Table 2.4.

Table 2.4. Product information

Specification	Standard Product	Luxury Product	Total
Revenue	110,000	120,000	230,000
Direct materials	40,000	60,000	100,000
Number of products	2,000	1,000	

In the activity-based costing system of ProduCo, the quantities of production activity drivers (mh, h, parts and setups) are collected in the MRP systems and are presented in Table 2.5.

Table 2.5. Product driver information

Activity	Driver	Standard Product	Luxury Product	Total
Machining	mh	3,000	2,000	5,000
Assembly	h	1,400	1,000	2,400
Materials handling	parts	10,000	10,000	20,000
Set-ups	setups	100	300	400

Based on the data above, the activity-based costing calculation is performed starting with the allocation of the Production building costs. First, the actual cost rate per square meter is calculated: costs rate = costs/actual capacity = $19,600 /1,800 m² = $10.89 /m². Based on the calculated rate, the costs of the Production building are allocated to Machining (1,000 m² * $10.89 /m² = $10,889) and Assembly (800 m² * $10.89 /m² = $8,711). Now, the secondary costs of the four production activities and General Administration can be added to the primary costs to establish the total costs. In the last lines of Table 2.6, the total costs are divided by actual capacity to determine the activity rates (for Machining: $55,889 /5,000 mh = $11.18 /mh). The activity rate is not determined for General Administration because this cost is regarded as a company sustaining cost (a company level activity) and is not allocated to products.

Table 2.6. Rate calculation for activities in ABC

Specification	Machining	Assembly	Materials handling	Setups	General administration
Depreciation	20,000	4,000	1,000	3,600	2,000
Salaries	8,000	5,000	3,000	6,000	5,000
Other	17,000	9,600	3,000	4,000	1,000
Primary costs total	45,000	18,600	7,000	13,600	8,000
Production building	10,889	8,711			
Secondary costs total	10,889	8,711	0	0	0
All costs total	55,889	27,311	7,000	13,600	8.000
Actual capacity	5,000	2,400	20,000	400	
Activity rate	11.18	1,138	0.35	34.00	

The activity rates estimated in Table 2.6 are used to allocate production activity costs to products, for example the total costs of Machining for the Standard Product are calculated as follows: $11.18 /mh * 3,000 mh = $33,533. The total cost of the activity is then divided by the number of products to establish unit cost ($33,533 /2,000 units = $16.77 /unit). The other activity costs are allocated in a similar manner and the profitability report based on activity-based costing is presented in the Table 2.7.

Table 2.7. Profitability report from ABC

Specification	Standard Product		Luxury Product		Total
	total	per unit	total	per unit	
Revenue	110,000	55.00	120,000	120.00	230,000
Direct materials	40,000	20.00	60,000	60.00	100,000
Contribution margin	70,000	35.00	60,000	60.00	130,000
% contribution margin	63.64	63.64	50.00	50.00	56.52
Indirect costs:					
Machining	33,533	16.77	22,356	22.36	55,889
Assembly	15,931	7.97	11,380	11.38	27,311
Materials handling	3,500	1.75	3,500	3.50	7,000
Setups	3,400	1.70	10,200	10.20	13,600
Indirect costs total	56,365	28.18	47,435	47.44	103,800
Gross margin	13,635	6.82	12,565	12.56	26,200
% gross margin	12.40	12.40	10.47	10.47	11.39
General administration	8,000				8,000
Net margin	18,200				18,200
% net margin	7.91				7.91

Activity-based costing takes a long-run view of the product costs meaning that, in the long run, all costs are variable. In that sense ABC can be perceived as a model identifying cost/effect relationships viable in the long term, and may be viewed as a long-run resource consumption accounting model (Grasso, 2005). Activity-based costing allows for better cost assignment to products than traditional costing but requires additional sophistication in gathering activity costs and allocating them to products with the use of different drivers (not necessarily proportional to production volume), for example Setup – a batch level activity in our example. Critics of ABC point out that companies implementing this approach have to run very detailed costing systems and have to gather a lot of operational data on activity drivers which is both time consuming and costly. What is more, ABC systems functioning in practice are usually based on actual capacity which, with the share of fixed costs in indirect cost pools, means that excess capacity costs are not separated but they are allocated to products (long ago Kaplan and Cooper (1998) advocated for excess capacity cost identification but companies in practice generally do not do this). The drawback of the ABC system is also that it fails to distinguish between fixed and variable costs in the short term, so it is suitable for long-term decisions with a no excess capacity situation, but is not suitable in short-term decision making in conditions of excess capacity where a contribution margin criterion should be used.

2.2.2. Time-driven activity-based costing

Suppose now that ProduCo implemented a more advanced version of activity-costing, namely time-driven activity-based costing. As the example is simple, suppose that basic data on activities and their costs, use of production building space, product information and product driver information are the same as in the ABC example (as in Tables 2.3, 2.4 and 2.5). As was mentioned at the beginning of the example, the case is kept simple so we do not show the time equations in TD ABC but concentrate on the detailed illustration of excess capacity calculation. The basic difference between ABC and TD ABC in practice is that the activity rates in the former are based on actual capacity (although Kaplan and Cooper postulated practical capacity) whereas the later are based on practical capacity, making it possible to show costs of excess capacity. The basic data on activity capacity (theoretical, practical and actual) is presented in Table 2.8.

Table 2.8. Activity capacity

Activity	Driver	Theoretical	Practical	Actual
Machining	mh	10,000	6,850	5,000
Assembly	h	3,000	2,644	2,400
Materials handling	parts	25,000	23,333	20,000
Set-ups	setups	600	500	400
Production building	m²	2,000	2,000	1,800
General administration	–	–	–	–

In TD ABC, as in "traditional" ABC, it is necessary to begin with calculating the cost rate per square meter for allocating Production building costs to activities (Machining and Assembly). The basic calculations are similar to those in ABC with one difference, however: they are based on practical and not actual capacity: costs rate = costs/practical capacity = $19,600 /2,000 m² = $9.80 /m². Then the established rate is used to allocate building costs to activities (e.g. for Machining – $9.80 /m² * 1,000 m² = $9,800) and to excess capacity pool – $9.8 /m² * 200 m² = $1,960. After allocating secondary costs to activities one get total costs, and by dividing them by practical capacity it is possible to estimate the cost rate for each activity (Table 2.9).

Table 2.9. Rate calculation for activities in TD ABC

Specification	Machining	Assembly	Materials handling	Setups	General administration
Depreciation	20,000	4,000	1,000	3,600	2,000
Salaries	8,000	5,000	3,000	6,000	5,000
Other	17,000	9,600	3,000	4,000	1,000
Primary costs total	45,000	18,600	7,000	13,600	8,000
Production building	9,800	7,840			
Secondary costs total	9,800	7,840	0	0	0
All costs total	54,800	26,440	7,000	13,600	8,000
Practical capacity	6,850	2,644	23,333	500	
Activity rate	8.00	10.00	0.30	27.20	

It is necessary to note that activity rates in TD ABC (Table 2.9) are lower than in ABC (Table 2.6) because of different activity levels used in both systems (practical and actual). Activity rates are then used to allocate indirect costs to products, shown in Table 2.10, for example total Machining costs for the Standard Product are calculated as follows: $8.00 /mh * 3,000 mh = $24,000. The total cost is then divided by the number of the Standard Product units manufactured to establish the activity cost per unit ($24,000 /2,000 units = $12.00 /unit. The rest of the activity costs (Assembly, Materials Handling and Setups) are calculated in a similar way, however, the cost of unused capacity is clearly shown in the report. It can be seen that excess capacity costs are calculated at both the support activities/resources level e.g. Production building ($9.8 /m^2 * 200 m^2 = $1,960$) and also the production activity level e.g. Machining ($8.00 /mh * 1,850 mh = $14,800$).

Table 2.10. Profitability report from TD ABC

Specification	Standard Product		Luxury Product		Total
	Total	Per unit	Total	Per unit	
Revenue	110,000	55.00	120,000	120.00	230,000
Direct materials	40,000	20.00	60,000	60.00	100,000
Contribution margin	70,000	35.00	60,000	60.00	130,000
% contribution margin	63.64	63.64	50.00	50.00	56.52
Indirect costs:					
Machining	24,000	12.00	16,000	16.00	40,000
Assembly	14,000	7.00	10,000	10.00	24,000
Materials handling	3,000	1.50	3,000	3.00	6,000
Set-ups	2,720	1.36	8,160	8.16	10,880
Indirect costs total	43,720	21.86	37,160	37.16	80,880
Gross margin	26,280	13.14	22,840	22.84	49,120
% gross margin	23.89	23.89	19.03	19.03	21.36
Excess capacity:					
Production building	1,960				1,960
Machining	14,800				14,800
Assembly	2,440				2,440
Materials handling	1,000				1,000
Set-ups	2,720				2,720
Excess capacity total	22,920				22,920
General administration	8,000				8,000
Net margin	18,200				18,200
% net margin	7.91				7.91

Time-driven activity-based costing is in many aspects similar to the "traditional" ABC system with all its benefits and drawbacks. Two basic differences should be mentioned, however. The first is the use of time equations for simplicity in data gathering (the measurement of activity drivers) and the second is the identification of excess capacity costs (these two differences address the two most important problems in ABC implementation). Thus TD ABC can be more easily constructed, maintained and updated and it enables the identification of unused resource capacity, so altogether it can be more easily implemented than the classic ABC in an entire, large and complex organization (trading, service or a production company). One general drawback of TD ABC, also characteristic of ABC, is still present – this is the lack of separation of fixed and variable costs, so the system is generally suitable for long-run decisions only and may be misleading when used for short-term decision making.

2.2.3. Resource consumption accounting

If our case company ProduCo decides to implement resource consumption accounting, two basic changes in cost gathering are required – separation of the resources and the division of their costs into two pools: fixed and proportional. In RCA the term "variable costs", popular in traditional variable costing systems, is not typically used, as variable costs are supposed to move with the changes of product volume and proportional costs move with the changes of resource driver volume which could, but does not necessarily have to, move in a way proportional to product units. In the ProduCo example there are resources whose quantity is used proportionally to the number of products – unit level activities (MD People, MD Production line, AD People, AD Production line and Materials handling) and also resources whose quantity is not used proportionally to product units (Setups – this resource use is proportional to the number of product batches). In the costing system of a company using RCA, costs of the separate resources are presented with their division into fixed and proportional, which is shown in Table 2.11.

Table 2.11. Resource costs

A. MD People

Costs	Fixed	Proportional	Total
Depreciation	0	0	0
Salaries	6,000	2,000	8,000
Other	3,000	2,000	5,000
Primary costs total	9,000	4,000	13,000

B. MD Production line

Costs	Fixed	Proportional	Total
Depreciation	20,000	0	20,000
Salaries	0	0	0
Other	4,000	8,000	12,000
Primary costs total	24,000	8,000	32,000

C. AD People

Costs	Fixed	Proportional	Total
Depreciation	0	0	0

Salaries	3,000	2,000	5,000
Other	2,400	1,600	4,000
Primary costs total	5,400	3,600	9,000

D. AD Production line

Costs	Fixed	Proportional	Total
Depreciation	4,000	0	4,000
Salaries	0	0	0
Other	800	4,800	5,600
Primary costs total	4,800	4,800	9,600

E. Materials handling

Costs	Fixed	Proportional	Total
Depreciation	1,000	0	1,000
Salaries	3,000	0	3,000
Other	1,000	2,000	3,000
Primary costs total	5,000	2,000	7,000

F. Setups

Costs	Fixed	Proportional	Total
Depreciation	3,600	0	3,600
Salaries	6,000	0	6,000
Other	0	4,000	4,000
Primary costs total	9,600	4,000	13,600

G. Production building

Costs	Fixed	Proportional	Total
Depreciation	10,000	0	10,000
Salaries	3,000	0	3,000
Other	3,000	3,600	6,600
Primary costs total	16,000	3,600	19,600

H. General administration

Costs	Fixed	Proportional	Total
Depreciation	2,000	0	2,000
Salaries	5,000	0	5,000
Other	1,000	0	1,000
Primary costs total	8,000	0	8,000

Resource rates in RCA are usually based not on actual capacity (which is usually the case in ABC) nor on practical capacity (which is the case in TD ABC) but on the theoretical capacity of resources (see Table 2.12). It should to be stressed that the number of resources is, in our example, bigger than the number of activities, so our case company has to collect some more data on the resources (fixed and proportional costs of resources). Companies using RCA differ somewhat in how they define pools of indirect costs. Usually resources are used where a resource is a piece of machinery, building or homogeneous group of people (in our example MD People, MD Production line, AD People, AD production line, Production building), but in other cases they can group indirect costs into activity pools (in our example Materials handling and Setups). Only one indirect resource cost pool in ProduCo does not have a driver – it is the General Administration cost pool which, like in other versions of costing systems (ABC and TD ABC), comprises only fixed costs which were not allocated to products.

Table 2.12. Resource capacity

Resource	Driver	Theoretical	Practical	Actual
MD People	h	6,000	5,000	4,000
MD Production line	mh	10,000	6,850	5,000
AD People	h	3,000	2,644	2,400
AD Production line	mh	8,000	7,000	6,000
Materials handling	parts	25,000	23,333	20,000
Set-ups	setups	600	500	400
Production building	m2	2,000	2,000	1,800
General administration	–	–	–	–

As the example is simple, let us suppose that basic data on the use of production building space and product information are the same as in the ABC and TD ABC examples (as in Table 2.4). Resource driver information is, however, collected differently for every resource (or activity) – the amount of data which is needed to run RCA is greater than in ABC or TD ABC and it is typically required that the company implementing resource consumption accounting has to have a good ERP system (e.g. SAP).

Table 2.13. Product driver information for RCA

Resource	Driver	Standard Product	Product luxury	Total
MD People	h	2,000	2,000	4,000
MD Production line	mh	3,000	2,000	5,000
AD People	h	1,400	1,000	2,400
AD Production line	mh	2,000	4,000	6,000
Materials handling	parts	10,000	10,000	20,000
Set-ups	setups	100	300	400

As in other versions of costing systems, ProduCo has to begin allocations with calculating the cost rate per square meter for allocating Production building space to resources (MD Production line and AD Production line). Basic calculations are similar to those in ABC or TD ABC with two differences, however, i.e. they are done separately for fixed and proportional costs, and the rate for fixed costs is based on theoretical capacity and the rate for proportional costs is based on actual capacity:

fixed costs rate = fixed costs/theoretical capacity = $16,000 /2,000 m^2 = $8.00 /m^2

proportional costs rate = proportional costs/actual capacity = $3,600 /1,800 m^2 = $2.00 /m^2

Then the established rates are used to allocate building costs to activities (e.g. for MD Production line: fixed costs – $8.00 /m^2 * 1,000 m^2 = $8,000 and proportional costs – $2.00 /m^2 * 1,000 m^2 = $2,000) and to excess capacity pool – $8.00 /m^2 * 200 m^2 = $1,600 (Table 2.14).

Table 2.14. Allocation of production building costs

Resource	Fixed	Proportional	Total
MD Production line	8,000	2,000	10,000
AD Production line	6,400	1,600	8,000
Excess capacity	1,600		1,600
Total	16,000	3,600	19,600

Two things characteristic of RCA should be stressed. First, the costs of the Production building are divided into fixed and proportional (proportional costs change with the number of square meters used – the example of these costs could be cleaning materials) but then allocated to Production lines these costs became fixed costs, meaning that they do not change with the number of machine hours of production on the lines. The second important change in allocating Production building costs is that costs of excess capacity are comprised only of fixed costs ($8.00 /m^2 * 200 m^2 = $1,600 $) – costs of excess capacity are than lower than in the case of TD ABC where the total cost rates (fixed and proportional) were used to calculate excess capacity costs ($9.80 /m^2 * 200 m^2 = $1,960). Calculation of excess capacity costs in RCA is better because no proportional costs are allocated to the excess capacity pool.

After allocating secondary costs to activities one get total costs, and by dividing them by theoretical capacity it is possible to estimate the cost rate for each activity (Table 2.15).

Table 2.15. Rate calculation for resources

A. MD People

Specification	Fixed	Proportional	Total
Depreciation	0	0	0
Salaries	6,000	2,000	8,000
Other	3,000	2,000	5,000
Primary costs total	9,000	4,000	13,000
Production building			0
Secondary costs total	0	0	0
All costs total	9,000	4,000	13,000
Theoretical capacity	6,000		
Actual capacity		4,000	
Resource rate	1.50	1.00	

B. MD Production line

Specification	Fixed	Proportional	Total
Depreciation	20,000	0	20,000
Salaries	0	0	0
Other	4,000	8,000	12,000
Primary costs total	24,000	8,000	32,000
Production building	10,000		0
Secondary costs total	10,000	0	0
All costs total	34,000	8,000	42,000
Theoretical capacity	10,000		
Actual capacity		5,000	
Resource rate	3.40	1.60	

C. AD People

Specification	Fixed	Proportional	Total
Depreciation	0	0	0
Salaries	3,000	2,000	5,000
Other	2,400	1,600	4,000
Primary costs total	5,400	3,600	9,000
Production building			0
Secondary costs total	0	0	0
All costs total	5,400	3,600	9,000
Theoretical capacity	3,000		
Actual capacity		2,400	
Resource rate	1.80	1.50	

D. AD Production line

Specification	Fixed	Proportional	Total
Depreciation	4,000	0	4,000
Salaries	0	0	0
Other	800	4,800	5,600
Primary costs total	4,800	4,800	9,600
Production building	8,000		0
Secondary costs total	8,000	0	0
All costs total	12,800	4,800	17,600
Theoretical capacity	8,000		
Actual capacity		6,000	
Resource rate	1.60	0.80	

E. Materials handling

Specification	Fixed	Proportional	Total
Depreciation	1,000	0	1,000
Salaries	3,000	0	3,000
Other	1,000	2,000	3,000
Primary costs total	5,000	2,000	7,000
Production building			0
Secondary costs total	0	0	0
All costs total	5,000	2,000	7,000
Theoretical capacity	25,000		
Actual capacity		20,000	
Resource rate	0.20	0.10	

F. Set-ups

Specification	Fixed	Proportional	Total
Depreciation	3,600	0	3,600
Salaries	6,000	0	6,000
Other	0	4,000	4,000
Primary costs total	9,600	4,000	13,600
Production building			0
Secondary costs total	0	0	0
All costs total	9,600	4,000	13,600
Theoretical capacity	600		
Actual capacity		400	
Resource rate	16.00	10.00	

G. General administration

Specification	Fixed	Proportional	Total
Depreciation	2,000	0	2,000
Salaries	5,000	0	5,000

Other	1,000	0	1,000
Primary costs total	8,000	0	8,000
Production building			0
Secondary costs total	0	0	0
All costs total	8,000	0	8,000

The calculated resource rates (Table 2.15) are used to allocate indirect costs to products, but fixed and proportional rates are used separately, for example fixed MD Production line costs for the Standard Product are calculated as follows: $3.40 /mh * 3,000 mh = $10,200 and proportional costs: $1.60 /mh * 3,000 mh = $4,800 $. The total fixed cost is then divided by the number of the Standard Product units manufactured to establish the resource cost per unit of product: $10,200 /2,000 units = $5.10 /unit (the unit proportional cost is established in a similar manner: $4,800 /2,000 units = $2.40 /unit). The rest of the resource costs are calculated in similar way, however, the cost of excess capacity shown in the report (Table 2.16) is calculated only with the use of fixed costs rates (no proportional costs are allocated to the excess capacity cost pool).

Table 2.16. Profitability report from RCA

Specification	Standard Product		Luxury Product		Total
	Total	Per unit	Total	Per unit	Total
Revenue	110,000	55.00	120,000	120.00	230,000
Direct materials	40,000	20.00	60,000	60.00	100,000
Contribution margin 1	70,000	35.00	60,000	60.00	130,000
% contribution margin 2	63.64	63.64	50.00	50.00	56.52
Proportional costs:					
MD People	2,000	1.00	2,000	2.00	4,000
MD Production line	4,800	2.40	3,200	3.20	8,000
AD People	2,100	1.05	1,500	1.50	3,600
AD Production line	1,600	0.80	3,200	3.20	4,800
Materials handling	1,000	0.50	1,000	1.00	2,000
Set-ups	1,000	0.50	3,000	3.00	4,000
Proportional costs total	12,500	6.25	13,900	13.90	26,400
Contribution margin 2	57,500	28.75	46,100	46.10	103,600
% contribution margin 2	52.27	52.27	38.42	38.42	45.04
Fixed costs:					
MD People	3,000	1.50	3,000	3.00	6,000
MD Production line	10,200	5.10	6,800	6.80	17,000
AD People	2,520	1.26	1,800	1.80	4,320
AD Production line	3,200	1.60	6,400	6.40	9,600

Materials handling	2,000	1.00	2,000	2.00	4,000
Set-ups	1,600	0.80	4,800	4.80	6,400
Fixed costs total	22,520	11.26	24,800	24.80	47,320
Gross margin	34,980	17.49	21,300	21.30	56,280
% gross margin	31.80	31.80	17.75	17.75	24.47
Excess capacity:					
Production building	1,600				1,600
MD People	3,000				3,000
MD Production line	17,000				17,000
AD People	1,080				1,080
AD Production line	3,200				3,200
Materials handling	1,000				1,000
Set-ups	3,200				3,200
Excess capacity total	30,080				30,080
General administration	8,000				8,000
Net margin	18,200				18,200
% net margin	7.91				7.91

Resource consumption accounting is an even more detailed approach to costing than both ABC and TD ABC. It concentrates on resources and attempts to identify the capacity of the resources, use of this capacity and excess capacity as well as costs which are fixed and proportional to the resource level (costs at the resource level typically comprise primary costs and secondary costs, which in fact is not so typical in "traditional" ABC implementations). It should to be mentioned that RCA could be implemented in practice vertically through the cost centers, or horizontally through activities – this distinction could be lost in practice, however, e.g. in the ProduCo case study, a mixed approach was used, meaning that four resources (MD People, MD Production line, AD People and AD Production line) and two activities (Setup and Material handling) were separated from the indirect costs of production. Wherever the implementation of RCA takes place, vertically or horizontally, fixed and proportional costs should be strictly separated. A distinguishing feature of RCA is that fixed costs rates are determined by dividing costs by theoretical capacity (thus allowing for excess capacity cost identification) and proportional cost rates are estimated by dividing costs by actual capacity (no proportional costs are allocated to the excess capacity cost pool). By separating fixed and proportional costs, RCA could be suitable both for short and long-term decision making. It can also be used for planning purposes and flexible budget preparation with variance analysis at the resource level (volume variance). The allocation of fixed costs only to the excess capacity cost pool allows for better estimation of its "true" cost (this cost is definitely more precise than in TD ABC, where no distinction between fixed and proportional cost is made).

2.3. Summary and conclusions

On the basis of the investigation presented in chapter two, it is possible to formulate the following general conclusions, which support the main research thesis and specific theses:

1. TD ABC as well as RCA emerged as possible solutions to the shortcomings of activity-based costing but represent different philosophies regarding the development of cost allocation and management systems. The purpose of time-driven activity-based costing was to simplify the process of ABC implementation and operation whereas the purpose of RCA was to recognize complex relationships between resources and cost objects by relying on integration with ERP systems.

2. The origins of time-driven activity-based costing may be found in Anderson's works, who in 1997 used time equations in his work for a consulting company, Acron. The TD ABC method was later supplemented by capacity costs calculation (Kaplan & Anderson, 2004). According to the creators of time-driven activity-based costing, the system overcomes the difficulties in the implementation process of classic ABC.

3. Resource consumption accounting emerged around the year 2000. The concept developed and in 2009 International Federation of Accountants recognized RCA as a costing method which attains higher level of accuracy than traditional ABC. RCA is a costing system based on two concepts – activity-based costing and *Grenzplankostenrechnung*. Resource consumption accounting concentrates on resources with the use of activity-based costing, activity-based resource planning, absorption costing, variable costing, actual costs, standard costs, segmented profitability reports, primary and secondary costs, and is usually a part of organizations' enterprise resources planning system (resource consumption accounting integrates the best cost management concepts to create information intended to support management decision making in a company).

4. The most important differences between TD ABC and RCA are the cost behavior patterns they employ and the separation of excess capacity costs. It should be stressed that in TD ABC there is no distinction between variable and fixed costs, whereas in RCA, the costs of resources are separated into proportional and fixed components. Both models do not allocate costs of unused capacity to cost objects but in the TD ABC model, resource cost allocations are driven by activity levels which in turn are driven by output level, whereas in RCA, resource cost allocation is driven by usage of each resource separately.

5. The TD ABC approach to cost management could be beneficial for organizations with standardized, homogeneous operations, especially for those

with a large proportion of employee costs in their cost structure (e.g. service organizations with a lot of human costs). RCA is thus a more universal system suitable to use in organizations with heterogeneous resources driven by multiple drivers and not only by time e.g. by complex manufacturing organizations where time is only one of the resource drivers.

CHAPTER 3

THE DEVELOPMENT OF ACTIVITY-BASED COSTING/MANAGEMENT JOURNAL LITERATURE IN POLAND 1994–2011[1]

3.1. Introduction

Companies all over the world have been interested in the concept of activity-based costing and activity-based management and have implemented it for more than twenty years. Enormous preoccupation with the concept is also mirrored in the literature. There are many publications on ABC/M, especially for practitioners (e.g. *Journal of Cost Management*, *Management Accounting* – the United States, *Management Accounting* – the United Kingdom etc.) but also, although to a lesser extent, there are academic publications[2] (*Management Accounting Research* and *Journal of Management Accounting Research*). Interestingly, a vast number of publications have been written by practitioners, specifically two groups of practitioners: those working for companies where activity-based costing is used, or those working in consulting companies specializing in ABC/M.

The analysis of ABC/ABM literature published in professional and scientific accounting journals in the United States and in the United Kingdom between 1987 and 2000 was presented by Björnenak and Mitchell (2000). The research shows that the majority of articles were published in professional journals (89% of all articles published). Björnenak and Mitchell research shows a loss of interest in ABC/ABM in the late 1990s (measured in the volume of publications). The

---

[1] This chapter is a modified and enhanced version of the paper by Joanna Domagała and Tomasz Wnuk-Pel (2011).

[2] Shields (1997) observed the phenomenon; he noticed that the number of professional publications on ABC/M was incomparably higher than the number of academic publications.

maximum level of publications in the United States and the United Kingdom journals was reached in the years 1996–1997, when more than 180 articles per year on ABC/ABM were published, from that time the volume of articles decreases and reaches about 50 articles per year in 1999–2000. After the 2000 the number of publications in the journals seems to further decrease which confirms the decline in ABC literature in the last years of the 1990s.

The decline in the volume of ABC/ABM literature in scientific journals is evident from the mid-1990s and it occured in advance of the number of publications in the professional journals. While in 1991 12% of the articles published in scientific journals dealt with ABC, it dropped to 4.2% in 1996 (Carmona, Gutierrez, 2003). The results of the studies by Björnenak and Mitchell (2000, 2002) and Carmona and Gutierrez (2003) show, trough decline of the number of articles published on subject, the evolution in the interest for ABC/ABM in the United States and the United Kingdom.

The research examining the same phenomenon of the ABC/ABM literature diffusion in France was presented by Alcouffe (2004). The aim of his paper was to generate evidence which can enrich and support the studies of communication structures in accounting research by Björnenak and Mitchell (2000, 2002), Lukka and Granlund (2000) and Carmona and Gutierrez (2003). The paper presents an analysis (quantitative and qualitative) of activity-based costing literature in French accounting journals. The results of Alcouffe's (2004) research show a volume dominance of the output of consulting and basic genres and their location primarily outside the academic research literature. The results of the literature research in France were different than in the United States and the United Kingdom, because they demonstrated that academics were not critical of ABC/ABM but instead they focused on the propagation of the idea (method).

The birth and development of the ABC/M concept greatly influenced academic and professional literature on management accounting. The number of ABC/M publications shows that not many concepts have raised comparable interest among practitioners and theoreticians so far. Numerous publications on management accounting, presenting the subject of ABC/M, undoubtedly popularized its concept knowledge among practitioners, consultants, researchers and students. The publications also shed some light on the problems with activity-based costing systems in companies and have spread the concepts based on activity-based costing in practice. It can be stated that publications on activity-based costing and activity-based management have greatly influenced the development of education, research and practice of management accounting equally in Poland and in the world. One can consider the literature as a chronological record of ABC/M development and its influence on companies' practices.

The majority of activity-based costing literature in developing countries was published during the last decade, so research on that phenomenon and comparative analysis of ABC literature in those countries and highly-developed countries has only been possible in recent years. The problem, like in other developing countries, is evident in Poland. Due to historical conditions, the development of the management accounting literature in Poland was less intense and delayed in comparison to highly-developed countries; the trend is also noticeable in the ABC literature.

So far, however, there has been no research in Poland aimed at creating evidence which could support and broaden studies of communication structures in management accounting research (Lukka, Granlund, 2000; Björnenak, Mitchell, 2000, 2002; Alcouffe, 2004). Additionally there is a clearly expressed need for the replication, extension and refinement of the studies on ABC diffusion which have been done so far in more developed countries. In the light of the presented facts, it is important to fill in the identified research gap i.e. to analyze journal literature on ABC/ABM accumulated in Poland during the last eighteen years since the first article on ABC emerged.

In the context of the ABC/M literature, the aim of the chapter was formulated – it aims to analyze existing Polish literature on ABC/M, especially its amount and structure, subject area and research methods, as well as to analyze the views presented by authors. In order to realize the aim of the study, the research has been divided into three parts. The first part presents the research method i.e. justification of the sample choice, justification of the variables choice, and presentation of the research hypothesis. The results of the research are presented in the second part i.e. the analysis of the distribution of publications over time, the views expressed by the authors, the research methods and the subject areas. The last part presents a short recapitulation and conclusions.

3.2. Characteristics of the research method

The research concerning Polish literature on the subject of ABC/M was based on a selected set of articles published in the key journals and cyclical publications on accounting. The following were excluded from the study:

- textbooks[3], specialist books[4], books which have been translated[5] (including even those which, to some degree, deal with the subject of ABC/M);
- published academic dissertations (including collections of articles or PhD theses and postdoctoral dissertations published by universities and colleges[6]);

---

[3] See e.g. Jaruga *et al.* (2001); Sobańska (2009).

[4] See e.g. Leszczyński, Wnuk-Pel (2004); Piechota (2005); Wnuk-Pel (2006c).

[5] See e.g. Kaplan, Cooper (2000); Miller (2000).

[6] To the authors' knowledge (source SYNABA), up to now in Poland three postdoctoral dissertations (Karmańska, 2001; Piosik, 2002; Mielcarek, 2008), and eight PhD theses on ABC/M have been written.

- specialist journals dealing with the area of accounting and taxes (e.g. *Monitor Księgowego, Rachunkowość Finansowa i Audyt, Serwis F-K* etc.);
- specialist journals not dealing with the area of accounting where some articles on ABC were published (e.g. *Gazeta Prawna, Businessman Magazine* etc.);
- daily papers (for example *Rzeczpospolita* where, in the time period considered, one would find a few popular science articles on activity-based costing and activity-based management).

The above-mentioned journals were excluded from the research as they do not deal with the subject of management accounting. Articles on ABC/M published in those journals were sporadic therefore their contribution to the development of ABC/M literature in Poland was minor. Exclusion of the books from the research is motivated by the fact that they are not published consistently but they appear at a certain moment in time (the majority of the book publications on ABC/M emerged in Poland between 2000 and 2003) therefore it is impossible to follow the track of changes in the issue of the presentation of ABC/M. From the research aim point of view, books have yet another drawback – the latest theoretical and practical issues are usually first presented in articles and subsequently in book publications.

It needs to be emphasized that the majority of writers whose literature has been excluded from the research are simultaneously authors of articles which are analyzed here, hence one can know their standpoint on the issue of ABC/M. It has been decided to limit the research to three main sources (see Table 3.1).

Table 3.1. Journals used in the research

Title	Profile	Time of research
Controlling i Rachunkowość Zarządcza (*Controlling and Management Accounting*)	Practice (management accounting)	1998–2011
Rachunkowość (*Accounting*)	Practice (accounting)	1994–2011
Zeszyty Teoretyczne Rachunkowości (*Theoretical Journal of Accounting*)	Theory (accounting)	1994–2011

Controlling and Management Accounting (CMA) has been included in the study since it is the sole journal in Poland on management accounting for practitioners. However, the journal was not published over the whole period of time analyzed in the research but between the years 1998 and 2011. Despite the fact that *Accounting* is mainly a journal dealing with the issue of financial accounting, it was chosen for the study because: (a) according to the author it is the most prestigious and opinion forming journal among accountants i.e. its publications reach a wide group of accountancy practitioners who hold high positions in their companies,

(b) it quite regularly publishes articles on management accounting and finance. *Theoretical Journal of Accounting* constitute the third periodical included in this research. This title deals in general with the subject area of accounting, yet the issue of management accounting is extremely important there. This research analyzed the typical editions (usually four) as well as some special issues published mainly because of annual, country-wide conferences of departments of accounting.

The time frame of the research has been set for the years 1994–2011. The beginning of the analyzed period of time is marked by the publication of an article dedicated to the concept of activity-based costing written by Jaruga and Szychta (1994) – it was the first article on that subject in Poland. September 2011 closes the period, as it was the latest possible date of collecting information for the research.

Four basic groups of variables have been used:
- variables characterizing a specific publication in terms of quantity;
- variables characterizing the author of the publication and his views;
- variables characterizing the research method;
- variables characterizing the subject area of the publications.

Bearning in mind the aims of the research, the specific variables were chosen; they were selected in order to reliably characterize the analysis of the literature on ABC/M in terms of content, structure and significance. The presentation and justification of the choice of individual variables follows below.

The quantitative characteristics of the publications in the researched period of time are the most evident area of the analysis. It will enable a general presentation of the literature on ABC/M from selected journals in terms of e.g. prevalence of certain subject areas. In the quantitative characteristics of the literature, the number of ABC/M publications in the given time period, in terms of individual journals and in general, will be presented. The simplest quantitative characteristic of the publications on ABC/M together with the other researched variables will make the analysis more extensive and will enable the identification of the possible trends.

Determining the author of the ABC/M publication is yet another research variable which allows one to identify the professional group being the most interested in the concept of ABC/M; it also enables the identification of the professional group which helped to spread the idea in Poland. In the management accounting research, usually three groups of professionals are distinguished: university researchers, consultants and practitioners.

The ratio between the enthusiasts and objectors to the ABC/M concept is another research variable used in the study. Authors' points of view have been grouped into three categories: (a) ABC/M enthusiasts, (b) its objectors, (c) neutral. The authors were allocated to individual categories on the basis of the content of the publication, the author's conclusions and evaluations as well as their opinions expressed in the literature. Enthusiasts of the ABC/M concept emphasize its technical advantage over conventional methods of cost calculation and economic impact resulting from the use of the new method. One can observe such opinion in the works of Cooper (1988a), Shank and Govindarajan (1988), Cooper and Kaplan (1991) or Dolinsky and Vollman (1991). Opposing expert opinion stating that the ABC/M concept is not new and that it is only a fashionable trend in management accounting can be found in publications by Horngren (1990), Staubus (1990) or Malmi (1997). The analysis of the publications in terms of positive and negative opinions towards the ABC/M concept will enable this author to determine whether Polish publications are enthusiastic or pessimistic about the method. The ratio between enthusiasts and objectors to the concept, bearing in mind the professional group they come from, might prove interesting. One might assume that consultants are advocates of the idea, whereas the academics should be more sceptical about the method.

The research method used is another variable which has been taken into account in this study; it helps to determine the way the information on the ABC/M concept is acquired. Classifications of the research methods are different yet they mainly agree[7]. The research methods in this study have been classified as follows:

• review (of literature, history etc.) – this type of research usually analyzes the literature to determine who writes about ABC/M, to determine the subject area, and the use of research methods (Björnenak, Mitchell, 2000; Lukka, Granlund, 2000);

• research (survey, questionnaire etc.) – this type of research concentrates on: (a) the analysis of the degree of prevalence the ABC/M method, (b) the analysis of the ABC/M systems' structure, (c) opinion examination among companies using ABC/M systems, (d) the analysis of positive implementations of ABC/M systems[8];

• case study – this research relies on an examination of individual companies, the reasons for their interest in the concept of ABC/M, a comparison between ABC/M and the system which had been previously used, an analysis of the consequences resulting from the ABC/M implementation which influence the decision-making process in the company or analysis of the factors behind the positive or negative implementations of the systems[9];

---

[7] In the research of accounting, different authors, depending on the subject of the analysis, use different classifications (see: Prather, Rueschoff, 1996; Shields, 1997).

[8] Examples of the analysis of the ABC/M diffusion degree, the analysis of the ABC/M systems' structure or the opinion examination among the companies which use the ABC/M system are e.g. Bescos, Mendoza (1995); Innes, Mitchell (1995). The issue of analysis of the positive implementations of ABC/M is treated in the works of Shields (1995) or Foster, Swenson (1997).

[9] In the case study research movement, one can distinguish two directions. The first one focused on the influence of ABC/M on the product cost, pricing policy, process and product design, make or buy decisions, and transfer prices. Examples of such works are: Foster, Gupta (1990); Kovac, Troy (1989); Spicer, (1992). The second direction of the research, in the form of case studies, addresses the problem of ABC/M in more detail and focuses on the factors which influence the process of

• descriptive research – it typically presents the general rules of the functioning of activity based costing or activity based management;

• analytical research (mathematical modeling) – the research is based on the mathematical analysis of the cost behavior as a reaction to the change of the activity drivers; the research aims to analyze systematically the cost behavior and to construct mathematical models used for forecasting cost behavior[10].

Distinguishing the above research categories will constitute the basis for the analysis of how different research methods have been used in time including the shift from descriptive research to survey research or case study analysis.

In order to explain the significance of Polish and international publications on ABC/M, an additional variable has been taken into consideration – the number of Polish and foreign publications listed in the bibliography of the researched articles.

The characteristics of the subject area of ABC/M publications provide further possibilities for analysis. An attempt to characterize the birth and the process of changes in ABC/M publications in Poland will be based on this analysis. In order to specify the subject area of publications on the issue of the ABC/M concept, a division into strictly activity-based costing publications (usually earlier ones) and publications extended by the activity-based management subject (usually published later) has been made. This evolution in the ABC/M publications has been observed in American and western literature since the late eighties, through the nineties until the beginning of the 21st century.

Another variable which has been taken into account in this research was the type of business sector. It has been decided not to distinguish the industries (e.g. telecommunications, construction etc.) but to make a distinction between production and services.

The third variable used in this research of the detailed subject areas was the type of process (e.g. logistics) where the concept of ABC/M could be used. According to Porter (1985) two groups of processes in a company can be distinguished i.e. main processes and supporting processes. In the group of the main processes Porter itemized: internal logistics, main business activity, external logistics, sales and marketing and post-sales service. However in the group of supporting processes he listed: infrastructure maintenance, human resources management, technological development and buying. For the purposes

---

ABC/M implementation in a positive or negative way. Examples of such works are: Gietzmann (1991); Cobb, Mitchell (1993); Cobb, Helliar, Innes (1995); Anderson (1995).

[10] Research in the form of a mathematical modelling is typically theoretical, though it is possible to find some research based on empirical material. Journals constitute the majority of such literature: *The Accounting Review, Journal of Accounting and Economics, Journal of Accounting Research* or *Journal of Management Accounting Research*. Examples of this type of research are e.g. Noreen (1991); Foster, Gupta (1990); Babad, Balachandran (1993); Datar, Gupta (1994); Dillon, Nash (1978); Zimmermann (1979); Lere (1986).

of this research, Porter's list has been modified and the following processes or their groups were distinguished:

- main activity process (e.g. manufacturing goods or providing services);
- logistics process (internal and external);
- sales and marketing process;
- remaining processes (post-sale process, infrastructure maintenance, human resources management, technological development and buying).

The connection between ABC/M and other concepts and tools of management accounting constitute another variable[11]. These type of publications typically appear later than the first activity-based costing publications and usually later than the ABM literature. This relation displays a wider perspective in which one can observe the possibilities resulting from using all the innovative management accounting concepts i.e. ABM.

A detailed characteristic of the subject areas of ABC/M publications will provide answers to such questions as: (a) are the publications' subject areas only restricted to ABC or do they treat the issue with a wider perspective?, (b) what sectors and processes do they apply to?, (c) are other innovative concepts and tools of management accounting linked to the concept of ABC/M? The characteristics of the subject area will enable further analyses e.g. the connection between the subject and author's affiliation and placing it in time. In turn, it may lead to interesting findings about the evolution of the publications as well as authors' and readers' interests and knowledge.

Five hypotheses have been suggested in order to analyze the quantity and structure, subject areas, research methods and authors' views contained in the Polish publications on ABC/M between the years 1994 and 2011.

Due to historical conditions, the development of management accounting in Poland was less intense and delayed in comparison to the theory and practice in highly-developed countries; the trend is also noticeable in the ABC/M literature. Hypothesis 1 – The development of ABC/M literature in Poland is considerably delayed in comparison to the publications from United States, Great Britain and other highly-developed countries.

The studies conducted in the United States, the United Kingdom and in France (Lukka, Granlund, 2000; Björnenak, Mitchell, 2000; Alcouffe, 2004) claim that vast majority of ABC/M articles are published in journals for practitioners. The notion is also evident in Poland. Hypothesis 2 – There are more publications on the ABC/M concept in journals for practitioners than in university publications, and the authors of those publications are mainly university researchers.

---

[11] Björnenak and Mitchell (2000) have researched the link between the ABC/M publications in professional British and American journals with such concepts and tools of management accounting as the theory of constraints, continuous improvement, global quality control, just in time, business process reengineering, economic value added, transfer pricing, product life cycle management, financial reporting, environmental accounting, product attributes, zero based budgeting, functional analysis, benchmarking, capital budgeting, and target costing.

The author's viewpoint on the concept of ABC/M may depend on his professional interests. There exists a confirmed hypothesis, which has been presented in numerous articles, that a for or against attitude towards the ABC/M concept is strictly related to one of the professional groups the author represents – academic researchers, consultants or practitioners[12]. It has been proved that university researchers were sceptical about the ABC/M concept, consultants appeared to be boundless enthusiasts and practitioners' opinions seemed moderate. This research formulates the hypothesis that the views presented by academic researchers, consultants and practitioners will not be diverse to such an extent. Hypothesis 3 – The percentage of the ABC/M enthusiasts among consultants is close to the highest possible level, yet the ratio among practitioners and university researchers is only slightly lower.

As already mentioned, due to the delays in familiarity and application of the modern management accounting methods in Poland, the research concerning this issue is simultaneously less advanced. The notion also applies to the research methods in use. Hypothesis 4 – Among the research methods used in the publications, it is more common to encounter descriptive works, surveys and case studies than literature reviews and analytical papers.

In accordance with world trends, the subject area of publications on the concept of ABC/M also evolved in Poland. The last research hypothesis claims that the direction of changes in Poland was similar to the world tendencies. Hypothesis 5 – The subject area of the publications evolved from activity-based costing in production companies and only in the main area of activity, into ABM in production and service companies in the main and supporting processes with reference to other concepts and tools of management accounting.

3.3. Analysis of the research findings

3.3.1. Quantitative characteristics of the publications

The study shows that the number of ABC/M publications in the researched time was so high that each reader of the analyzed journals must have come across them (see Figure 3.1). After the initial stage, when the ABC/M publications were sporadic (1994–1998), a noticeable increase in their number can be observed. It was mainly related to the birth of the first, and so far the only, Polish journal fully dealing with the issue of management accounting – the monthly *Controlling and Management Accounting* (CMA). In Poland, as well as in the United States and United Kingdom, the majority of publications on ABC/M appeared in a specialist

---

[12] The notion about the role of consultants and consulting companies in the process of ABC/M publicizing is presented by e.g. Macintosh (1998) and Noreen (1987).

journal for practitioners, a journal dealing with the subject of management accounting (CMA). In general, in the time given, 145 articles on ABC/M were published; 112 of them (77.3%) appeared in *Controlling and Management Accounting*, 5 of them (3.4%) were published in *Accounting* and 28 of them (19.3%) in *Theoretical Journal of Accounting* (TJA). Over the years 1999–2009, the number of publications on ABC/M has been stable, somewhere in the 8–16 bracket annually, from the year 2010 it dropped.

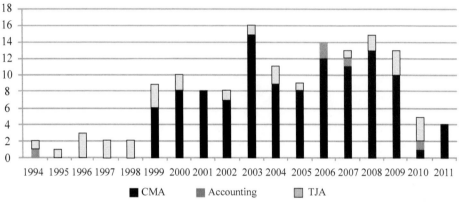

Figure 3.1. Publications on ABC/M

On the basis of the conducted research, one may distinguish certain differences in the time arrangement of the ABC/M publications in Poland and in such countries as the United State or Great Britain (Gosselin, 2007):

• the first publications on the concept of ABC/M appeared in the *United States* and Great Britain in 1988, and in Poland six years later i.e. in 1994;

• in the United States and the United Kingdom, the majority of publications on ABC/M appeared between 1993 and 1997 (the number of publications was up to 170–190 per year), whereas in Poland the noticeable increase in the number of publications was evident six years later in 1999;

• similar to the United States and the United Kingdom, where after the increase period (1993–1997) a significant fall in the number of publications could be observed (70–90 publications in 2000), Poland also witnessed the phenomenon and the number of publications dropped from the year 2010.

3.3.2. Characteristics of the authors of the publications

The analysis shows that ABC/M publications are mainly written by academic researchers. The percentage of their works reaches annually 55.9%, whereas, in the case of consultants, the percentage equals 31% and in the case of practitioners

13.1%. The arrangement of publications in time (see Figure 3.2) shows that during the first five-year period (1994–1998) only academic researchers published papers on the ABC/M concept; in the following years they also constituted the largest professional group among authors. Publications by consultants appeared in 1999 and became a large part of publications with the special year 2007 when they comprised the majority. Excluding 2000 when only one publication by practitioners appeared, their works started to be published more regularly commencing from 2003, but more often from 2006. The analysis of the authors of the publications in the time given, shows that consultants, but mainly practitioners, started writing about the concept of ABC/M later which stands in opposition to the American and British trends. Research conducted by Björnenak and Mitchell (2000) proved that publications by consultants and practitioners started to appear in 1988 and from that time they constituted a substantial percentage of all publications on ABC/M.

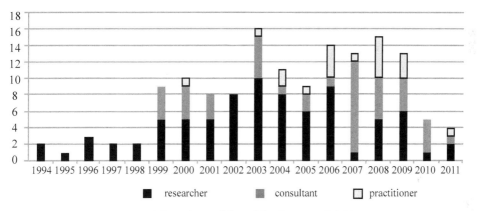

Figure 3.2. Authors of the publications on ABC/M

Publications by consultants have recently become a very important source of information about the new management accounting concepts especially about ABC/M. The tendency stems from the fact that consulting companies, which specialize in the area of management accounting, have gained importance and they have also become means of promoting the development of management accounting practices (Granlund, Lukka, 1998). Such companies often treat magazines as a way of advertising their services[13]. The publications by consultants are seen as means of promotion and advertising of a certain consulting company's services rather than

---

[13] Macintosh (1998) presents quite an extreme opinion that the advertisements of consulting companies are the main reason behind the popularity of ABC/M. A similar view is expressed by Noreen (1987) who claims that one can read the ABC/M publications as if they were 'advertisements of consulting companies'.

means of promotion of the new management accounting tools and concepts. In order to address practitioners, who constitute the most important group of readers, these type of publications characterizes a simplified approach towards the subject area. The research methods presented in those publications are not their strongest advantage; the publications also lack critical arguments and appropriate empirical evidence. The publications by consultants express their professional and practical interests in the subject of ABC/M, therefore one may expect that their works will only emphasize the positive aspects and implementation successes, neglecting the possible problems and failures in certain implementation processes. Despite the tendentiousness of the publications, it is worth stressing that if it had not been for the consultants' papers and works, academic researchers would not have had many new concepts to investigate (Lukka, Granlund, 2000).

Publications on the subject of ABC/M by practitioners are rare. It probably results from the fact that people who are controllers or management accounting experts in companies are busy, and secondly, they are disinclined to disclose the solutions which make their companies more competitive (especially the detailed information, potential problems and ways of avoiding them and results of implementations). On the other hand, those scarce publications by practitioners stress their personal successes and present the company's achievements. Despite the very few publications by practitioners, the concept of ABC/M was developed by practitioners themselves, before it was widely presented by Cooper and Kaplan (1988a, b; Cooper, 1985) in the *Harvard Business Review*. Due to the previously presented restrictions (lack of time and reluctance to disclose the sources of competitive advantage), the contribution of practitioners' publications to the development of ABC concept may be underestimated in the research.

One may agree with the opinion of Bromwich (1998) that recently all the new concepts of accounting (including management accounting) come from practitioners and consultants. Undoubtedly, academic researchers come up with a smaller number of new ideas and concepts, although Lukka and Shields (1999) draw our attention to the fact that more and more university researchers participate in the process of designing and implementing the latest management accounting innovations.

The conducted research helped to draw attention to the fact that the percentage of academic researchers, consultants and practitioners publishing in individual magazines was diverse (see Table 3.2). As anticipated, the largest percentage of consultants and practitioners write for the journal aimed at practitioners (*Controlling and Management Accounting*), whereas the publications from the journal aimed at the academic community (*Theoretical Journal of Accounting*) were almost exclusively authored by university researchers. It should be stressed that the percentage of publications by consultants and practitioners in *Controlling and Management Accounting* exceeded 50%, similar to the American and British journals dedicated to the area of management accounting (45%)[14].

Table 3.2. Authors of ABC/M publications in individual journals

Specification	CMA		Accounting		TJA		Overall	
	n	%	n	%	n	%	n	%
Researcher	55	49.1	3	60.0	22	91.7	80	56.7
Consultant	38	33.9	2	40.0	2	8.3	42	29.8
Practitioner	19	17.0		0.0		0.0	19	13.5
Overall	112	100.0	5	100.0	24	100.0	141	100.0

Additional and detailed analysis proved that publications in individual journals were substantially diverse in terms of length. The articles published in *Controlling and Management Accounting* and in *Accounting* were rather short (respectively 4.9 and 6.6 pages long) whereas publications from *Theoretical Journal of Accounting* were significantly longer (the average length reached 16 pages), which might imply their more thorough character.

Table 3.3. Examples of opinions expressed by the ABC/M enthusiasts, and those who were neutral

Enthusiasts	Neutral
• "A modern concept of cost control may enable improvement in hospitals' performance […], activity-based budgeting is a concept which will help to improve cost management in hospitals" (Kludacz, 2006, pp. 48–50) • "Activity-based costing eliminates all the defects of conventional accounting systems in terms of correct cost calculation and customer and product profitability; it is managerial cost accounting which logically helps to support management of budgeting processes in a company" (Zieliński, 2007, p. 36) • "The use of activity-based costing will enable the correct calculation of actual costs instead of calculating them through arbitrary allocation of overheads" (Ozgowicz, 2008, pp. 4–5) • "Activity-based costing […] helps to correctly allocate costs to certain objects which need different activity inputs" (Ossowski, 2009, p. 28)	• "Accountants cast some doubt on the efficiency of the activity-based costing, activity-based costing was too complicated […], there were difficulties in forecasting and forecast evaluation […], activity-based costing does not overcome problems connected with the inefficiency of the current registration systems and cost calculation" (Ohl, 1995, pp. 113–114) • "The method is used in cases when the cost units do not change, primarily in multi-series and mass production" (Polak, 2003, p. 41) • "Activity-based costing is difficult to maintain, update and extend […], it is extensively static so its utility is restricted in companies working in a dynamic and changeable environment" (Przytuła, 2007, p. 27) • "Activity-based costing needs large financial expenses, time and labour […], the use of ABC is not always necessary" (Widera, 2008, pp. 19–20)

---

[14] See: Björnenak, Mitchell (2000).

The research revealed that an overwhelming majority of the authors were ABC/M enthusiasts (similar to France, see Alcouffe, 2004). Having analyzed 145 publications, 139 of their authors were activity-based costing and activity-based management enthusiasts and only 6 of them remained neutral in their views. None of the analyzed writers expressed a firm critical opinion. The profession of the authors did not influence their approach towards the ABC/M issue, yet practitioners, in 100% of cases, turned out to be ABC/M enthusiasts (probably because they had implemented the ABC/M system in their own companies). Examples of opinions expressed by the ABC/M enthusiasts, and those who were neutral, are presented in Table 3.3.

3.3.3. Research method used in the publications

The analysis proved that different research methods i.e. descriptive works, literature reviews, analytical works, surveys and case studies, have been used in the publications on ABC/M (see Figure 3.3). The methods were implemented in different manners. Descriptive works, presenting the general rules behind activity-based costing and activity-based management, were the most common (98 articles, 67.6%). The second method most commonly used, especially from 2006, was case studies (32 articles, 22.1%). The first survey research on the subject of ABC/M appeared in 2002. Over the following years, approximately every second year, from one to three articles using this method were published. Generally, this research method has been used 11 times which constitutes 7.6% of all the publications. Publications in the form of a literature review and analytical work were published sporadically – respectively three times and once. The study shows that there is a similarity between the use of research methods in Poland and in the United States and the United Kingdom – in all the countries methods such as surveys and case studies were implemented in a later period (Björnenak, Mitchell, 2000).

The analysis of research methods used in the publications may be difficult due to the fact that exact determining of the research method in the journals for practitioners (especially *Controlling and Management Accounting*) was sometimes difficult. Additionally, articles from *Theoretical Journal of Accounting* were analyzed. Their more theoretical and formal character (the process of reviews) helped to determine the research method in a more precise manner.

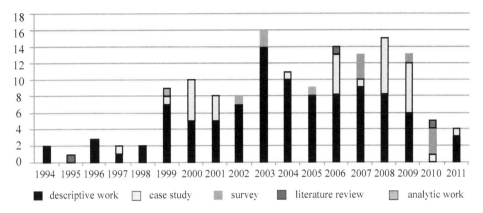

Figure 3.3. ABC/M research methods

The percentage of the research methods used in the publications is displayed below:

- descriptive (17 articles, 60.7%);
- literature review (2 articles, 7.1%);
- analytical (1 article, 3.6%);
- survey (3 articles, 10.7%);
- case study (5 articles, 17.9%).

The study showed substantial differences in bibliography references, depending on the type of journal and the author's affiliation. As one might expect, the biggest number of bibliography references (20 on average, 6.8 national and 13.2 foreign) was found in the articles published in *Theoretical Journal of Accounting*. In *Controlling and Management Accounting* and *Accounting*, the number of bibliography references was respectively 2.4 and 4. Regardless of the type of journal, the largest number of bibliography references prevailed in the articles by academic researchers (7), and the least number in the works by consultants and practitioners (2).

The publications by academic researchers seem better in terms of methodology and arguments which support the presented theses. The publications are also more objective, as their authors are not pressured to present views compliant with the character of their working environment (unlike consultants). Yet it needs to be emphasized that at least some part of university researchers who publish ABC/M articles are simultaneously consultants. Thus it may lead to a conflict of interests and it burdens their publications with problems specific to the work of consultants.

3.3.4. Subject area of the publications

One of the most interesting phenomena of the ABC/M diffusion is the fact that there are substantially more and more publications which fall outside activity-based costing (ABC) and focus more on activity-based management (ABM). In the researched articles, 71.7% was devoted to ABC and 28.3% to ABM (see Table 3.4). Interestingly, the area of ABM was presented more often in *Controlling and Management Accounting* (33.9% of publications) rather than in *Theoretical Journal of Accounting* (7.1%).

Table 3.4. Subject area of ABC/M publications, depending on the journal

Specification	CMA		Accounting		TJA		Overall	
Problem	n	%	n	%	n	%	n	%
ABC	74	66.1	4	80.0	26	92.9	104	71.7
ABM	38	33.9	1	20.0	2	7.1	41	28.3
Overall	112	100.0	5	100.0	28	100.0	145	100.0

The diffusion of activity-based costing and activity-based management can be observed in their spreading across various fields of business activity as well as processes realized by companies. Bearing in mind the distinction of companies into production and service firms (see Figure 3.4), the ABC/M concept, in the early years (1994–1999) was almost exclusively presented in the context of production companies, whereas later (2000–2009) a large number of publications were devoted to companies offering services. A similar pattern i.e. writing about production companies in the first stage and later about services companies (both private and public sectors), can be observed in the analysis of American and British publications (Björnenak, Mitchell, 2000).

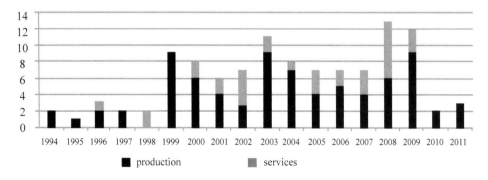

Figure 3.4. ABC/M publications in the context of production and service companies

A detailed analysis proved that the subject of ABC/M, in terms of production companies, was more often covered in the journals for practitioners (32.1% of publications) rather than in *Theoretical Journal of Accounting* (19.2% of publications).

In terms of processes realized in companies, it is worth noting that from the beginning (1994) the ABC/M publications related to all the significant processes realized, starting from main processes through logistics, sales and marketing and ending with other remaining processes (see Figure 3.5). The analysis showed that the publications frequently did not focus on only one process but presented ABC/M in the context of a few processes, often in the context of all the processes realized in companies. A detailed anlysis proved that the ABC/M subject in the context of various processes was presented in journals for practitioners (*Controlling and Management Accounting, Accounting*) and in *Theoretical Journal of Accounting* with similar frequency. An analysis of publications from the United States and the United Kingdom resulted in different findings (Björnenak, Mitchell, 2000); it showed that the issue of ABC/M in the context of many processes and management functions was mainly discussed in articles from journals on management accounting and aimed at to practitioners.

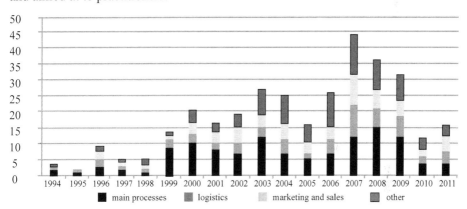

Figure 3.5. ABC/M publications in the context of processes

The study helps to form the statement that, over time, the growing number of ABC publications was accopmanied by a rise in the number of articles on ABM. Between 1994–1999 there were no publications on ABM but between 2000–2002, their number almost equaled the number of ABC publications and later between 2003–2011 it dropped in relation to ABC publications. It should be stressed here that the growth in the number of publications about ABC and ABM was accompanied by the growth in the number of references of ABC/M to other management accounting tools e.g. budgeting, transfer pricing etc. The vast number of references to other management accounting methods indicates an innovative manner of ABC and ABM applications as well as enthusiasm for the use of the methods (see Figure 3.6).

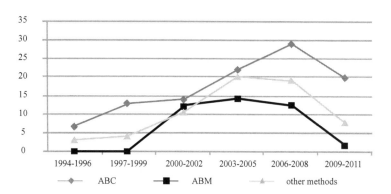

Figure 3.6. Diffusion of ABC and ABM and connections with other management accounting techniques and tools

A detailed analysis of ABC/M connections in the researched publications revealed that the references to other tools of management accounting are more frequent in *Controlling and Management Accounting* (51.9% of articles contain such references) than in *Theoretical Journal of Accounting* (29.2% of articles relate to other tools). Academic researchers more often refer to other methods of management accounting. Such references are evident in 51.3% of their articles whereas the percentage of publications by consultants and practitioners is 39.3%.

3.4. Summary and conclusions

ABC/M is undoubtedly one of the most important innovations in the field of management accounting in the 20th century. A diffusion of activity-based costing and activity-based management was observed in practice in many countries, including Poland. In order to understand better the process of ABC/M diffusion, 145 articles published in three Polish journals (*Controlling and Management Accounting, Accounting, Theoretical Journal of Accounting*) between 1994–2011 have been analyzed. On the basis of the research carried out, bearing in mind the hypotheses formulated at the beginning of the study, the following conclusions can be drawn:

1. The emergence and the significant rise in the number of ABC/M publications in Poland is approximately 6 years delayed in comparison to American or British publications. Like the United States or the United Kingdom, the number of ABC/M publications in Poland, after the growth phase (8–16 articles a year between 1999–2009), dropped from the year 2010.

2. In Poland, similar to the United States, the United Kingdom and France, the largest number of ABC/M publications appeared in specialist magazines for practitioners (80.7%) but they were mainly authored by academic researchers (55.9%).

3. The overwhelming majority of the authors can be described as enthusiasts of ABC/M (95.9%). None of the articles was written by ABC/M objectors and only 6 authors remain neutral. The author's approach to the issue of ABC/M is not influenced by the fact that they are academic researchers or consultants (practitioners were enthusiasts in 100% of cases). In this respect the research has similar results as the research in France (Alcouffe, 2004).

4. Descriptive works prevail among the research methods (67.6%), with case studies in second place (22.1%). Research in the form of surveys, literature reviews or analytical works are sporadic.

5. The growing number of ABC publications was accompanied by the growth in the number of ABM publications as well as references and connections with other tools of management accounting. The huge number of connections with other methods of management accounting indicates, the innovative character of the concept and manifests enthusiasm for it.

As in developing countries the majority of ABC/M literature was published during the last decade, so research on that phenomenon and comparative analysis of ABC literature in those countries and the highly developed countries was only possible in the last few years. In Poland due to historical conditions, the development of management accounting literature and especially ABC/M literature was less intense and delayed in comparison to the United States, the United Kingdom or France. As there has not been any research so far in Poland aiming to analyze ABC/M literature, the study attempted to fill in the identified research gap i.e. to analyze journal literature on ABC/ABM accumulated in Poland during the last seventeen years since the first article on ABC emerged. These research results support and broaden the studies of the communication structure in management accounting research (Björnenak, Mitchell, 2000, 2002; Lukka, Granlund, 2002; Carmona, Gutierrez, 2003; Alcouffe, 2004). It may be continued so as to examine the diffusion of different innovative methods of management accounting in Poland e.g. balanced scorecard, target costing etc.

CHAPTER 4

DIFFUSION AND USE OF ACTIVITY-BASED COSTING IN POLAND IN THE LIGHT OF QUESTIONNAIRE RESEARCH

4.1. Introduction

At the turn of the 20th and the 21st centuries research into activity-based costing became extremely popular. As empirical studies reveal – the diffusion of ABC in companies in different countries varies significantly. On the one hand, the research is descriptive and shows degree of the diffusion as well as the characteristic features of ABC systems in practice in the different countries. On the other hand, empirical research concentrates on the influence of such factors as company size, cost structure, competitive strategy or level of competiveness on the implementation, shape, functioning and use of activity-based costing systems.

However, most of the empirical research investigated the percentage of companies in different countries which: use activity-based costing, consider its implementation in the future, rejected activity-based costing implementation after analyzing its pros and cons, or never thought of implementing ABC system. Table 4.1 presents the results of the key research into the diffusion of ABC carried out both in developed countries (the United States, Canada, Australia, New Zealand, Great Britain, Ireland, Norway, Sweden, Finland, Germany, France, Italy) and in developing countries (China, India, Saudi Arabia, the Czech Republic and Slovakia).

Table 4.1. Comparison of results of questionnaire research into activity-based costing use

Research	Companies (in %)			
	using ABC	considering implementation of ABC	which rejected ABC implementation	which never considered ABC implementation
US				
NAA (1991)[a]	11.0	19.0	–	70.0
IMA (1993)	36.0	14.0	–	50.0
IMA (1995)	41.0	24.0	–	35.0
IMA (1996)	49.0	–	–	–
IMA (1997)	39.0	–	–	–
Grott (1999)[b]	17.0	–	–	–
Ho, Kidwell (2000)[c]	50.0[d]	15.0[e]	–	–
Kianni, Sangeladij (2003)	11.8	40.0[f]	0.0	48.2
Lawson (2005)[g]	14.0	–	–	–
Kennett et al. (2007)	16.0	24.0[h]	–	–
Canada				
Armitage, Nicholson (1993)	14.0	15.0	4.0	67.0
Gosselin (1997)	30.4	–	–	–
Bescos et al. (2002)	23.1	9.3	13.9	53.7
Australia				
Clarke et al. (1997)[i]	10.0	–	–	–
Askarany, Yazdifar (2007)[j]	14.0	11.0	–	–
Askarany, Yazdifar (2007)	28.0[k]	21.0	13.0	38.0
Baird et al. (2004)	41.9	–	–	–
New Zealand				
Love, Brader (1994)	17.0	21.0	–	–
Hoque (2000)	41.0	–	–	–
Cotton et al. (2003)	20.3	11.1	10.8	42.2
Great Britain				
Innes, Mitchell (1991)	6.0[l]	33.0	9.0	52.0
Davies, Sweeting (1991)	60.0[m]		–	–
Nicholls (1992)	10.0	18.0[n]	–	62.0
Bright et al. (1992)	32.0	62.0	–	–
Drury, Tyles (1994)	4.0	46.0[o]	5.0	45.0
Innes, Mitchell (1995)	21.0	29.6	13.3	36.1
Innes, Mitchell (1997)	54.0[p]	–	–	–

Table 4.1 (cont.)

Research	Companies (in %)			
	using ABC	considering implementation of ABC	which rejected ABC implementation	which never considered ABC implementation
Innes *et al.* (2000)	17.5	20.3	15.3	46.9
Kennedy, Affleck- -Grave (2001)	20.1	–	–	–
Al-Omiri, Drury (2007)	15.0	–	–	–
Ireland				
Clarke *et al.* (1999)	11.8	20.6	12.7	54.9
Clarke, Mullins (2001)	19.0	13.0	5.0	63.0
Pierce (2004)	27.9	9.0	10.7	52.4
Norway				
Björnenak (1997)	56.6^r	–	20.8	22.6
Sweden				
Ask, Ax (1992)	23.0^s	–	–	–
Finland				
Lukka, Granlund (1996)	5.0^t	25.0	–	–
Laitinen (1999)	15.0	–	–	–
Kallunki, Silvola (2008)	28.0	–	–	–
Germany				
Hauer (1994)	3.2	–	–	–
Horvath *et al.* (1998)	46.6	14.2	–	39.2
France				
Bescos *et al.* (2002)	23.0	22.9	11.9	42.2
Italy				
Cinquini *et al.* (1999)	10.7	31.0^u	11.9	46.4
Cinquini *et al.* (2008)	17.9	23.9^w	20.2	38.0
China				
Firth (1996)	17.2	–	–	–
Nanjing (2001)	9.0	–	–	–
Chow *et al.* (2007)	52.2	–	–	–
Parkinson (2009)	29.4	–	–	–
India				
Anderson, Lanen (1999)	0.0	–	–	–
Joshi (2001)	20.0	–	–	–
Anand *et al.* (2005)	28.3	–	–	–
Saudi Arabia				
Khalid (2005)	33.3	7.7	23.0	35.9

Table 4.1 (cont.)

Research	Companies (in %)			
	using ABC	considering implementation of ABC	which rejected ABC implementation	which never considered ABC implementation
The Czech Republic and Slovakia				
Novák (2009)[y]	5.0	–	–	–
Novák (2009)	6.0	–	–	–

[a] Research of NAA from 1991, as well as all the following IMA research was conducted among the members of NAA and IMA.

[b] The research investigated only companies operating in the food industry.

[c] The research by Ho and Kidwell (2000), as well as the later one by Kennett et al. (2007), were carried out on a sample of large cities.

[d] Among the companies, 20% used ABC globally, and 80% used it at least in one area of their operation.

[e] Those were the companies which considered ABC implementation.

[f] The research embraced companies which had already begun the process of activity-based costing implementation.

[g] The research by Lawson (2005) involved companies operating in the healthcare sector.

[h] Among the companies, one-third were planning implementation and two-thirds were considering implementation in the future.

[i] The research was carried out in 1991.

[j] The research was conducted in 1997.

[k] Two-thirds of the companies used activity-based costing on a daily basis and one-third used it from time to time.

[l] In the research by Innes and Mitchell, this category embraced both companies which were implementing ABC and those which were supposed to implement it soon.

[m] Those were the companies which used activity-based costing as well as those which planned its implementation within the next three years.

[n] Those were the companies which experimented with ABC implementation.

[o] In Drury and Tyles' research, this category embraced both companies that were planning to implement ABC (9%) and those which were considering ABC implementation (37%).

[p] This research was conducted on a sample of the biggest financial institutions.

[r] Companies which were implementing ABC but also firms which intended to implement ABC were listed among companies that were using activity-based costing.

[s] Those were the companies which were planning activity-based costing implementation.

[t] Those were the firms, which during the research, were implementing activity-based costing.

[u] Companies which were planning implementation and those which considered it were listed here.

[w] Companies which were planning implementation and those which considered it were listed here.

[y] The research was carried out in 2007.

The analysis of the empirical research which is presented in Table 4.1 helps to notice that the early research on activity-based costing investigating its diffusion in the early 1990s indicated a great interest in ABC among managers in most of the highly-developed countries (NAA, 1991; Innes, Mitchell, 1991; Davies, Sweeting, 1991; Ask, Ax, 1992; Nicholls, 1992; Bright *et al.*, 1992; IMA, 1993; Drury, Tyles, 1994; Hauer, 1994; Love, Brader, 1994; IMA, 1995; Innes, Mitchell, 1995; Armitage, Nicholson, 1993). However, the percentage of companies which implemented and used activity-based costing was relatively low at that time. Some of the researched companies were implementing ABC, while relatively a larger group of companies was planning or intending to consider implementation.

Research carried out in the late 1990s showed that activity-based costing was used in a larger group of companies (IMA, 1996; Lukka, Granlund, 1996; Björnenak, 1997; Clarke *et al.*, 1997; Gosselin, 1997; IMA, 1997; Innes, Mitchell, 1997; Horvath *et al.*, 1998; Cinquini *et al.*, 1999; Clarke *et al.*, 1999; Grott, 1999; Laitinen, 1999; Ho, Kidwell, 2000; Hoque, 2000; Innes *et al.*, 2000). What seems significant is that, more and more companies were planning implementation or were considering activity-based costing implementation. On the other hand, the cases of abandoning ABC implementation after analyzing the costs and benefits or rare cases of abandoning ABC after its implementation and use for some time were evident. Despite the fact that the percentage of companies using activity-based costing or companies interested in its future implementation was higher than a few years earlier, the diffusion rate of the new system was lower than expected. Interestingly, the tendency was noted at a time when a record number of articles on activity-based costing was published and when the issue of ABC was included in the leading academic textbooks, university curriculums and vocational courses for management accounting specialists, and when consulting and computer companies competed in the promotion of the new system. The phenomenon was called the ABC-paradox.

The research into activity-based costing diffusion which was carried out in highly-developed countries in the first decade of the 21st century revealed that the percentage of companies using ABC was not growing and it remained at an average level, lower than anticipated (Clarke, Mullins, 2001; Kennedy, Affleck-Graves, 2001; Bescos *et al.*, 2002; Cotton *et al.*, 2003; Kianni, Sangeladij, 2003; Baird *et al.*, 2004; Pierce, 2004; Lawson, 2005; Al-Omiri, Drury, 2007; Askarany, Yazdifar, 2007; Kennett *et al.*, 2007; Cinquini *et al.*, 2008; Kallunki, Silvola, 2008). Moreover, the percentage of companies planning activity-based costing implementation or thinking about it in the future fell whereas the number of firms abandoning the implementation after analyzing its costs and benefits rose.

Analyzing the results of questionnaire research, it should be stressed that the results differ significantly. The percentage of companies using activity-based costing varies from zero to several dozen percent, and may stem from the following:

• the inadequacy of ABC in some companies – the adoption of ABC in many companies may not provide significantly better results than a traditional cost accounting systems in areas such as: saving time, labor input, implementability (people making decisions about ABC implementation are not convinced whether this method is better than traditional techniques). Such an interpretation complies with Chenhall and Langfield-Smith's conclusions which suggest that benefits resulting from the implementation of modern methods of management accounting still do not surpass the benefits resulting from implementation of traditional methods. Such an interpretation also explains the behavior of companies which began implementation of an innovation however at some point ceased it (Innes, Mitchell, 1991);

  • different understanding of ABC – the results of all the research into diffusion of activity-based costing should be analyzed carefully because there is not any single and commonly accepted, definition of ABC either in theory or in practice. Gosselin (1997) and Baird et al. (2004) emphasize that respondents are not exactly sure of what activity-based costing really is. The conclusions are also mirrored in the research of companies using ABC – the research proves that activity-based costing systems functioning in those companies are significantly different (Gosselin, 2007);

  • the level of management accounting development – in general, in countries which are economically more developed, the use of management accounting methods is higher than in countries which are less developed or are still developing;

  • sampling method – the studies into diffusion of activity-based costing were carried out both among large and small companies, manufacturing and non-manufacturing companies, financial institutions etc.;

  • time of collecting information – in general, earlier studies show a significantly smaller percentage of companies using ABC. In all the countries where the research on the diffusion of activity-based costing was carried out, the percentage of companies using ABC was increased until the end of the 20th century and it later stabilized in the first decade of the 21st century.

In general, the presented research into the diffusion of activity-based costing may overestimate the percentage of companies using ABC because there was a smaller percentage of answers among companies which did not use ABC. Companies that do not adopt activity-based costing more often tend not to respond to survey research in comparison to companies using activity-based costing. The overestimated percentage of companies using ABC may also stem from the fact that the majority of the research was carried out among management accounting specialists – their perception of ABC might vary from the one expressed by other managers.

The situation was different in developing countries. In the 1990s, cases of activity-based costing implementation in those countries were incidental and apart from a few exceptions (e.g. Firth, 1996; Anderson, Lanen, 1999), no research on the diffusion of ABC was carried out there. The interest in activity-based costing in developing countries increased at the beginning of the 21st century when cases of ABC implementation became more frequent and, therefore, studies of ABC diffusion in companies operating in the countries started to emerge (Nanjing, 2001; Joshi, 2001; Anand et al., 2005; Khalid, 2005; Chow et al., 2007; Novák,

2009; Parkinson, 2009). Unlike in highly developed countries, where the interest in activity-based costing decreased and the percentage of companies with functioning ABC stopped to growing (some studies stated that the percentage fell), in developing countries companies implemented activity-based costing more often. Yet, it needs to be stressed that the percentage of companies using ABC in developing countries (including Poland) is significantly lower than in companies operating in more developed countries.

The first study which proved that ABC was present in the practice of Polish companies was conducted by Sobańska and Wnuk (2000). Other research carried out by different researchers revealed rare cases of activity-based costing use or its elements (Jarugowa, Skowroński, 1994; Szychta, 2001, 2002; Karmańska, 2003; Januszewski, Gierusz, 2004; Januszewski, 2005[1]; Wnuk-Pel, 2006a; Szychta, 2006, 2007a). Sometimes, the studies signalized that the researched companies were implementing or were considering implementation of ABC (Dyhdalewicz, 2000, 2001; Szychta, 2001, 2002; Karmańska, 2003; Januszewski, Gierusz, 2004; Januszewski, 2005; Szychta, 2006, 2007a). The studies carried out quite often proved that not even a single company used activity-based costing or was planning its implementation, however those were the findings of some earlier research (Kinast, 1993; Sobańska, Szychta, 1995, 1996; Gierusz et al., 1996; Radek, Schwarz, 2000; Szadziewska, 2002, 2003). The summary of the previous research investigating the diffusion of ABC in Polish companies is presented in table 4.2.

More detailed studies on the popularity of activity-based costing in Poland were carried out by Karmańska (2003), Januszewski and Gierusz (2004; Januszewski, 2005) and Wnuk-Pel (2006a). These studies explored, among other, the knowledge of ABC concepts, the perceived benefits of ABC adoption, the problems anticipated by companies considering ABC implementation, the reasons for rejecting this system, and the problems which occurred in the implementation process.

The study by Karmańska (2003), in the form of a survey, examined a sample of 342 companies to find out the level of knowledge of activity-based costing among Polish managers. Nearly half of the respondents (48%) reported fairly good or limited understanding of the concept of ABC (only 20% declared very good knowledge). The rest of the respondents (52%) admitted never having heard of it or having heard but knowing nothing about it. These findings are consistent with the results of a survey of 101 large companies in northern Poland, conducted by Gierusz and Januszewski (2004; Januszewski, 2005): 44% of the interviewees declared good or very good knowledge of activity-based costing, 47% said to have only some vague information about it, and 9% – to have never heard of it. Gierusz and Januszewski also found that familiarity with the concept of ABC is much greater among managers in companies with foreign capital and privatised companies rather than in private companies with Polish capital.

---

[1] See Januszewski (2004a, b).

Table 4.2. Diffusion of activity-based costing in Poland based on the previous research

Authors	Research method	Number of companies studied	Companies			
			using ABC	using elements of ABC	implementing ABC	considering implementation of ABC
Kinast (1993)	Case Studies	9	0	–	–	–
Jarugowa, Skowroński (1994)	Case Studies	1	0	1	–	–
Sobańska, Szychta (1995, 1996)	Survey	20	0	–	–	–
Gierusz et al. (1996	Survey	60	0	–	–	–
Sobańska, Wnuk (1999, 2000, 2001); Sobańska (2002)	Survey And case studies	104	2	–	–	–
Radek, Schwarz (2000)	Survey	200	0	–	–	–
Dyhdalewicz (2000, 2001)	Case Studies	10	0	–	–	1
Szychta (2001, 2002)	Survey And case studies	60	0	3	1	–
Szadziewska (2002, 2003)	Survey	246	0	–	–	–
Karmańska (2003)	Survey	342	1	–	3	–
Januszewski, Gierusz (2004); Januszewski (2005)	Survey	101	3	5	1	29
Wnuk-Pel (2006a)	Survey	6	6	0	0	0
Szychta (2006, 2007a)	Survey	90	9	–	–	13

The study carried out in 2003 by Karmańska (2003) revealed that managers in the companies surveyed see the need for detailed analysis based on indicators other than accounting criteria, which they consider to be an argument in favour of adoption of ABC. Other factors conducive to ABC adoption were: (a) the urgent need to examine what we do in our company and how it is done (26.7%),

(b) the availability of sufficient funds and qualified personnel (21.9%), (c) ambitious, committed employees (10.3%), (d) management support (8.2%), (e) employees' capacity for quick learning (7.5%).

The research by Gierusz and Januszewski (2004; Januszewski, 2005) found that more than half of the respondents (55%) believed activity-based costing to be useful in managing a company, 17% regarded it as rather not useful, and 4% as quite useless. Among potential uses of ABC system in a company the respondents named: (a) measurement of efficiency of activities and processes (45 companies), (b) measurement of product cost and profitability (44 companies), (c) measurement of customer cost and profitability (43 companies), (d) cost budgeting (42 companies) (e) identification of non-value adding activities (23 companies).

The number of ABC implementations in companies operating in Poland is relatively low. Some of the companies gave up the idea of implementing this costing model after weighting the costs and benefits of its undertaking. A considerable part of the companies are considering ABC adoption. The major reasons for rejecting ABC adoption (13 of the 101 companies surveyed) were found to be, in order of importance: (a) very high cost in relation to anticipated benefits, (b) labour-intensity of the project, (c) lack of adequate knowledge of ABC, (d) lack of management support, (e) shortage of qualified staff, (e) lack of adequate information technology (Gierusz, Januszewski, 2004; Januszewski, 2005).

The same research (Gierusz, Januszewski, 2004; Januszewski, 2005) found that reasons for non-consideration of ABC adoption were (in order of importance): (a) satisfaction with information generated by the currently used costing system (26 companies), (b) lack of sufficient knowledge of ABC (5 companies), (c) lack of funds for a new information system implementation and for employee training, (d) consistency of existing cost system with the corporation's policy and standards (2 companies).

The study by Karmańska (2003) identified the problems that were expected in ABC implementation by companies considering adoption of this costing model. Major barriers mentioned by the respondents included: (a) insufficient knowledge of the ABC concept (31.4%), (b) resistance to change (18.6%), (c) lack of sufficient financial resources (17.4%), (d) absence of need for change because the company's performance is satisfactory (5.8%).

The application of activity-based costing systems in Polish companies was also examined on the basis of six ABC implementations (Wnuk-Pel, 2006a). The study identified, among others, major problems that were encountered during ABC implementations in the companies examined and their perceived importance. The problems included: (a) high labor input in ABC implementation and operation (important), (b) problems with model construction (e.g. selection of activities, drivers) (moderately important), (c) insufficient knowledge of ABC among employees (moderately important), (d) lack of management support (little importance), (e) high cost of ABC implementation and operation (little importance), (f) other priorities, e.g. implementation of ISO, TQM, ERP (little importance), (g) lack of adequate information resources (little importance).

To sum up, there is a considerable body of research on the popularity of ABC in Poland, the extent of its adoption and the functioning of ABC systems in Polish companies. Overall, it has been found that the percentage of companies using, installing or considering instalment of ABC is growing. Empirical research makes it possible, though to a limited degree, to identify factors affecting adoption/ rejection of this costing model and the problems in its implementation.

4.2. Research method

In terms of activity-based costing, so far in Poland there has been some questionnaire research carried out, which investigated, on the one hand, the degree of diffusion, and on the other hand, the way ABC systems functioned. The studies prove that the percentage of companies using activity-based costing, implementing it or considering its future implementation is growing. To some extent, the research allows the way ABC functions to be analyzed and how the information generated by the system is used. The author of this work with his research (surveys, case studies and action research) fits into the trend of such empirical studies.

Two questionnaires (A and B) were used in the research on the diffusion and use of activity-based costing. Survey A aimed to verify the hypothesis about the degree of modern methods of cost accounting diffusion in Polish companies, including in particular activity-based costing. The survey also aimed to investigate factors influencing the fact that most of the companies operating in Poland did not even consider the implementation of activity-based costing or thought about it, or after analyzing its potential costs and benefits rejected its implementation. Survey B was carried out to verify the hypotheses about the reasons underlying the implementation, as well as the ways activity-based costing functions in Polish companies (survey B was carried out only among companies which used activity-based costing). In particular, this survey was supposed to define the basic causes of ABC implementations and it aimed to identify the main problems related to activity-based costing implementation. The questionnaire additionally was to analyze the structure of activity-based costing and its functioning in Polish companies. What is more, the research carried out by means of survey B aimed to investigate the areas in which information from activity-based costing was used, and to define whether the implementation of activity-based costing was accompanied by the use of other modern methods of cost accounting and management accounting.

Within the empirical research project, carried out by means of questionnaires, several stages have were isolated: the formulation of hypotheses, selection of research methods and objects, research design, making sure that the study is credible and reliable, data collection, evaluation and analysis of data[2]. As previously mentioned, in order to reach the main objective of the work and to prove the main research thesis, two surveys were carried out. The surveys aimed to verify the following specific hypotheses:

a) companies operating in Poland mostly use traditional systems of cost accounting; modern systems such as target costing or activity-based costing are used sporadically and their diffusion is significantly lower than in Western countries;

b) implementation of activity-based costing is influenced by various factors; the most important are: headquarters' demand (e.g. parent company), rise of competition and the drive to expand into new sales markets, dissatisfaction with the previous cost accounting, change of organizational structure or strategy, implementation of new technologies, desire to reduce costs and improve results, change-oriented attitude of employees, and accessibility of financial and human resources;

c) among the most important problems related to the process of activity-based costing which companies are afraid of, one could mention: lack of management support, high implementation and maintenance costs, significant labor input during ABC implementation and maintenance, other priorities, insufficient knowledge of ABC, difficulties with system structuring, and lack of adequate resources;

d) lack of interest in implementation of activity-based costing or giving up ABC implementation are conditioned by: satisfaction with current cost accounting system, low indirect costs, lack of management support, high costs of ABC implementation and maintenance, high labor input during ABC implementation and maintenance, other priorities, insufficient knowledge of ABC among employees, difficulties with system modelling, and lack of adequate IT resources;

e) the most important factors which positively influence ABC implementation are: high direct costs, high competition, foreign capital share in the company and size of the company;

f) the structure of activity-based costing systems which function in Polish companies is consistent with the structure of systems functioning in foreign companies;

g) in companies which implemented activity-based costing, information obtained from the system is used in different ways by particular departments and it enables various decisions to be made;

---

[2] The stages of the study are compliant with the stages of empirical research in management accounting (see: Ryan *et al.*, 2002).

h) companies in which activity-based costing operates, simultaneously use other modern methods of management.

The pilot survey, conducted on a relatively small sample of 50 companies, helped to create the questionnaires which were later used in the research (questionnaires A and B). Initially, the author was aiming to conduct the research investigating the degree of activity-based costing diffusion in Polish companies by means of a questionnaire sent by mail to a group of 3,000 large companies. However, the author came across an extremely important problem during the research – out of 3,000 companies to which the questionnaire was sent, only 15 sent it back and that constituted 0.5% of all surveyed companies. The situation made the author change the way the questionnaire A was distributed. Those who were asked to complete the questionnaire included participants of MBA and postgraduate studies, as well as candidates for chartered accountants (during the training sessions, the issue of cost accounting and management accounting, especially activity-based costing were discussed) and participants of various specialist courses on cost accounting and management accounting and activity-based costing. Such a distribution of questionnaires made the sample unrepresentative. In order to analyze the way activity-based costing functioned in Polish companies (by means of questionnaire B), it was necessary to identify companies which had implemented ABC. According to the author's knowledge, the population of companies using activity-based costing is small, therefore, in order to reach as many companies using activity-based costing as possible, the author made use of every potential source he knew, especially:

• the findings of his own questionnaire research (questionnaire A), in which companies declared ABC use;

• ABC projects and implementations which the author completed during his consulting activity;

• every publication describing companies using activity-based costing known to the author;

• conference papers and training materials which mentioned companies using ABC;

• information from IT and consulting firms which participated in ABC implementations.

To analyze the degree of ABC diffusion in Polish companies (questionnaire A), three basic groups of variables were used: variables characterizing the researched company, variables characterizing the cost accounting system used within the company and variables characterizing the company's attitude towards ABC. In order to analyze the activity-based costing systems functioning in Polish companies (questionnaire B), three basic groups of variables were used: variables which generally characterize ABC in the researched company, variables characterizing the structure of ABC in the given company and variables characterizing the use of ABC within the researched company. The choice of groups and individual variables in both questionnaires (A and B) was made in compliance with the objectives of the study, and it was important to analyze the systems of activity-based costing functioning in Polish practice in its most competent and reliable way.

While preparing and conducting the surveys, the author undertook numerous activities, which were to ensure the structural reliability of the research, internal and external reliability, as well as the validity of the study. The activities may be summarized as follows:

- structural reliability – the conducted research was preceded by extensive literature studies, which enabled the choice of adequate theoretical concepts and proper research methods to the analyzed phenomenon (research into activity-based costing in Polish companies). The literature study included the use of survey method for analysis of activity-based costing diffusion and its functioning in Poland and in the world;

- internal reliability – in order to maintain the internal reliability of the research, it was ensured that the respondents who answered the questionnaire had knowledge of the analyzed phenomenon i.e. cost accounting functioning within the researched companies; conducting the studies in such a way was done to prove the existence of a cause-and-effect relationship between the data and the findings;

- external reliability – in order to maintain external reliability, the results of the conducted research were compared to the results produced by other authors (from Poland and other countries). Due to the fact that the choice of sample was non-random, the findings of the research cannot be statistically referred to all the companies within the investigated population (companies operating in Poland);

- validity – to ensure the validity of the study, adequate procedures and means of documenting (filing of the reviewed surveys, entering data to the database etc.) had been established prior to the research.

The research into the diffusion of activity-based costing in Polish companies (survey A) included 1,267 respondents. The author received 531 questionnaires, out of which 495 qualified for further research (incomplete surveys were rejected and repeated questionnaires – two or more from the same company were also not taken into consideration). The percentage of correctly filled in surveys (questionnaire A) was 39.1%. For the purpose of the analysis of activity-based costing implementation process and ABC functioning in Polish companies (by means of questionnaire B), 71 companies were identified which used activity-based costing (46 companies were identified by means of the author's own questionnaire research, and 25 by other means). The author contacted the companies in person, by telephone or via e-mail, he sent them a detailed questionnaire investigating the problems related to the ABC implementation process, the structure of ABC systems and how ABC is used (questionnaire B). The companies responded with

33 correctly filled in questionnaires. The author checked to make sure that the respondents had practical knowledge of activity-based costing use – the people were responsible for the process of ABC implementation and modifications of activity-based costing in their companies. The percentage of correct surveys received in the research (questionnaire B) was 46.5%. The percentage of correctly filled in surveys (questionnaire A – 39.1% and questionnaire B – 46.5%) was quite high because the author had direct, personal contact with the respondents.

The analysis and evaluation of the gathered documentation, in the form of questionnaires (A and B), constituted the last stage of the empirical research. The amassed research material was verified in terms of cross-compliance. The questionnaire research verified the surveys in terms of internal integrity, it was analyzed e.g. if a respondent marked in one of the questions that the company used activity-based costing, and in another question that the company was just considering ABC implementation. Both descriptive analysis and tests of statistical significance for average values, as well as chi-square tests were applied[3]. The results of the research are presented in sections 4.3 and 4.4.

4.3. Diffusion of ABC in Poland

4.3.1. General description of the companies covered by the survey

The survey respondents (questionnaire A) represented both manufacturing and non-manufacturing companies, with a slight predominance of non-manufacturing firms (268, i.e. 54.1% of the 495 companies covered by the survey). The manufacturing firms made up 45.9% (227). Nearly half of the surveyed companies (46.6%) pursued the cost strategy, supplying mass-produced goods to their customers, while the rest (53.4%) followed the differentiation strategy, providing their customers with special products. 46.7% of the survey respondents regarded competition in their company's main area of activity as strong, while other respondents believed it to be moderate (31.9%) or weak (21.3%). As far as the source of equity capital in the companies in question is concerned, in 299 firms (60.5%) it is solely domestic capital, 77 firms (13.6%) have mixed capital, and 128 (25.9%) have only foreign capital. Nearly half of the companies (45.8%) sell their products in domestic markets only, and the remaining companies (54.2%) – both in the country and abroad. It is worth noting that for 16.4% export sales constitute more than half of their total sales, and 12 companies (2.5%) are solely engaged in export sales. The number of employees – a variable used in this research project to define the size of the companies – is presented in Table 4.3.

---

[3] Such statistical tools are quite often used when the diffusion of activity-based costing and evaluation of cost accounting systems are studied (e.g. McGowan, 1998; Byrne et al., 2009).

Table **4.3.** The number of employees in the companies surveyed

Specification	n	%
1–100 employees	185	37.4
101–500 employees	192	38.8
501–1000 employees	51	10.3
More than 1000 employees	67	13.5
Total	495	100.0

It should be noted that small entities were the dominant group among non-manufacturing enterprises (48.5%), compared with 24.2% for manufacturing companies. In the remaining size categories (medium, large and very large companies) manufacturing entities dominated – 45.8% employed 101–500 people, 14.5% had 501–1000 employees and 15.4% had more than 1000 employees. In the group of non-manufacturing companies 32.8% were medium-sized entities (101–500 employees), 6.7% were large entities (501–1000 employees) and 11.9% were very large entities (more than 1000 employees).

4.3.2. Characteristics of cost accounting systems used in the companies

The findings of the questionnaire survey suggest that the actual shape of the cost accounting systems used currently in these enterprises is defined by their management in more than half of the cases – of the 486 companies which provided answers to this question, as many as 270 (55.5%) responded in this way. In 114 enterprises (23.5%) the shape of cost accounting is determined in part by the management and in part by the headquarters (e.g. parent company), and in 102 (21%) it depends solely on the head office (e.g. parent company).

As regards the time that existing cost accounting systems were implemented, there are considerable differences among the sample enterprises. In 188 (39.7%), the systems used currently are relatively "young" – they had been implemented not earlier than three years before this questionnaire. In nearly half of the enterprises (229, 48.3%) costing systems had been implemented 4 to 10 years earlier, and in 57 (12%) they are "older" than 10 years. It is interesting to note that in as many as 88% of cases there was a change of the costing system in the last ten years. In the majority of the companies surveyed the proportion of indirect costs in total costs grew in the last ten years – in 52 cases (36.4%) the rise was insignificant, and in 79 (18.9%) it grew significantly. In 96 enterprises (23%) no change in the proportion of indirect costs was observed, and in 91 (21.8%) it was reported to have decreased. The majority of the enterprises (392, 79.2%) apply actual cost accounting (full or variable),135 (27.3%) use standard costing (full or variable), and 60 (12.1%) use multi-step and multi-bloc costing. More advanced costing methods are applied to a rather limited extent – target costing was reported to be used only in 9 companies and ABC in 46.

It has to be stressed however that the question about companies using activity-based costing is not an easy one to answer because there is some confusion around ABC and the concepts that are relevant to it. ABC systems used in practice differ one from the other, for example the research conducted by Gosselin and Mevellec (2004) which interviewed managers from 42 companies from France and Canada revealed that none of the ABC systems analyzed were similar[4]. Because there is no single definition of ABC, the results of the present survey and all the surveys on ABC have to be analyzed cautiously (Gosselin, 1997; Baird *at al.*, 2004). What is even more important is that it is possible that in most ABC surveys (this one not being an exception), the rate of ABC implementation could be overestimated because (a) respondents from companies not using ABC may not be inclined to answer ABC surveys and (b) the sample was based on companies which were taking part in accounting courses which could cover firms interested more than average in new costing techniques. Similarly Baird *et al.* (2004) stressed that questionnaire surveys overstated the level of ABC implementation and that there was a gap between the leading edge practices described in the literature and current practices within organizations.

4.3.3. Analysis of attitudes towards ABC

The first question in this section of the questionnaire asked respondents about their company's attitude to activity-based costing. As anticipated, the majority of the companies (302, 65.1%) had not so far considered adopting ABC, and 19 (4.1%) had considered its adoption and decided against it, so 69.2% of the examined companies had not implemented ABC and were not planning to do so. 46 firms (9.3%) have implemented activity-based costing and 97 (20.9%) are considering its adoption in the future. The subsequent part of the chapter analyzes, successively:

1) problems envisaged by companies which have never considered ABC adoption or rejected it after cost-benefit analysis;

---

[4] Confusion is even greater because academics and practitioners use multiplicity of expressions and abbreviations for activity-based costing methods and models: activity accounting (Brimson, 1991), ABM – activity-based management (Turney, 1992; Reeve, 1996), AA – activity accounting (Gosselin, 1997), ACA – activity cost analysis (Gosselin, 1997), CDA – cost driver analysis (Gosselin, 2007), some authors use also the term of ABCM – activity-based cost management (Foster, Swenson, 1997). Companies using ABC use more or less complex system, and Gosselin (1997) distinguished four levels of complexity: activity analysis, activity cost analysis, pilot ABC and full ABC, which is the ultimate level of activity-based costing implementation meaning the costing system in which all products are valued on the basis of the output of the ABC system, ABC information is used both for managerial purposes and financial reporting as well as for the purposes of transfer pricing, make or buy decisions, performance measurement or strategic decisions. There is no evidence in the research that such a system exists in practice.

2) problems envisaged by companies considering ABC adoption;
3) problems encountered by companies during ABC implementation;
4) reasons for ABC implementation.

Table 4.4. Reasons for non-consideration or rejection of ABC

Specification	Mean[a]	Standard deviation	Variability coefficient	Dominant value
Other	4.31	1.18	0.27	5
Insufficient knowledge of ABC among employees	4.05	1.09	0.27	5
High labor input in ABC implementation and operation	3.99	0.96	0.24	4
High cost of ABC implementation and operation	3.82	1.00	0.26	4
Difficulty with model construction (e.g. selection of activities)	3.64	1.06	0.29	4
Lack of adequate IT resources	3.29	1.41	0.43	5
Lack of management support	3.17	1.46	0.46	5
Other priorities (e.g. implementation of ISO, ERP)	2.87	1.47	0.51	1
Low levels of indirect costs	2.49	1.21	0.49	3
Satisfaction with existing cost system	2.46	1.31	0.53	1

[a] The respondents evaluated the importance of reasons for non-consideration or rejection of ABC using the following scale: 1 – unimportant, 2 – little importance, 3 – moderately important, 4 – important, 5 – very important.

The next question asked the respondents to evaluate the importance of possible reasons for lack of interest in ABC implementation or its rejection (see Table 4.4). The five top ratings among factors (these factors statistically and significantly (more than the average rating 3) impeded ABC implementation) believed to be important in this respect were given to:

1) other – the respondents listed here lack of guidelines from headquarters abroad, the need to measure profitability at the level of headquarters (located abroad), too small scope of activity, fast and not completely predictable growth of the company, inadequate financial resources, lack of awareness of the need for proper cost calculation, negative attitude of the accounting department (average rating 4.31; $t = 3.99$ statistical significance 0.01);

2) insufficient knowledge of ABC among employees (average rating 4.05; $t = 9.47$ statistical significance 0.01);

3) high labour input in ABC implementation and operation (average rating 3.99; $t = 10.03$ statistical significance 0.01);

4) high cost of ABC implementation and operation (average rating 3.82; t = 7.78 statistical significance 0.01);

5) difficulty with model construction (average rating 3.64; t = 5.55 statistical significance 0.01).

The factors regarded as moderately important include lack of adequate IT resources (3.29), lack of management support (3.17) and other priorities (2.87). Low levels of indirect costs (2.49) and satisfaction with the costing system used currently (2.46) were considered to be the least important. Previous research among companies in Poland (Gierusz, Januszewski, 2004; Januszewski, 2005) found similar reasons for rejecting ABC adoption – the three major reasons were very high cost in relation to anticipated benefits, labour-intensity of the project, and lack of adequate knowledge of ABC. The same research (Gierusz, Januszewski, 2004; Januszewski, 2005) found that major reasons for non-consideration of ABC adoption were satisfaction with information generated by the currently used costing system, lack of sufficient knowledge of ABC, and lack of funds for a new information system – the same reasons were identified in the present research.

Similar problems to those anticipated by the companies considering activity-based costing implementation and identified in this research, can be found in other studies conducted in different countries e.g.:

1) in Great Britain (Cobb et al., 1992), the lack of decision about the implementation of activity-based costing was caused by high labour input in ABC implementation and existence of priorities other than the ABC implementation;

2) in Sweden (Ask, Ax, 1992), the key problems related to implementation of new systems of costs accounting included other management priorities, familiarity with the current cost accounting system, lack of knowledge and understanding of the alternative methods of cost accounting and lack of adequate data;

3) in Saudi Arabia (Clarke, Mullins, 2001), the analysis of companies not using ABC enabled to define the reasons for rejection or non-consideration of ABC implementation – among the basic causes one may find satisfaction with the existing cost systems, as well as the lack of sufficient knowledge required for implementation of activity-based costing;

4) in Australia (Askarany, Yazdifar, 2007), the variables which condition the slow diffusion of ABC are: the lack of adequate IT resources, high cost of ABC implementation and operation, high cost of information gathering, lack of information about modern methods of cost accounting, management policy and priorities and lack of knowledge of cost accounting.

With regard to potential problems envisaged by companies considering ABC adoption (see Table 4.5), the three top ratings were assigned to[5]:

---

[5] Factors number two and three may according to the respondents statistically and significantly (more than the average rating of 3) impede implementation of ABC. The influence of factor one on the ABC implementation is significant yet not statistically important.

1) other – the problems cited here by the respondents include telecommunications law and energy law requirements, corporate directives, implementation of an integrated information system, fear of novelty, and lack of teaching materials addressing ABC implementation in their particular industry (average rating 4.00);

2) insufficient knowledge of ABC among employees (average rating 3.97; t = 9.13 statistical significance 0.01);

3) high labour input in ABC implementation and operation (average rating 3.66; t = 5.73 statistical significance 0.01).

Table 4.5. Problems expected by companies considering ABC adoption

Specification	Mean[a]	Standard deviation	Variability coefficient	Dominant value
Other	4.00	0.71	0.18	4
Insufficient knowledge of ABC among employees	3.97	0.95	0.24	4
High labour input in ABC implementation and operation	3.66	0.97	0.27	4
Difficulty in model construction (e.g. selection of activities)	3.45	0.86	0.25	4
High cost of ABC implementation and operation	3.13	0.93	0.30	3
Lack of adequate IT resources	2.88	1.29	0.45	4
Other priorities (e.g. implementation of ISO, ERP)	2.51	1.27	0.51	1
Lack of management support	2.11	1.12	0.53	1

[a] The respondents indicated the perceived importance of the factors listed above by assigning ratings according to the following scale: 1 – unimportant, 2 – little importance, 3 – moderately important, 4 – important, 5 – very important.

Potential problems regarded as moderately important include difficulty with ABC model designing (3.45), high cost of ABC implementation and operation (3.13), lack of sufficient IT resources (2.88), and other priorities (2.51). Lack of management support for ABC implementation is believed to be the least important problem. Previous research among companies in Poland (Karmańska, 2003) identified that most important problems that were expected in ABC implementation by companies considering adoption were insufficient knowledge of ABC concept, resistance to change, and lack of sufficient financial resources – the same reasons were identified in the present research (with the exception of resistance to change). Similar problems to those identified in the present research and anticipated by companies considering activity-based costing implementation were observed in studies carried out in other countries, e.g. in Ireland (Pierce, 2004). Among the main problems, respondents enumerated insufficiency of resources needed for implementation and its high costs along with the vague implementation benefits, which were difficult to evaluate.

Table 4.6. Main problems during ABC implementation

Specification	Mean[a]	Standard deviation	Variability coefficient	Dominant value
High labour input during ABC implementation and operation	3.55	0.97	0.27	4
Insufficient knowledge of ABC among employees	3.42	0.99	0.29	4
Problems with model (selection of activities, drivers etc.)	3.25	0.92	0.28	3
Other	3.00	2.00	0.67	1
Lack of adequate IT resources	2.68	1.44	0.54	1
High cost of ABC implementation and operation	2.33	1.09	0.47	3
Lack of support from management/head office etc.	1.81	1.14	0.63	1
Other priorities (implementation of ISO, TQM, ERP etc.)	1.80	1.12	0.62	1

[a] The respondents assessed the significance of problems according to the following scale: 1 – no problem, 2 – insignificant, 3 – moderately significant, 4 – significant, 5 – very significant.

As far as problems with ABC implementation are concerned (see Table 4.6), high labour input in implementation and maintenance were named considerable problem (average grade – 3.55; t = 3.23 statistical significance 0.01). None of the problems listed in the survey questionnaire was assessed as significant or very significant. The respondents named four problems assessed by them as moderately important:

1) insufficient knowledge of ABC among employees (average grade 3.42);

2) difficulties with model designing, e.g. choice of activities, drivers etc. (average rating 3.25);

3) other problems, such as resistance to change (foodstuffs manufacturing company) or mutual antagonism caused by disclosure of individual divisions' profitability as a result of activity-based costing implementation (service company) (average rating 3);

4) inadequate IT resources (average rating 2.68).

Problems evaluated as insignificant included: high costs of ABC implementation and maintenance (2.33), lack of management/headquarters etc. support (1.81), and other priorities, e.g. adoption of ISO, TQM or ERP (1.80). Previous research among companies in Poland (Wnuk-Pel, 2006a) identified major problems that were encountered during ABC implementations – the problems included: high labour input in ABC implementation and operation (important), problems with model construction (moderately important), insufficient knowledge of ABC among employees (moderately important), lack of management support (little importance), high cost of ABC implementation and operation (little importance), other priorities, e.g. implementation of ISO, TQM, ERP (little importance), and lack of adequate IT resources (little importance). Exactly the same problems and in the same order of importance were identified in the present study.

Similar problems to those observed in the present research were also evident in other studies on the diffusion of activity-based costing carried out in different countries. In Great Britain, Innes and Mitchell (1998) observed that the high labor input related to the implementation process and later to the operation of the system is perceived as a problem. Apart from that, four other problems connected with the activity-based costing implementation were isolated: the difficulty with cost driver data collection, problems with the identification of processes performed by many organizational units, other priorities and the substantial workload of financial and accounting employees. Nicholls (1992) observed that the companies enumerate among the key difficulties related to the implementation of ABC such issues as: little access to data, insufficiency of resources, negative attitude to changes and lack of training[6]. Friedman and Lyne (2000) noticed a variety of organizational consequences related to the implementation of activity-based costing, among them: behavioral problems stemming from the division of activities into value and non-value adding, the new way of discussion companies' problems and the change of attitude and relationship between the management accounting specialists and operational managers.

In Ireland, the study by Clarke et al. (1999) showed that among the most important problems connected with the ABC implementation there were: defining activity costs (50%), identification of cost drivers (42%), inaccessibility of adequate software (38%) and difficulty in defining activities (33%). On the other hand, the study by Clarke and Mullins (2001) enabled the identification of conceptual and institutional problems that companies implementing activity-based costing come across. The major conceptual problems were: problems with data collection about cost drivers (89%), problems with the identification of drivers for the calculation of costs for products (78%), difficulties in the calculation of activity costs (56%) and problems with the defining activities (56%). Among the main institutional

---

[6] Research conducted among organizations operating within the healthcare sector in the United States (Lawson, 2005) showed that, similar to other sectors of the economy, the main problems related to the process of ABC implementation (according to companies which had implemented ABC) are: difficulties with the definition of activities, activity drivers and means of cost calculation for activities, and insufficiency of resources (including IT resources). The research also stressed that, unlike other sectors, there were problems with involvement and management support in the implementation process.

problems, there were: poor education of managers and accountants (67%), lack of time (56%), insufficiency of adequate resources (44%) and lack of guidelines for ABC implementation (44%).

In research conducted in developing countries e.g. India (Anand *et al.*, 2005), companies implementing activity-based costing enumerated among the major problems such issues as: difficulties in gathering information about costs in new cross-sections (42.3%) and difficulties in defining activities (34.6%)[7]. In research carried out in Saudi Arabia (Khalid, 2005), the main problems with activity-based costing implementation included insufficient knowledge and difficulties in calculating cost drivers.

Analyzing problems related to the process of activity-based costing implementation, perceived from the point of view of companies which rejected the implementation or never considered it (Table 4.4), or companies which are considering implementation (Table 4.5) and companies which have already implemented ABC (Table 4.6), one may notice that all the problems are similar. A more detailed analysis reveals that, in reality, the problems were less significant in companies that have already implemented ABC than the expected problems in companies that considered implementation or companies that did not consider implementation or those companies that abandoned implementation. In conclusion, it may be stated that companies, which do not use activity-based costing, overestimate the expected problems. Misunderstanding of problems related to the process of activity-based costing implementation by companies which do not use the system was identified by Clarke *et al.* (1999). The researchers, while studying Irish companies, noticed that the companies which abandoned implementation, among the least important problems enumerated difficulties in calculation of costs and activity drivers, as well as insufficiency of IT resources, and that contradicts opinions of companies which had already implemented ABC.

The next question asked respondents to indicate which of the factors listed in the questionnaire had influenced the decision to implement ABC in their enterprises and to what extent. The results (see Table 4.7) suggest that four factors were vitally important or important for ABC adoption (these factors are statistically significant and significantly (more than the average rating of 3) influenced ABC implementation):

1) other reasons – the respondents cited factors such as the need to value non-standard products and to obtain accurate information for managing activities, or the application of an ABC system by their competitors (average rating 4.80; t = 9.00 statistical significance 0.01);

---

[7] Studies on the diffusion of activity-based costing in a developing country i.e. China (Parkinson, 2009) enabled isolation of the key factors behind a successful ABC implementation; the factors were: management support, sufficient financial resources, quality of support information systems and knowledge as well as dedication of middle management. The lack of involvement from the top management was identified as the main difficulty.

2) the need for cost reduction and performance improvement (average rating 4.03; t = 6.70 statistical significance 0.01);

3) changed management information needs (average rating 3.91; t = 5.91 statistical significance 0.01);

4) the need for improvement of management control (average rating 3.62; t = 3.56 statistical significance 0.01).

Table 4.7. Reasons for implementation of activity-based costing

Specification	Mean[a]	Standard deviation	Variability coefficient	Dominant value
Other	4.80	0.45	0.09	5
Need for cost reduction and performance improvement	4.03	0.94	0.23	4
Changed management information needs	3.91	0.90	0.23	4
Need for improvement of control	3.62	1.06	0.29	4
Dissatisfaction with existing cost system	3.25	1.13	0.35	4
Increased competition	3.19	1.13	0.35	4
Headquarters' demands	3.12	1.68	0.54	5
Desire to gain new markets	2.78	1.29	0.46	3
Change of strategy	2.48	1.44	0.58	1
Availability of financial resources	2.47	1.25	0.51	2
Change in organisational structure	2.47	1.35	0.55	1
Availability of human resources	2.35	1.20	0.51	1
Implementation of new technologies	2.30	1.31	0.57	1
Change of management	2.14	1.44	0.67	1
Favourable attitude among employees	1.91	0.96	0.50	1

[a] The respondents indicated the importance of the factors listed above by assigning the following ratings: 1 – unimportant, 2 – little importance, 3 – moderately important, 4 – important, 5 – very important.

The factors believed to have contributed to ABC adoption to a slightly lesser degree include dissatisfaction with the cost accounting system used currently (3.25), increased competition (3.19), headquarters' demand (3.12), and seeking to gain new markets (2.78) – the respondents rated the importance of these factors as moderate. The least importance was attached to change of strategy (2.48), availability of financial resources (2.47), change in organisational structure (2.47), availability of human resources (2.35), the implementation of new technologies (2.30), change of management (2.14) and favourable atmosphere among employees (1.91).

Analyzing the factors that encouraged companies to undergo the difficult process of activity-based costing implementation Nicholls (1992) identified the need for more accurate data about costs (65% of respondents), dissatisfaction with the current cost system (65% of respondents) the need for cost reduction (45% of respondents) and an increase of indirect costs in the company's cost structure (32%). The research carried out by Innes and Mitchells (1995) revealed that respondents included the need for cost reduction, the need for profitability analysis, improvement of performance and improvement of cost management[8] among the main reasons for the implementation of ABC. Similar reasons for activity-based costing implementation were identified in other countries, for example in Germany (Horvath *et al.*, 1998) the need for improvement of business processes, the need for a more reliable product cost calculation and the need to signalize the problem of unused capacity were mentioned. In developing countries like India (Anand *et al.*, 2005), the main notion underlying ABC implementations were the need for precise information about value adding and non-value adding activities, the necessity to improve company competitiveness and usefulness in budgeting.

Available empirical research carried out around the world prove that the benefits resulting from adoption of ABC observed in companies which use the system are higher than the benefits expected prior to implementation. The research carried out by Clarke *et al.* (1999) points out that respondents derived better benefits than expected in all of the areas analyzed (improvement of product cost calculation for pricing, improvement of control and cost management, better understanding of reasons for cost formation, better performance evaluation, more accurate analysis of customer profitability, positive influence on employee performance). The observations were also proved by later studies (Clarke, Mullins, 2001).

4.3.4. Contextual factors influencing the implementation of ABC

The attitude of companies included in the research towards activity-based costing is one of the most important issues of the questionnaire research. It is worth analyzing then what kind of companies use ABC or consider its implementation in the future, and what companies, after analyzing the costs and benefits of

---

[8] The reasons for the implementation of activity-based costing in different sectors of the economy are quite similar. The research conducted among organizations operating in the healthcare sector in the United States (Lawson, 2005) showed that, like other sectors, the main benefits expected in the process of ABC implementation included better understanding of the realized processes and improvement of information about product costs as well as information used for improvement of processes. On the other hand, research carried out on a sample of American cities (Ho, Kidwell, 2000) showed that the basic benefits expected in terms of ABC implementation (both by the users of the system and organizations which do not use ABC) included its usefulness in decision-making in terms of external auxiliary units, business units, administrative units and units related to safety maintenance. It should be noted that the usefulness of activity-based costing in the areas above was ranked higher by the cities where the system was used than by the cities which do not have ABC.

implementation rejected it and what kind of companies never considered ABC implementation. Selected results of the analysis of the relationship between the company's attitude towards activity-based costing and some characteristic features of the researched companies are presented in Table 4.8.

Table 4.8. Attitude towards activity-based costing and selected features of the companies researched

Features	Uses or considers implementation of ABC (in %)	Rejected or did not consider ABC implementation (in %)
Type of operation		
Manufacturing company	33.1	66.9
Non-manufacturing company	28.8	71.2
Capital origin		
Non-foreign capital companies	27.3	72.7
Foreign capital companies	36.2	63.8
Number of employees		
1–100	23.8	76.2
101–500	29.2	70.8
501–1000	44.9	55.1
Above 1000	42.3	57.7

Analysis of the information presented in Table 4.8 enables the formulation of the following observations in terms of the companies researched:

1. A comparable percentage of manufacturing and non-manufacturing companies implemented or are considering implementation of activity-based costing (the differences are statistically insignificant). The findings are similar to those received by Innes and Mitchell (1995) as well as Innes et al. (2000), who noticed that the percentage of companies using ABC was actually the same among manufacturing companies and service companies – it seems interesting due to the fact that, initially, ABC was perceived as a method which was useful for manufacturing firms[9]. Some research (e.g. Cotton et. al., 2003) proves that the diffusion of ABC is greater among manufacturing companies (25.5%) than among non-manufacturing companies (18.8%).

2. Companies with foreign capital used ABC or considered its implementation more often than companies with only domestic capital (because $\chi^2 = 4.10 > 2.71 = \chi^2_{0.1;1}$, significance level of 0.1 therefore it may be assumed that the relationship is statistically significant, although the relationship is weak (V Cramer coefficient = 0.094)). The findings of the present research are confirmed by results of other research carried out in different countries. Clarke et al. (1999), who studied an

---

[9] Research conducted by Lawson (2005) in organizations operating in healthcare showed that ABC was used more often in profit-oriented enterprises (33%) than in non-profit-oriented organizations (8%).

Irish companies sample, claimed that the international status (capital) of the company was one of the key variables conditioning implementation of activity-based costing. Joshi (2001) obtained similar results studying Chinese companies.

3. The larger the company, the more likely it is that the company adopts ABC or considers its use in the future (because $\chi^2 = 12.51 > 11.34 = \chi^2_{0.01;3}$, significance level of 0.01 therefore it may be assumed that the relationship is statistically significant, although the relationship is weak (V Cramer coefficient = 0.165)). The positive relationship between the size of a company and ABC implementation has been shown by most empirical research (Armitage, Nicholson, 1993; Innes, Mitchell, 1995; IMA, 1996; Lukka, Granlund, 1996; Björnenak, 1997; Gosselin, 1997; Clarke et al., 1997; Van Nguyen, Brookes, 1997; Krumwiede, 1998; Clarke et al., 1999; Innes et al., 2000; Hoque, 2000; Joshi, 2001; Baird et al., 2004; Khalid, 2005; Kallunki, Silvola, 2008). Yet there are studies, which did not observe such a relationship (Booth, Giacobbe, 1998).

4. The research did not prove any statistically significant relationship between the company's attitude to activity-based costing and the business sector the company operated in, competitiveness in the main area of operation and sales direction. With regard to the relationship between those factors and implementation of activity-based costing, the research carried out in the world does not provide firm results. Björnenak (1997) for example proved that companies operating in an environment that is characterized by high competitiveness do not use activity-based costing (Van Nguyen and Brooks (1997) came to a similar conclusion). A positive influence of competitiveness on activity-based costing implementation was shown by e.g. research carried out by Anderson (1995), Innes and Mitchell (1995), Krumwiede (1998) or Malmi (1999). Booth and Giacobbe (1998) proved that there was no relationship between ABC implementation and the level of competitiveness. Björnenak (1997) noticed that the companies which rejected ABC implementation operated in a more competitive environment, in comparison to companies which had already implemented ABC, were implementing or were considering implementation (which was not compliant with the subject literature and hypotheses formed at the beginning of the research). His research additionally proved that differentiation of products, measured by the number of variants, was greater in the companies using activity-based costing than in the companies which did not adopt the system. Malmi (1999) showed that companies which offer a wide variety of products and those which sell most of their products abroad tend to implement activity-based costing (Krumwiede (1998), Clarke et al. (1999) and Khalid (2005) proved similar results in terms of product differentiation). The lack of relationship between product differentiation and activity-based costing implementation was exhibited in the research by Lukka and Granlund (1996) as well as Van Nguyen and Brooks (1997), however, Clarke et al. (1997) observed a negative relationship in that matter[10].

---

[10] Research carried out by Baines and Langfield-Smith (2003) on a sample of Australian companies proved that replacing the cost strategy with differentiation strategy has a positive

The relationship between the company's attitude towards ABC and selected features of their cost structure was the last issue analyzed in the present questionnaire research (questionnaire A). The results are presented in Table 4.9.

Table 4.9. Attitude towards activity-based costing and cost structure in the companies researched

Features	Uses or considers implementation of ABC (in %)	Rejected or did non consider ABC implementation (in %)
Up to 20% of indirect costs	26.2	73.8
From 21% to 40% of indirect costs	34.8	65.2
From 41% to 60% of indirect costs	39.4	60.6
Over 60% of indirect costs	65.0	35.0

Analysis of the data presented in Table 3.9 enables the formulation of the observation that, in the case of the companies researched, the percentage of companies which had already implemented activity-based costing is directly proportional to the share of indirect costs in the cost structure of the company analyzed (because χ^2 = 14.69 > 11.34 = $\chi^2_{0.01;3}$, significance level of 0.01, therefore it may be assumed that the relationship is statistically significant, although the relationship is weak (V Cramer coefficient = 0.199))[11]. The observations are compliant with the subject literature, which supports the positive relationship between the implementation of ABC and the percentage of indirect costs in the company's cost structure.

Some research carried out in the world proves the results of the present study to be correct. For example Björnenak (1997), who investigated factors influencing implementation of activity-based costing in Norway stated that the only variable which proved to be statistically significant in terms of ABC implementation was the company's cost structure. A similar conclusion was drawn in research into the diffusion of activity-based costing in Saudi Arabia (Khalid, 2005). However, some research did not observe any significant relationship between the company's cost structure and implementation of activity-based costing (Van Nguyen, Brookes, 1997; Booth, Giacobbe, 1998; Clarke et al., 1999).

---

influence on the use of advanced management tools in general, especially ABC – the findings are compliant with research conducted e.g. by Gosselin (1997).

[11] Out of the companies which had no more than 20% of indirect costs, only 7.1% used ABC, among companies which had 21–40% of indirect costs the percentage was 10.9%, and among enterprises with 41–60% of indirect costs it was 15.2%. The highest percentage of companies using activity-based costing (20%) was among firms whose indirect costs constituted more than 60% of total costs (it should be stressed that a further 45% of companies with such a high share of indirect costs were considering implementation of ABC).

4.4. Functioning and use of ABC in Poland

4.4.1. General description of the companies covered by the survey

Out of the 33 enterprises (ABC adopters) that were surveyed (questionnaire B), 19 were manufacturing companies (57.6%), and 14 were non-manufacturing companies (42.4%). The companies covered by the survey served varying numbers of customers and pursued both cost strategy and a product differentiation strategy. The classification of ABC adopters by these two characteristics is presented in Table 4.10.

Table 4.10. Main areas of activity of the companies surveyed

Specification	n	%
Provision of mass-produced goods to many customers (cost strategy)	11	36.7
Provision of mass-produced goods to a small number of customers (cost strategy)	0	0.0
Provision of special products to many customers (differentiation strategy)	17	56.7
Provision of special products to a small number of customers (differentiation strategy)	2	6.7
Total	30	100.0

Table 4.11. Competition in the companies' main areas of activity

Specification	n	%
Weak competition	3	9.1
Moderate competition	7	21.2
Strong competition	23	69.7
Total	33	100.0

Nearly two-thirds of the companies (65.4%) followed a product differentiation strategy, and slightly over one-third (36.7%) pursued a cost strategy. As many as 93.4% sold their products to many customers and only 6.7% (2 companies) serve a limited number of customers. The companies also differed in respect of competition in their main areas of activity (Table 4.11).

More than two-thirds of the companies surveyed (69.7%) described competition in their basic area of activity as strong (the percentages for manufacturing and non-manufacturing companies were similar – 68.4% and 71.4%, respectively), 7 companies stated that competition was moderate, and only three companies assessed it as weak. As regards the source of equity capital, 17 (51.5%) companies declared only domestic capital, 9 companies (27.3%) mixed capital and 7 companies (21.2%) only foreign capital. 13 companies

(39.4%) in the sample of ABC adopters sold their products only in domestic markets, while the remaining 60.6% operated both in their country and abroad. It should be noted that for 15.2% of these companies exports constituted over half of the total value of sales, and that none of them was engaged solely in export activities.

The number of employees – a variable used in this research project to define the size of the companies – is presented in Table 4.12.

Table 4.12. The number of employees in the companies surveyed

Specification	n	%
1–100 employees	5	15.2
101–500 employees	13	39.4
501–1000 employees	7	21.2
More than 1000 employees	8	24.2
Total	33	100.0

The research has shown that in over half of the companies the form of the activity-based costing system depended solely on the independent decisions of management (18 companies, i.e. 54.5%); in 12 companies (36.4%) it was determined in part by the management and in part by the headquarters (e.g. parent company), and only in 3 cases did it depend wholly on the headquarters.

Of the 33 companies surveyed, 100% use activity-based costing (which is self-evident because of the character of the sample); 26 companies (78.7%) also employed traditional actual cost systems (full or variable costing), 14 companies (42.4%) used standard costing (full or variable), and only 5 companies made use of target costing parallel with ABC. 9 companies stated that they applied activity-based costing only in a limited form, the comments expressed by the companies were as follows:

- "the company uses ABC in a limited form" (chemical industry);
- "the company uses ABC in a part of its operation" (pharmaceutical company);
- "ABC embraces only selected areas of the company's operation" (construction company);
- "activity-based costing is used for preparation of ad hoc analyses e.g. calculation of a minimal production batch, calculation of costs of transportation, logistics, bonuses etc." (food industry company);
- "ABC is exclusively used for profitability analysis of individual financial products" (financial services company);
- "activity-based costing functions in its very basic form, i.e. its structure is not well developed" (company manufacturing household goods);

- "the company uses elements of ABC" (electronics industry company);
- "ABC is used in its simplified version – a significantly limited number of activities" (bank).

The sample companies varied considerably as regards the cost structure (direct and indirect costs) – the proportions of indirect costs in total costs are shown in Table 4.13.

Table 4.13. The share of indirect costs in cost structure of the companies surveyed

Specification	n	%
Up to 10% of indirect costs	4	14.8
From 11% to 20% of indirect costs	6	22.2
From 21% to 30% of indirect costs	5	18.5
From 31% to 40% of indirect costs	5	18.5
From 41% to 50% of indirect costs	2	7.4
From 51% to 60% of indirect costs	3	11.1
From 61% to 70% of indirect costs	2	7.4
Total	27	100.0

In the majority of the companies the proportion of indirect costs grew over the last 10 years – in 10 companies (37%) it increased only slightly, and in 5 companies (18.6%) the increase was quite significant. In 3 of the firms (11.1%) no change in the percentage of indirect costs was reported, and in 9 cases (33.3%) it was stated to have decreased. Several respondents did not give answers to this question.

4.4.2. General description of ABC systems

In response to the question whose initiative it was to adopt ABC more than half of the respondents (54.5%) stated that the idea came from the owner/head office/ management. In 13 cases (49.4%) it was the initiative of the economic section. In 2 companies adoption of ABC was stated: (a) to have been the consequence of implementing SAP/R3 (manufacturing company), (b) to have been postulated by the Purchasing Department (company producing household goods).

The activity-based costing systems functioning in the companies in question were implemented at various times. In 22 companies (66.7%) they had been functioning no longer than three years (in 7 of them for less than a year, and in 15 it was between 1–3 years). Only 11 companies (33.3%) had been using ABC for longer than three years. The mode of activity-based costing implementation is presented in Table 4.14.

Table 4.14. The mode of ABC implementation in the companies surveyed

Specification	n	%
By employees without external assistance	14	42.4
By employees with external consulting	13	39.4
By employees with headquarters' assistance	6	18.2
Total	33	100.0

In most cases ABC was implemented by the companies' employees with outside assistance – 13 companies (39.4%) used the services of external consultants, and in 6 firms (18.2%) the head offices provided assistance. In 14 enterprises (42.2%) no outside help was needed. The key role of the company's employees in the process of activity-based costing implementation was stressed by the research carried out in Great Britain (Innes *et al.*, 2000) and New Zealand (Cotton *et al.*, 2003). The analysis of activity-based costing implementation in New Zealand showed that accountancy professionals were the key to the implementation – 91.7% (90.3% in Great Britain), consultants' role was lesser in that respect – 28.3% (48.4% in Great Britain), then IT specialists – 30% (22.6% in Great Britain) and production personnel – 28.3% (16.1% in Great Britain). The role of marketing personnel, sales personnel and employees from other departments in the implementation of ABC was significantly limited.

The number of employees engaged in ABC implementation varied from company to company: (a) 1–3 employees in 9 companies (27.3%), (b) 4–10 employees in 16 companies (48.5%), (c) 11–30 employees in 5 companies (15.2%), (d) more than 30 employees in 3 companies (9.1%). The number of employees taking care of the systems maintenance and operation after completion of the implementation process is shown in Table 4.15.

Table 4.15. The number of employees engaged in operation of ABC systems

Specification	n	%
1 employee as part of responsibilities	14	43.8
1 employee as main responsibility	2	6.2
2–3 employees	11	34.4
4 or more employees	5	15.6
Total	32	100.0

Research on companies which have adopted ABC in such countries as the United States or Great Britain indicates that it is extremely rare that activity-based costing completely replaces the existing cost systems. The usual practice in such cases is to use the existing system for external reporting and ABC for management purposes (Armitage, Nicholson, 1993). Research into the relation between ABC and other cost accounting systems used in parallel with it will make it possible to establish whether the practices found in western countries are equally common in Poland. Analysis of the sample population of Polish ABC adopters reveals that after ABC implementation 24 companies (72.7%) have not given up the formerly used costing system and are using it parallel with ABC. In 5 companies (15.5%) the old system continues to function, but has been marginalized (ABC has the primary importance). In only 4 cases (12.1%) has the old system been given up entirely.

The next of the selected variables, i.e. success of ABC implementation, was to indicate not so much the objective success or otherwise of this system implementation, but rather the way it is perceived by the employees – whether the 'climate' in the company is favourable to the new system. Shields (1995) has demonstrated a relationship between the perceived success of ABC implementation and six variables: management support, integration with strategic initiatives strengthening competitiveness such as TQM or JIT, performance evaluation and rewarding, project management by non-accounting personnel, training during ABC design, implementation and application, and availability of resources necessary for implementation. Shields also found that variables such as the type of software used or designing the ABC model without external assistance have no impact on the implementation success. Research carried out by McGowan and Klammer (1997) confirms a connection between three variables identified by Shields with perceived success of ABC implementation. These factors are: management support, performance evaluation and rewarding, and training during ABC design, implementation and application. Foster and Swenson (1997) found that success of ABC implementation depended primarily on integration with the performance evaluation and reward system, links with quality improvement projects, management support, training during implementation, and availability of resources. The findings of the three research projects mentioned above roughly agree as to the factors that have the greatest impact on ABC implementation success. To identify factors conditioning a successful implementation of ABC Friedman and Lyne (2000) conducted research in Great Britain using the long-term case study method. The results of this research coincide for the most part with the results of research carried out in the United States – the success of ABC implementation was found to depend on: the recognized need for implementation, wide support for implementation, especially from management, close cooperation between accounting and non-accounting staff during ABC implementation and use, incorporation of ABC into organizational structure and practice, availability of resources, and links with other projects such as TQM. Innes *et al.* (2000) explored the importance for successful implementation of factors such as management support, engagement of consultants, involvement of accounting team and production personnel, and companies' prior experience with ABC models. The findings suggest that only management support had a significant influence on the implementation's success.

The respondents were asked in the present survey (questionnaire B) to assess the implementation of activity-based costing systems in their companies on a 5-grade scale, from total failure through partial failure, moderate success and success to great success. None of the companies considered implementation as a complete failure or partial failure. Only one company declared great success, and 31 (of the 32 companies which answered this question) evaluated ABC implementation as a moderate success (19) or success (12).

Table 4.16. Main problems during ABC implementation

Specification	Mean[a]	Standard deviation	Variability coefficient	Dominant value
High labor input during ABC implementation and operation	3.55	0.97	0.27	4
Insufficient knowledge of ABC among employees	3.42	0.99	0.29	4
Problems with model (selection of activities, drivers etc.)	3.25	0.92	0.28	3
Other	3.00	2.00	0.67	1
Lack of adequate IT resources	2.68	1.44	0.54	1
High cost of ABC implementation and operation	2.33	1.09	0.47	3
Lack of support from management/head office etc.	1.81	1.14	0.63	1
Other priorities (implementation of ISO, TQM, ERP etc.)	1.80	1.12	0.62	1

[a] The respondents assessed the significance of problems according to the following scale: 1 – no problem, 2 – insignificant, 3 – moderately significant, 4 – significant, 5 – very significant.

As far as problems with ABC implementation are concerned (see Table 4.16), high labour input in implementation and maintenance were named as significant problem (average grade – 3.55). None of the problems listed in the survey questionnaire was assessed as very significant. The respondents named four problems considered by them as moderately significant:

1) insufficient knowledge of ABC among employees (average grade – 3.42);
2) difficulties with model design, e.g. choice of activities, drivers etc. (3.25);
3) other problems, such as resistance to change (foodstuffs manufacturing company) or mutual antagonism caused by disclosure of individual divisions profitability as a result of activity-based costing implementation (service company) (3);
4) inadequate IT resources (2.68).

Problems evaluated as insignificant included: the high costs of ABC implementation and maintenance (average rating – 2.33), lack of management/ headquarters etc. support (1.81), and other priorities, e.g. adoption of ISO, TQM or ERP (1.80).

Innes and Mitchell (1998) observed that high labour input is regarded as presenting a problem not only before but also after ABC implementation. It was named as one of five main problems encountered by companies using ABC, the remaining four problems being: difficulties with collecting data on cost drivers, processes crossing divisional boundaries, other priorities, and great time load placed on the accounting personnel.

4.4.3. Analysis of the structure of ABC systems

Activity-based costing systems employed in sample companies operate in various IT applications (see Table 4.17).

Table 4.17. IT environment of ABC models in the companies surveyed

Specification	n	%
Spreadsheet or database (EXCEL, ACCESS etc.)	19	57.6
Specially written computer program	5	15.2
Ready-made specialized software adapted for specific needs of the company	4	12.1
Ready-made (adjusted for specific needs) module in an integrated system	5	15.2
Total	33	100.0

The lack of appropriate software is among the chief problems connected with ABC implementation in Poland, which has often been pointed out by practitioners. There are two kinds of tools most commonly used for this purpose: ready-made, specialized programs, customized for individual company's needs (this mode of ABC informatization is mostly adopted by large enterprises) and in-house designed models of ABC using spreadsheets and databases (this way is usually chosen by small enterprises, which on the one hand, do not have sufficient resources to buy specialist software and on the other hand, do not need very sophisticated systems, because the structure of ABC in such companies normally is relatively simple). Rather rarely are used such modes of informatization as individually developed information systems and ready-made, modules adapted for the individual needs of the integrated systems. The research carried out in Great Britain (Innes et al., 2000) and in New Zealand (Cotton et al., 2003) showed that the respondents pointed out the use of diversified software for the implementation of activity-based costing systems, although they were mainly specialized programs for ABC. Such software was applied by 58% of companies in Great Britain, 47% in New Zealand but only 12.1% in Poland[12].

ABC includes five basic elements, i.e. resources, resource drivers, activities, activity drivers and cost objects. This is a simplified model, but it provides a good indication of the ABC structure in particular companies and the degree of the model's complexity. Activity-based costing systems functioning in the companies covered by the survey vary widely in respect of the elements identified (see Table 4.18).

Table 4.18. Number of elements identified in ABC systems

Elements	Number					
Resources	3	12	4	1	1	21
	14.3%	57.1%	19.0%	4.8%	4.8%	100.0%
Resource drivers	6	11	3	1	0	21
	28.6%	52.4%	14.3%	4.8%	0.0%	100.0%
Activities	4	12	9	4	0	29
	13.8%	41.4%	31.0%	13.8%	0.0%	100.0%
Activity drivers	6	12	7	1	0	26
	23.1%	46.2%	26.9%	3.8%	0.0%	100.0%
Cost objects (products, customers etc.)	2	3	8	5	11	29
	6.9%	10.3%	27.6%	17.2%	37.9%	100.0%

Analysis of the data presented in Table 4.18 reveals that:

1) in most of the companies, activity-based costing systems have the following numbers of elements: 6–100 resources (76.1% of companies), 1–20 resource drivers (81% companies), 6–100 activities (72.4%), 6–100 activity drivers (73.1%) and over 500 cost objects (37.9%);

2) in 2 cases activity-based costing had more than 100 resources (101–500 and over 500);

3) only 1 company used more than one hundred different resource cost drivers;

4) only 4 companies (13.8%) identified more than 100 activities, and only 1 company (3.8%) more than 100 various activity cost drivers;

5) the majority of the companies (55.1%) identified over 100 cost objects (products, customers etc.);

6) several respondents stated that their ABC systems used a maximum 5 resources, resource drivers, activities, activity drivers or cost objects – it indicates that their systems' level of detail is rather low (it should be noted that 9 companies had declared earlier that they used activity-based costing to a limited extent).

---

[12] Research carried out on a sample of 552 companies using activity-based costing (Nair, 2000), showed that two-thirds of respondents stressed the necessity of integrating ABC/M systems with ERP systems, the percentage of such answers grew along with the size of the company.

Table 4.19. Number of calculations for different cost objects in the companies surveyed

Objects	Number					
Products	5 20.8%	3 12.5%	8 33.3%	2 8.3%	6 25.0%	24 100.0%
Groups of products	6 25.0%	12 50.0%	5 20.8%	1 4.2%	0 0.0%	24 100.0%
Customers	2 15.4%	3 23.1%	3 23.1%	3 23.1%	2 15.4%	13 100.0%
Groups of customers	7 43.8%	7 43.8%	1 6.3%	1 6.3%	0 0.0%	16 100.0%
Sales regions	7 46.7%	7 46.7%	1 6.7%	0 0.0%	0 0.0%	15 100.0%
Distribution channels	10 66.7%	4 26.7%	1 6.7%	0 0.0%	0 0.0%	15 100.0%
Organizational units	9 47.4%	4 21.1%	5 26.3%	1 5.3%	0 0.0%	19 100.0%
Projects	7 46.7%	5 33.3%	3 20.0%	0 0.0%	0 0.0%	15 100.0%

With respect to the complexity of activity-based costing systems, empirical research carried out around the world provide different results. Research done in Great Britain (Innes *et al.*, 2000) revealed that usually in the activity-based costing there were 40 cost objects isolated and 52 activities concentrated in 22 cost pools calculated by means of 14 activity drivers. According to the empirical research conducted in New Zealand (Cotton *et al.*, 2003), the systems of activity-based costing functioning there are less complex than the systems functioning in British companies. On average, there are 4 cost objects and 15 activities concentrated in 6 cost pools calculated by means of 5 activity drivers isolated within a New Zealand company. Additionally, research done in Italy (Cinquini *et al.*, 2008) proves that, like in New Zealand, Italian systems of ABC are less complex than those in British companies. In 93.3% of cases (Cinquini *et al.*, 2008), the system does not use more than 10 different drivers (research carried out in 1999 showed that 40% of companies used more than 10 drivers). The authors came to the conclusion that the systems of activity-based costing which have been implemented recently are less complex than the systems implemented before.

It needs to be emphasized that the differences in the minuteness of activity-based costing systems functioning in different countries stems from the fact that the British research investigated larger companies than in other countries, and that, with time (British research was the earliest), the awareness of high implementation costs and maintenance of complex systems grew[13].

---

[13] The degree of complexity of cost systems (including ABC) may depend on a variety of

The respondents were next asked about the number of cost calculations done for different objects (products, customers etc.) as part of activity-based costing (see Table 4.19).

Analysis of the data presented in table 4.19 reveals that:

1) the highest proportion of the companies (33.3%) calculate costs for 21–100 products; 25% for over 500 products;

2) 98.5% of the companies make cost calculations for up to 100 groups of products; only one company for between 101–500 groups;

3) cost calculations are made for 6–20 customers (23.1% of the companies), 21–100 customers (23.1%) or 101–500 customers (23.1%);

4) 87.6% calculate costs for 1–20 groups of customers;

5) costs are also calculated for 1–20 sales regions (93.4% of the companies);

6) 66.7% calculate costs for several (1–5) distribution channels;

7) calculations for 1–5 organisational units are done in 47.4% of the companies, and 46.7% calculate costs for several (1–5) projects.

The number of profitability analyses based on ABC carried out in individual company cases was addressed in the next question. The answers showed that the numbers of profitability analyses coincided with the numbers of cost calculations, which means that, generally, profitability analyses were prepared for those cost objects for which cost calculations were done.

Of the 33 sample companies, as many as 27 classify costs into fixed and variable; only 7 companies (18.2%) do not make such a division. Less than half of the enterprises (13, 41.9%) identify unused capacity costs, of which a few use one of two alternative variants of cost allocation: (a) only indirect costs of used capacity are assigned to products, customers etc. and costs of unused capacity are charged directly to income, (b) all costs, including costs of unused capacity, are allocated to products, customers etc.

Table 4.20 shows how activity-based costing modifications are done in the companies concerned.

---

variables such as importance of cost information for management, the cost structure or product differentiation. Research carried out by Cinquini *et al.* (2008) on a sample of 84 Italian companies revealed that there was a statistically significant and positive relationship between the importance of the cost data and the cost structure and the degree of activity-based costing system's complexity. It means that the more important information about costs for management and the more indirect costs in the company's cost structure, the higher complexity of activity-based costing system. No earlier research (apart from the research by Björnenak, 1997) had proved the relationship between the cost structure and the degree of cost system complexity. On the other hand, the relationship between the importance of information about costs and the system's complexity was previously exhibited, although the relationship was statistically insignificant (Baird *et al.*, 2004; Drury, Tyles, 2005; Al-Omiri, Drury, 2007).

Table 4.20. Modifications of ABC systems in the companies surveyed

Specification	n	%
No modification so far	7	21.9
From time to time, as necessary	19	59.3
At regular intervals	6	18.8
Total	32	100.0

Nearly four-fifths of the companies (25, 88.1%) modify their activity-based costing systems: 6 do it on a regular basis and 19 from time to time, as need arise. In 7 companies (21.9%) no modification had been done (it should be noted that in 66.7% of these firms ABC systems were not "older" than 3 years). In responding to this question several companies offered the following explanations:

1) "regular modifications are carried out once a year together with work on the preparation of the budget for the next year" (large foodstuffs manufacturing company);

2) "modifications are carried out regularly, but their frequency is largely connected with the identification of new cost centers, projects or groups of projects; such modifications are done from two to five times per year" (medium-sized commercial company);

3) "modifications are done on an annual basis, although at times they were done more frequently, e.g. after the introduction of a new division of sales segments, because of the profitability reporting to management requirement" (large telecommunications company).

4.4.4. Analysis of the utilisation of information generated by ABC systems

The subsequent part of the survey was dedicated to the users of ABC information in the companies studied and the use that is made of it (see Table 4.21).

Information from activity-based costing systems is used very frequently by departments such as purchasing department (company producing household goods) or engineering department (telecommunications company). Frequent use was reported to be made by management accountants (average rating 4.28) and top management (average grade 3.71[14]). Occasional use is made by: (a) marketing and sales department (3.41), (b) operational departments, e.g. manufacturing department (3.10), (c) accountants (2.63).

Activity-based costing has a number of applications, as reported below on the basis of a literature review:

• research conducted by Innes et al. (2000) showed that, respectively, 24.2% (1994) and 16.1% (1999) of the companies which they studied used ABC for

---

[14] The results are statistically significant at a significance level of 0.01 for: management accounting specialists (t = 5.49) and top management (t = 3.25).

inventory valuation in financial statements – it is an area of the most limited of the ABC uses that were tested by these authors;

Table 4.21. Utilisation of ABC information in the companies surveyed

Specification	Mean[a]	Standard deviation	Variability coefficient	Dominant value
Other divisions	4.50	1.00	0.22	5
Management accountants	4.28	1.25	0.29	5
Top management	3.71	1.22	0.33	4
Sales and marketing departments	3.41	1.27	0.37	4
Operational departments (e.g. production)	3.10	1.21	0.39	3
Accountants	2.63	1.47	0.56	1

[a] The respondents were asked to assign a rating on a five-grade scale; 1 – information not used, 2 – information used sporadically, 3 – information used from time to time, 4 – information used frequently 5 – information used very frequently.

- ABC can provide a basis for determining long-term variable costs and for making decisions on the volume and structure of sales in the longer term (Johnson, Kaplan, 1987);
- budgeting by activities can be used for improving responsibility accounting in a company (Brimson, Fraser, 1991);
- information about costs of activities and demand for products can be used in the process of designing goods and services (Jonez, Wright, 1987; Dolinsky, Vollman, 1991);
- customer profitability analysis is one of the most frequently used types of ABC information; for instance, research carried out by Innes *et al.* (2000) in 1994 and 1999 revealed that the percentages of companies making use of customer profitability information were 51.4% and 51.6%, respectively for these years;
- traditional analysis of profit sensitivity, leverage analysis and breakeven analysis are based on the precept of classification of costs into fixed and variable; Cooper (1994) proposed an extension of this type of analysis by repartition of costs into four levels: unit of product, batch, type and company as a whole.

Information supplied by activity-based costing in the analyzed companies is used, to a varying extent, in various areas (see Table 4.22[15]).

Activity-based costing information was found to be very important (average rating 4.50) in the following areas: (a) "making investment decisions, setting minimum batch size etc." (foodstuffs manufacturing company), (b) "management

---

[15] The results are statistically significant at a significance level of 0.01 for: cost reduction (t = 7,88), pricing decisions (t = 3.85), budgeting (t = 2.84), performance measurement and improvement (t = 2.86) and sales plan optimalization (t = 2.85).

remuneration" (commercial company), (c) "establishment of break-even points in investment projects appraisal" (telecommunications company).

Table 4.22. Significance (applicability) of ABC information in the companies surveyed

Specification	Mean[a]	Standard deviation	Variability coefficient	Dominant value
Other	4.50	1.00	0.22	5
Cost reduction	4.16	0.82	0.20	5
Price decisions	3.81	1.17	0.31	5
Budgeting (ABB)	3.75	1.29	0.35	5
Performance measurement and improvement	3.65	1.16	0.32	4
Sales plan optimization	3.56	1.01	0.28	3
Customer profitability analysis	3.52	1.37	0.39	5
Cost modelling (e.g. sensitivity analysis)	3.41	1.01	0.30	4
Goods and services designing	2.88	1.30	0.45	3
Inventories valuation (for financial reporting)	2.40	1.63	0.68	1

[a] The respondents were asked to assign a rating on a five-grade scale: 1 – information is insignificant, 2 – information is not very significant, 3 – information is fairly significant, 4 – information is significant, 5 – information is very significant.

Research into the diffusion of activity-based costing showed similar results with respect to the use of activity-based costing information:

- in the United States (IMA, 1996) companies used activity-based costing for making decisions in areas such as production and marketing (53% of companies using ABC). 32% used ABC for making operational and strategic decisions and 15% made use of activity-based costing in financial reporting (in these companies, traditional systems of costing were replaced by activity-based costing in financial reporting)[16]. Research conducted on a group of 552 enterprises using activity-based costing (Nair, 2000) revealed that the main areas where information from activity-based costing was used included: product pricing (58%), analysis of processes (51%), performance management (49%), profitability analysis (38%) and value management (18%). Later studies (Nair, 2000) showed that managers noticed that information from ABC could be used in areas such as budgeting or performance management. Such use of information generated by ABC/M systems required the integration of activity-based costing IT systems with ERP systems and data warehouses; the integration enabled effective data collection and its analysis and reporting within entire organization;

---

[16] Another piece of research carried out by IMA (1997) showed that companies mainly used information from activity-based costing in product pricing (54%), performance measurement (36%) and pricing policy (32%).

• in Great Britain (Innes *et al.*, 2000) and New Zealand (Cotton *et al.*, 2003) ABC was mainly used to reduce costs and manage costs, to price goods and services, to revise pricing policy, and to measure and improve activities in modelling costs and in budgeting. Another piece of research (Friedman, Lyne, 2000) proved cost management (cost reduction), product pricing and budgeting to be the prevailing areas in which information generated by activity-based costing was used. The information was used on a moderate level in making make-or-buy decisions or decisions related to process reorganization. The information was less frequently used for product pricing, capital budgeting or financial reporting;

• in developing countries e.g. China (Parkinson, 2009), information from activity-based costing was basically used in areas such as product pricing and widely-understood decision-making (usefulness of the system's information was ranked high with respect to investment decisions and risk evaluation). Surprisingly, indirect cost allocation was an area where ABC the information was not often used. Information provided by ABC systems is used in the liquidation of investment expenditure, reduction of expenditure, expansion of expenditure or making new investments (see Table 4.23).

Table 4.23. Types of decisions in which ABC information is used

Specification	Liquidation	Reduction	Expansion	New investment
Products	9	12	15	12
Groups of products	4	11	19	11
Customers	4	3	10	5
Groups of customers	2	7	12	3
Sales regions	2	9	14	5
Distribution channels	2	9	11	4
Organisational units (e.g. divisions)	2	11	8	7
Projects	3	5	7	8

Analysis of the data from Table 4.23 indicates that ABC information is mainly used for making decisions concerning the expansion of expenditure (96) and, to a lesser extent, the reduction of expenditure (67) and new investments (55). The least use is made of this information in decisions on liquidation (28).

The degree of application of ABC information in performance measurement and evaluation was the subject of the next question (see table 4.24).

According to the respondents, activity-based costing information is often used for the valuation of activities and processes (average rating 3.59[17]) and performance measurement of the company as a whole (3.50). From time to time it is used for measuring the performance of responsibility centers (3.15) and for employee performance measurement (2.93).

---

[17] The results are statistically significant at significance level of 0.01 (t = 2.74).

Table 4.24. Application of ABC information in performance measurement and evaluation

Specification	Mean[a]	Standard deviation	Variability coefficient	Dominant value
Measurement and evaluation of activities and processes	3.59	1.15	0.32	4
Company performance measurement and evaluation	3.50	1.21	0.35	4
Responsibility center performance measurement and evaluation	3.15	1.52	0.48	4
Management and employee performance measurement and evaluation	2.93	1.46	0.50	4

[a] The respondents were asked to assign a rating on a five-grade scale: 1 – information is insignificant, 2 – information is not very significant, 3 – information is fairly significant, 4 – information is significant, 5 – information is very significant.

The complexity of activity-based costing systems depends, apart from the number of identified elements (resources, resource drivers, activities, activity drivers and objects) on whether a given system includes activities with particular characteristics. The survey revealed that:

1) in 14 of the companies surveyed (42.4%) activities were classified into primary, supporting and general; this classification (Bellis-Jones, Hand, 1989) can be used for the estimation and then reduction of costs of activities other than primary;

2) in 13 companies (39.4%) activities were identified at the level of product unit, batch, type of product and company as a whole (Cooper, Kaplan, 1991);

3) in 7 companies activities were divided into strategic and operational;

4) only 6 companies stated that they identified activities creating value to the customer and not creating value to the customer; this classification is related with a very important area of ABC application, namely cost reduction (Brimson, 1991).

17 of the 33 companies employ *activity-based budgeting*. The respondents were asked to state what benefits their companies derived from this type of budgeting[18] (see Table 4.25).

The respondents whose companies applied activity-based budgeting stated that it significantly (there was a considerable benefit): (a) improved variance analysis (average rating 3.88), (b) improved the performance measurement system (average rating 3.87), (c) ensured relating costs to responsibility (average

---

[18] Piosik (2002, p. 70) points out that "the main benefit of using activity-based budgeting is the integration of the system with strategic level of ABM, as well as integration with the Genka Kikaku and Kaizen concept. It means that there is the possibility of enclosing programs of reduction of expected demand for activities and costs of resources in the budgeting".

rating 3.87) and (d) enabled more realistic budgets (average rating 3.80) [19]. The companies see a moderate benefit of using activity-based budgeting in three areas: (a) better identification of the demand for resources (average rating 3.43), (b) greater involvement of employees in budgeting (average rating 3.32) and (c) better acceptance of budgets (average rating 3.29).

Table 4.25. The benefits of using activity-based budgeting in the companies surveyed

Specification	Mean[a]	Standard deviation	Variability coefficient	Dominant value
Improved variance analysis	3.88	1.02	0.26	4
Improved performance measurement system	3.87	1.46	0.38	5
Relating costs to responsibility	3.87	1.13	0.29	4
More realistic budgets	3.80	1.08	0.28	4
Identification of demand for resources	3.43	1.16	0.34	4
Greater involvement of employees in budgeting	3.31	0.95	0.29	4
Better acceptance of budgets	3.29	1.33	0.40	4

[a] The respondents were asked to assign a rating on a five-grade scale: 1 – no benefit, 2 – little benefit, 3 – moderate benefit, 4 – considerable benefit, 5 – great benefit.

It should be stressed that the great majority of the 17 companies which have implemented activity-based budgeting apply it only in certain areas of activity, while in other areas they use traditional budgeting – this is the case with 15 (88.2%) of the companies which declared the use of ABB. Only 2 of them (11.8%) gave up traditional budgeting after ABB implementation.

There are a number of ABB applications that companies can benefit from, for instance: (1) the availability of historical data at the levels of resource drivers or activities will support making rational decisions at the level of resources necessary e.g. for future expansion of the company, (2) activity-based variance analysis can be useful in monitoring the causes of variances, (3) provision of information on utilisation of production capacity through comparison of the actual level with available capacity potential (Yoshikava *et al.*, 1992; Kaplan, 1994a).

Research conducted by Innes *et al.* (2000) found that about 60% of the largest British companies using ABC had implemented ABB as well. The following benefits deriving from ABB were identified: better identification of centres' demand for resources, preparation of more realistic budgets, greater involvement of employees in budget preparation, improved systems of performance

---

[19] The results are statistically significant at a significance level of 0.01 for: improvement of variance analysis (t = 3.42), relating costs to responsibility (t = 2.98) and calculation of more realistic budgets (t = 2.86).

measurement, improved connection between costs and responsibility, better acceptance of budgets, enhanced quality of variance analysis.

Information from activity-based costing systems is used in relations with customers in a variety of ways (see Table 4.26).

Table 4.26. Application of ABC information in customer relations

Specification	Mean[a]	Standard deviation	Variability coefficient	Dominant value
Improves customer service cost control	3.35	1.35	0.40	4
Provides information for price policy formulation	3.23	1.21	0.37	4
Provides information for marketing strategy development	3.08	1.20	0.39	3
Provides information for customer policy formulation	3.04	1.22	0.40	4
Provides a basis for negotiations with customers	2.73	1.25	0.46	4
Provides a basis for giving up customers	2.60	1.29	0.50	4

[a] The respondents were asked to assign a rating on a five-grade scale: 1 – no benefit, 2 – little benefit, 3 – moderate benefit, 4 – considerable benefit, 5 – great benefit.

Analysis of the data in Table 4.26 shows that as regards customer relations, ABC information is used to a moderate extent in all the areas specified. It is interesting to note that the majority of the respondents stated that ABC information is used in customer relations to a considerable extent (predominant rating – 4); only for the development of marketing strategy was the rating 3. Research on the diffusion of activity-based costing proved that ABC implementation improves customer profitability analysis (e.g. in research by Clarke *et al.* (1999), improvement of customer profitability analysis was recorded in 25% of companies using ABC).

The enterprises which have implemented activity-based costing also use other advanced management methods (see Table 4.27). Some of the sample companies made use of advanced management methods in addition to ABC – some used many such methods while others only a few. It was found that:

1) one company used eight methods, one company – six and one company – five,
2) six companies used three methods;
3) seven companies used two methods and seven used one method;
4) ten companies did not use any advanced management methods other than ABC.

In the last question of the survey, the respondents were asked to express their opinion on the expected modifications of ABC system in their companies.

8 (25.8%) companies did not plan to introduce any modifications to the existing activity-based costing as the system was appropriate for their needs. 7 (22.6%) companies do not intend to modify the functioning system within the next year, although they think that the system should be modified but there is no change-oriented atmosphere, no sufficient financial resources, no time or there are other priorities.

Table 4.27. Application of advanced management methods in the companies surveyed

Specification	n	%
Just in time	3	9.1
Business process reengineering	7	21.2
Continuous improvement	9	27.3
Benchmarking	12	36.4
Target costing	5	15.2
Life cycle costing	4	12.1
Balanced scorecard	10	30.3
Economic value added	6	18.2
Other	2	6.1

More than half of the companies (51.6%) were planning to modify the functioning activity-based costing within the next year, the modifications included:
- "extension of range, improvement of automatic data entering into EXCEL spreadsheet" (chemical industry company);
- "changes will include introduction of cost division into fixed and variable, and take into account the costs of unused capacity" (food industry manufacturing company);
- "soon, the ABC system will undergo some major changes, however it depends on management's attitude and head office requirements" (company manufacturing household goods);
- "the system's adaptation to cost calculation of new services will cause changes" (consulting company);
- "modifications related to adaptation to changes in the organizational structure" (insurance company);
- "those will be annual or even more frequent changes, connected with product development, company strategy, structure reorganization – possible acquisitions, technical services outsourcing etc." (telecommunications company).

4.5. Summary and conclusions

The author's own questionnaire research into the diffusion of activity-based costing in Polish companies (495 companies, questionnaire A) and research on functioning of those systems within enterprises which use them (33 companies, questionnaire B) enabled the formulation of the following detailed conclusions, which support the main thesis and verify the hypotheses:

1. The research (questionnaire A) proved that Polish companies mainly use traditional cost accounting systems; modern systems (e.g. activity-based costing or target costing) are implemented sporadically and their diffusion is considerably smaller in comparison to Western countries. The majority of the companies surveyed, 392 companies (79.2%), use actual costing (full costing or variable costing), 135 companies (27.3%) use standard costing (full or variable) and 60 companies (12.1%) use multi-step and multi-dimensional costing. The use of modern methods of costing is not frequent – activity-based costing is used by 46 companies (9.3%) and target costing is used by merely 9 companies (1.8%). In several cases the respondents declared using other cost accounting systems, and a few companies admitted to using a combined system, which comprised of features characteristic of different cost accounting systems.

2. The respondents were asked to indicate which of the factors listed in the questionnaire research (questionnaire A) had influenced the decision to implement ABC in their enterprises and to what extent. After calculating the average rating done by the respondents, it turned out that the reasons for ABC implementation of important and very important significance mainly included: other reasons (e.g. the necessity to value non-standard products, the need to obtain accurate information for managing activities or to adopt a system used by the competitors) (4.80), the need for cost reduction and performance improvement (4.03), changed management information needs (3.91) and the need for improvement of management control (3.62). The factors believed to have contributed to ABC adoption to a slightly lesser degree included dissatisfaction with the current cost accounting system (3.25), increased competition (3.19), headquarters' demand (3.12), and seeking to gain new markets (2.78) – the respondents rated the importance of these factors as moderate. The least importance was attached to change of strategy (2.48), availability of financial resources (2.47), change in organisational structure (2.47), availability of human resources (2.35), the implementation of new technologies (2.30), change of management (2.14) and favourable atmosphere among employees (1.91).

3. With respect to companies which are considering the implementation of activity-based costing, the questionnaire research (questionnaire A) enabled identification of three 'significant' problems expected in the implementation process: other (e.g. changes in legal and corporate regulations, fear of novelty) (4), insufficient knowledge of ABC among employees (3.97), and high labour input in ABC implementation and operation (3.66). Potential problems regarded by the respondents as 'moderately' important included: difficulty with designing the ABC model (3.45), the high cost of ABC implementation and operation (3.13), lack of sufficient IT resources (2.88), and other priorities (2.51). Lack of

management support for ABC implementation is believed by the respondents to be the least important problem (2.11) – the problem was rated as 'slight'. In contrast to the above problems expected by companies considering implementation of ABC, the analysis of real problems which appeared during implementation in companies using activity-based costing provided interesting results. The companies researched (questionnaire B) rated high labor input in implementation and maintenance as a considerable problem (3.55). None of the problems listed in the survey questionnaire was assessed as 'very significant'. However, the respondents named four problems as 'moderately important': insufficient knowledge of ABC among employees (3.42), difficulties with model design (e.g. choice of activities, drivers etc.) (3.25), other problems (e.g. resistance to change or mutual antagonism) (3), and lack of sufficient IT resources (2.68). Problems evaluated as 'insignificant' included: high costs of ABC implementation and maintenance (2.33), lack of management (board, headquarters etc.) support (1.81), and other priorities (e.g. adoption of ISO, TQM or ERP etc.) (1.80). It needs to be stressed that the actual problems encountered during activity-based costing implementation were fewer (lower ratings) than the problems expected by the companies considering implementation.

4. The questionnaire research (questionnaire A) revealed the reasons for non-consideration or rejection of activity-based costing. Problems rated by respondents as 'significant' included: insufficient knowledge of ABC among employees (4.05), high labor input in ABC implementation and operation (3.99), the high cost of ABC implementation and operation (3.82), and difficulty with model construction (3.64). Among the problems of high importance, respondents named other problems e.g. lack of guidelines from headquarters abroad, the need to measure profitability at the level of the headquarters (located abroad), too small scope of activity, fast and not completely predictable growth of the company, inadequate financial resources, lack of awareness of the need for proper cost calculation, and negative attitude of the accounting department (4.31). The factors which influenced to a lesser degree rejection or non-consideration of ABC implementation included: lack of adequate IT resources (3.29), lack of management support (3.17) and other priorities (2.87) – respondents rated these problems as 'moderate'. Low levels of indirect costs (2.49) and satisfaction with the current costing system (2.46) were considered to be the least important problems.

5. The questionnaire research (questionnaire A) did not prove the positive relationship between activity-based costing implementation and level of competition in the company's main area of activity. However, it is possible to assume that:

a) the larger the company, the more likely that it uses ABC or is considering its implementation;

b) the higher the share of indirect costs within the company's cost structure, the more likely that the company uses activity-based costing or is considering its implementation;

c) activity-based costing is used or considered by a considerably higher percentage of companies with a larger share of foreign capital than by companies with domestic capital only.

6. ABC embraces five basic elements i.e. resources, resource cost drivers, activities, activity cost drivers and cost objects. The model is simplified, however it portrays well the ABC structure within the company surveyed and its degree of complexity. With regard to the number of elements identified, the systems of activity-based costing functioning in the companies researched (questionnaire B) vary considerably. In some small companies, the activity--based costing system was not well developed and it contained only a few resources, resource cost drivers, activities, activity cost drivers and cost objects (out of the companies analyzed, 9 declared that they used ABC in its limited scope). In four large companies, within the ABC system, between 100 and 500 activities were identified, but only in one of the companies 100 different activity cost drivers were distinguished. The questionnaire research enables to conclude that in most of the companies surveyed, the ABC system has the following number of elements: 6–100 resources (76.1% of companies), 1–20 resource cost drivers (81% of companies), 6–100 activities (72.4% of companies), 6–100 activity cost drivers (73.1% of companies) and from 21 to more than 500 cost objects (82.7% of companies). Cost calculations for different types of objects (products, customers, distribution channels, projects etc.) constitute a considerable part of activity-based costing. The highest proportion of the companies (72.2%) prepare cost calculations for products and group of products, 39.4% of companies prepare cost calculations for customers, and 48.5% of firms prepare it for groups of customers. Information from the ABC systems also provides the basis for cost calculation for sales regions, distribution channels or projects (45.5% of companies). It should be emphasized that the number of profitability analyses prepared by means of activity-based costing coincides with the number of cost calculations i.e. generally, profitability analyses were prepared for those cost objects for which cost calculations were made. The complexity of activity-based costing depends on the number of identified elements (resources, resource cost drivers, activities, activity cost drivers and objects) but also on certain features of the activities: (a) out of the companies surveyed, 14 (42.4%) divided activities into support, primary and general, (b) 13 companies (39.4%) isolated activities at the level of unit of product, batch of products, type of products and the entire company, (c) 7 companies (21.2%) divided activities into strategic and operational, (d) only 6 companies (18.2%) declared that they differentiate activities into value adding and non-value adding

activities for customers. Among the 33 companies researched, 27 (81.8%) enterprises divided indirect costs into fixed and variable. Less than half of the companies (41.9%, 13 companies) isolate costs of unused capacity.

7. In companies, where activity-based costing functions (questionnaire B), information generated by the system is used differently by individual departments and enables them to make various decisions, in particular:

a) information from activity-based costing systems in the companies researched is used 'very frequently' by such departments as the purchasing department or engineering department (4.50), 'frequent' use was reported to be made by management accountants (4.28) and top management (3.71), 'occasional' use was made by marketing and sales department (3.41), and operational departments (3.10) and 'sporadic' use was ascribed to accountants (2.63);

b) information from the system was used by the companies surveyed in making numerous decisions, the information was ranked as 'significant' in such areas as: cost reduction (4.16), price decisions (3.81), budgeting (3.75), performance measurement and improvement (3.65), sales plan optimalization (3.56) and customer profitability analysis (3.52). The information from ABC was regarded as 'fairly significant' for cost modelling (3.41) and product design (2.88), and it was rated 'not very significant' for inventory valuation for financial reporting (2.40);

c) ABC information is more frequently used for making decisions about the expansion of expenditure and to a lesser extent about the reduction of expenditure or about making new investments. Information provided by ABC systems is rarely used for making decisions about liquidation;

d) on the basis of the present research, it is possible to claim that information from ABC systems is 'frequently' used for the measurement and evaluation of activities and processes (3.59) and the whole company performance measurement and evaluation (3.50), and 'sometimes' it is used for responsibility centers' performance measurement and evaluation (3.15) as well as management and employee performance measurement and evaluation (2.93);

e) information from ABC in the companies studied is used to a 'moderate' extent in customer relations, in particular it: improves customer service cost control (3.35), provides information for price policy formulation (3.23), provides information for marketing strategy development (3.08), provides information for customer policy formulation (3.04), provides a basis for negotiations with customers (2.73) and provides a basis for giving up customers (2.60).

8. Companies, in which activity-based costing has been adopted additionally use other modern methods of management i.e. mainly benchmarking (36.4%), balanced scorecard (30.3%) and continuous improvement (27.3%). To a lesser extent, companies applied such methods as business process reengineering (21.2%), economic value added (18.2%), and target costing (15.2%). The methods

which were rarely used included: life cycle costing (12.1%) and just in time (9.1%). Two companies (6.1%) declared use of some other modern methods – the researched companies used the six sigma method (car parts manufacturer), lean management (car parts manufacturer) and strategic analysis (household goods manufacturer). Some of the surveyed companies, used numerous modern methods of management, apart from ABC, and others used fewer of them. 10 companies did not use any other method apart from activity-based costing.

CHAPTER 5

EXPLORING MANAGEMENT ACCOUNTING SYSTEM CHANGE IN THE LIGHT OF CASE STUDIES AND ACTION RESEARCH. THE CASE OF ACTIVITY- -BASED COSTING IN POLAND

5.1. Introduction

Change, especially change in management accounting, is a result of the interactions between environmental factors (e.g. technology, competition, globalization, culture, politics) and internal processes within organizations (e.g. management accounting). Analyzing change, it is possible to learn how this interaction happens, what the factors influencing change are (positive and negative), what the role of individuals in the change process is, and how change influences organizations (Wickramasinghe, Alawattage, 2007). Focusing on change enables us to realize that management accounting is much more than a set of technical tools used in practice. Management accounting relates to social systems of organizations within which the relationships are changing – old techniques are being replaced by new ones. Traditional management accounting techniques, like budgeting and control, are no longer sufficient (although they might still be very useful) to meet the needs of organizations; managers also need different techniques (e.g. ABC, BSC) suitable to support strategic business aspects.

The transformations taking place in the field of management accounting have contributed to the intensification of research and have made it possible to formulate theories which explain the process of change in management accounting. The interest in the process of change in management accounting is connected to understanding the reasons why the change occurred and it is also motivated by the fact that this process is not sufficiently presented in the literature. The management accounting literature does not cover the ways the change occurs in enough detail, how it is implemented or what the results of the implementation are (Mitchell, 1990; Cobb *et al.* 1995; Kasurinen, 2002) however, it contains attempts to develop a theoretical framework for understanding the factors promoting and obstructing change.

In the light of the above, this study aims to analyze the forces influencing the process of management accounting change and, in particular, the factors influencing change in a positive (motivators, catalysts and facilitators) and negative manner (barriers), and also the role of individuals in the implementation process. The rest of the chapter is organized as follows: first the methodology underlying this research is discussed, followed by a short presentation of the research method. Then case studies of management accounting change in four companies are briefly analyzed (the analysis in the first three companies is based on the case study method and in the fourth company it is in the form of action research). In the next part of the chapter, discussion of the management accounting change model's suitability to explain innovation implementation in the analyzed companies is presented. The chapter finishes with a short conclusion.

5.2. Research methodology

Different studies have attempted to analyze the factors influencing the change process. The first attempt to model the management accounting change process was made by Innes and Mitchell (1990) based on seven manufacturing companies in the electronics industry (comparative case studies). The research suggested that change in management accounting is the result of a set of factors including: production technology, a competitive and dynamic market environment, the organizational structure, deteriorating financial performance, product cost structure, and management influence. On the basis of their nature and timing of their influence, the factors influencing change were grouped into three categories, namely: motivators, catalysts and facilitators. According to the Innes and Mitchell model, motivators (e.g. production technology, product cost structure and level of competition in the market) influence the change process in a general manner. Catalysts are factors whose occurrence corresponds closely with the timing of the change and they are directly associated with the change (e.g. the launch of competing products, poor financial performance). Facilitators (e.g. availability of IT resources and accounting staff, authority of accountants) are factors which, although not sufficient, are necessary for the change to occur. Management accounting change takes place through the interaction of motivators, catalysts and facilitators which act positively promoting the process of change.

The model of Innes and Mitchell (1990) was further developed by Cobb *et al.* (1995) in a longitudinal case study of change in the management accounting system of a division of a large multinational bank (the study took place during a seven-year period). The research of Cobb *et al.* (1995) was influenced by Hopwood (1987), who stated that "the consequences of accounting interventions in the organization can disturb, disrupt and displace the organizational arena [...] having the power to transform rather than to modify the process of organizational change" (Hopwood, 1987, p. 230). Cobb *et al.* (1995) criticized Innes's and Mitchell's (1990) model for not including factors obstructing the change process and focusing too much on factors from the organization's environment. The main contribution of the Cobb *et al.*(1995) model was to develop the model of Innes and Mitchell (1990) by identifying one type of factors (barriers) which disturb the process of change (e.g. resistance towards change, great amount of labor, changing priorities, accounting staff turnover) and also factors which influence management accounting change when it occurs in the organization – namely leadership (influence of key individuals/change agents in the process of change) and momentum for change (expectation of continuing change). The model of change in management accounting improved by Cobb *et al.* (1995) stated that motivators, catalysts and facilitators create the potential for change but stressed the pivotal role of leaders in overcoming barriers of change and reinforcing the momentum for change over some time. The interplay of factors promoting and disturbing change with the influence of leaders in the process of change is suggested by the model to have a very strong influence on whether the change occurs or not. According to Cobb *et al.* (1995) the role of change agents is fundamental to the change process: "motivators, catalysts and facilitators may be necessary to create a potential for change but action by individuals is needed to overcome the barriers to change" (Cobb *et al.*, 1995, p. 173). They stressed that key individuals act as catalysts, initiating the change process. Management accounting change occurs when their efforts combine with a momentum for change (expectation for continuing change). The Financial Controller in the study of Cobb *et al.* (1995, p. 172) commented that "the process of change can only happen through people, even if the vital elements of motivators, catalysts and facilitators are in place, change will not occur without commitment through the management process".

Probably the most important contribution of the Cobb *et al.* (1995) model was the identification of factors which can obstruct the process of change. Potential barriers to implementation have been broadly discussed in the management accounting literature. Argyris and Kaplan (1994) stressed that education and sponsorship enable advocates of change to articulate the merits of innovation on the one hand, and to gain management support for change on the other. They also say that to overcome defensive routines in the change process the organization should create internal commitment for the innovation implementation. Argyris and Kaplan (1994) argue that inadequate education and sponsorship, and inadequate internal commitment could be important barriers for the process of change. Shields (1995) generally supported the conclusions of Argyris and Kaplan (1994) by indicating that success of the change process was associated with behavioral and organizational variables. Shields stated that a lack of top management support, inadequate linkage to competitive strategies and performance evaluation, lack of training, ownership by accountants and inadequate resources could be main barriers in the change process. Roberts and Silvester (1996) stated that difficulties in the change process could be caused by organizational structures not favoring changes. Markus and Pfeffer (1983) claim that success of innovation implementation depends on the extent to which the new system matches the existing organizational culture and power distribution. They also stress that inadequate agreement on the organization's goals and the technology required for achieving them could present an important barrier for the process of change. Scapens and Roberts (1993) present the view that the change process could be obstructed by a failure to secure the legitimacy of a new system and also an inability to find a workable relationship between the languages of production and accounting. Strebel (1996) stressed that barriers in the process of change could be caused by different views on change of individuals – while for top managers change could be an opportunity, for middle level managers and employees change could be neither welcomed nor desired. The inclusion of different barriers in the change process led to the development of the management accounting change models of Inness and Mitchell (1990) and Cobb *et al.* (1995).

The next step in the development of the management accounting change model was made by Kasurinen (2002). The research was based on a case study of balanced scorecard implementation in a manufacturing company in Finland and resulted in a refinement of both the models of Innes and Mitchell's (1990) and Cobb *et al.* (1995). According to Kasurinen, the previous model (Cobb *et al.*, 1995) was limited because it specified only one general category of barriers of change. He extended the model, classifying barriers to change in three categories: confusers, delayers and frustrators. The first category, confusers, contains factors that disrupt the change process. The examples in Kasurinen's case included divergence between the project goals of the division and the business unit management, and uncertainty about the project's future role in the organization. The second category of barriers in Kasurinen's model, delayers, covers more technical and temporary factors, often related to the implementation of the innovation. The examples of delayers in the study were a lack of clear-cut strategies and inadequate information systems. Frustrators, the third category, included factors that suppress the change process. An example of this kind of factors was the prevailing engineering culture (in Kasurinen's case it strengthened the perception of the balanced scorecard as a diagnostic instrument instead of a strategic planning device). Apart from a more detailed analysis of barriers than in the Cobb *et al.* (1995) model, Kasurinen perceived differently the role of key individuals in the change process. While Cobb *et al.* stressed the capacity of leaders to overcome the barriers for change, Kasurinen emphasizes that leaders and momentum for change are necessary to create the potential for management accounting change to occur. According to Kasurinen, the potential for change can be neutralized by the three categories of barriers (confusers, delayers and frustrators) which determine whether the management accounting change occurs or not. Kasurinen's model of management accounting change is presented in Figure 5.1.

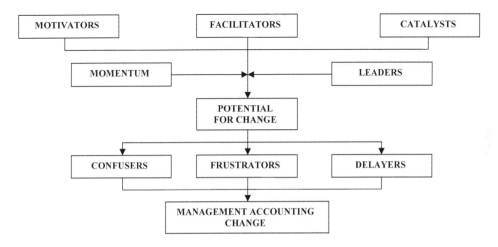

Figure 5.1. Management accounting change model

Source: Kasurinen, 2002, p. 338.

In 2008 Pimentel successfully tested Kasurinen's model on a longitudinal case study in a Portuguese service company. The analyzed company implemented BSC and the process turned out to be problematic – difficulties emerged in defining objectives and indicators, in regularly feeding the system and in creating a favorable organizational environment. The author identified factors that supported the change process, barriers to the process, the main factors of management accounting change, and their role in overcoming barriers to change and creating momentum for change. The research presented a contribution to Kasurinen's model by proposing a new category of barriers to change, the "negative questioners". Two "negative questioners" were observed – too much time devoted to implementation without significant results and an unfavorable cost-benefit ratio of the innovation. In his paper Pimentel argues that management accounting change should not be understood as a mere technical exercise but rather as an organizational and cultural process (Pimentel, 2008).

One more test of Kasurinen's model of management accounting change (the model was slightly revised) was conducted in the form of a questionnaire on the sample of Jordanian industrial companies (Nassar *et al.*, 2010; Nassar, 2012). The research proved the suitability of Kasurinen's model in explaining the forces driving the change process although the authors give up the classification of barriers into subcategories (as in Kasurinen's, 2002 and Pimentel's, 2008 research) and also did not analyze the role of individuals in the process of management accounting change implementation. The research was also different from previous work as it used a questionnaire which, on the one hand made it impossible to analyze the change process in such detail as the case study method, but on the other hand made it possible to test successfully the management accounting change model on a bigger sample (61 industrial companies). Table 5.1 summaries the previous studies investigating management accounting change.

Table 5.1. The development of management accounting change models

Author(s)	Catalysts	Motivators	Facilitators	Barriers
Innes, Mitchell, 1990	Loss of market share, poor financial performance, new accountants, organizational change	Competitiveness, production technology, organizational structure, product cost structure, short product life cycle	Accounting staff resources, authority of accountants, accounting computing resources	
Cobb *et al.*, 1995	Pressure on margins, individuals	Globalization, product innovation, increase in competition	IT, accounting staff	Changing priorities, accounting staff turnover, staff attitudes to change
Kasurinen, 2002	Pressure on margins, individuals	Globalization, product innovation, increase in competition	IT, accounting staff	Confusers: uncertainty, different views on change frustrators: existing systems, organizational culture delayers: lack of clear-cut strategy, inadequate information system

Pimentel, 2008	Pressure by the parent company, project of transformation, arrival of the champion, arrival of the process owner, conducted strategic analysis	Services cost structure, organizational structure, poor and financially oriented management accounting system, process of management and cultural change, participation of managers in implementation, product innovation	Staff availability, availability of data and information systems, authority of the planning and control function, existence of consultants, degree of authority from the parent company, strategically well-structured situation	Confusers: insufficient communication between managers, resignation of champion, resistance to top-down cascading of BSC, insufficient perception of BSC by the staff, cultural resistance frustrators: insufficient sponsorship, organizational structure changes, BSC not used for decision-making, lack of "quick-wins" delayers: inadequate data and information systems, inadequate measurement of indicators, lack of linkage with management system, insufficient perception of the BSC by the staff negative-questioners: long time gone, unfavorable cost-benefit ratio
Nassar et al., 2010; Nassar, 2012	Advice from consultants, we wished to try a new accounting innovation, to be seen as having a sophisticated costing system	Increasing proportion of overhead costs, increasing number of product variants, growing costs, increased competition	Adequate training was provided for designing ABC, operating data in the information system was updated in real time, adequate training was provided for using ABC, ABC received active support from top management	High cost of ABC implementation, high cost of ABC consulting, takes up a lot of computer staff's time

The majority of previous studies of management accounting change were based on one case study only and their validity was usually tested on companies in developed countries. In the light of the above, this research aims to make a contribution to Kasurinen's (2002) model in exploring the change process resulting from activity-based costing implementation in four companies in Poland. This paper is a response to the demand for studies on the implementation of management accounting innovations: "more case studies should be conducted in organizations which have successfully implemented the BSC or corresponding change. One aim of these studies could be to investigate the factors and implementation approaches which have made successful change possible. [...] the model could also be tested, and possibly further developed, by exposing it in other types of change projects" (Kasurinen, 2002, p. 341).

Using four cases this research makes a contribution to Kasurinen's model in explaining changes in the cost accounting systems in companies in Poland (especially in suggesting new factors which influence the change process and also underlying the role of controllers). The case study approach chosen for this research seems to provide the potential for analyzing the main forces influencing the implementation process of activity-based costing. The aim of the research will be fulfilled by analysis and understanding of individuals' actions in real-life companies.

5.3. Research method

It is possible to argue that research in the form of case studies enables the researcher to understand management accounting practice and to analyze how the practice is changing (Ryan *et al.*, 2002). Scapens (1990, p. 264) argues that "case studies offer us the possibility of understanding the nature of management accounting in practice; both in terms of the techniques, procedures, systems, etc. which are used and the way in which they are used." Yin (1989) states that a case study could be seen as "an empirical enquiry that investigates a contemporary phenomenon within a real-life context when the boundaries between phenomena are not clearly evident and in which multiple sources of evidence are used."

The need for more management accounting research in the form of case studies was advocated as far back as 30 years ago (Hopwood, 1983; Kaplan, 1993). Since then, the number of case studies has increased, but it still does not seem to be sufficient, especially where the case studies properly grounded in theory are concerned (these case studies seem to be most valuable for the theory development). Research in the form of case studies could be exploratory and explanatory of the change process and could also be the way to test and further develop models of management accounting change. Although the need for research in the form of case studies which could illustrate the nature of both internal and external forces of the change process is evident, there are still not enough such studies and especially studies developing already existing models of management accounting change on the sample of more than just one company.

The research on management accounting change in companies in Poland was organized in the form of a case study (four case studies) and followed the steps outlined for this type of research by Scapens (1990), Ryan *et al.* (2002) and Yin (2003). The research stages were as follows: (a) design of research questions, (b) selection of research methods and objects, (c) research design, (d) credibility of research assurance, (e) data collection, (f) report writing. The stages were followed interactively rather than sequentially:

• design of research questions – based on the literature on management accounting change, the following research questions were formulated: (a) what are the main factors positively influencing the ABC implementation process? (b) what are the main factors obstructing the process of ABC implementation? (c) what is the role of individuals in the change process and what creates momentum for change? (d) do the case studies fit in with Kasurinen's (2002) change model? (e) could any differences from Kasurinen's (2002) model be observed?

• the selection of research methods and objects – once research questions were formulated, the choice of companies was made, and the choice was deliberate – the selected companies had replaced their existing cost accounting system with ABC and therefore analysis of its implementation and implementation results was possible. Four enterprises were selected, which: (a) consented to participate in the research, (b) were different in terms of size, (c) were different in terms of area of operation. Due to trade secret, the names of the companies have not been disclosed, the companies were referred to as: ALPHA (a medium-sized manufacturing company), BETA (a large telecommunications company), GAMMA (a large insurance company), OMEGA (a medium-sized manufacturing and trading company). Some less significant features of the enterprises have been changed, and others were presented in a general manner, so that identification of the analyzed companies was impossible. Deliberate distortion of identification data was designed so as not to influence the analysis of results of ABC implementation and its use in the researched companies;

• research design – the research in the form of a case study (including action research in OMEGA) was based on two questionnaires followed by interviews with the management and employees of the companies analyzed, and analysis of internal documentation and data from the information systems of the companies. The research made it necessary to collect information allowing the analysis and explanation of the implementation and use of activity-based costing (case studies utilized multiple cost data (Yin, 2003)). In this analysis three general groups of variables were used. These were variables characterizing: (a) the analyzed organization, (b) factors promoting and obstructing the change of the costing system to activity-based costing and also the role of individuals in the process, (c) changes taking place as a result of activity-based costing implementation. The selection of variables was based being mindful of the purpose of the research, meaning fair analysis of activity-based costing implementation;

  • credibility of the research – during preparation of the research activities, which were to guarantee structural reliability, internal and external reliability as well as the validity of the research some actions were undertaken. All of the above activities implied in the case studies (conducted by means of questionnaires, interviews and action research) aimed to improve the quality of the present research. Data analysis and evaluation (in-house documentation of the analyzed companies, activity-based costing documentation and notes made during interviews) constituted the last stage of the empirical research conducted. The amassed documentation was verified in terms of cross-compliance; among other things, whether a given issue is confirmed by many sources was verified (e.g. ABC documentation and interviews);

  • data collection – the case studies were initiated by two questionnaires – information from the questionnaires was a starting point for further analysis of a given company. Information obtained by means of questionnaires was subsequently made more detailed in the course of the interviews; the information was also extended with problems which could not be covered in the questionnaire itself (e.g. methodological and institutional changes that occurred after implementation of the new management accounting concept – activity-based costing). In all the companies, interviews were conducted with workers employed in the operational and financial departments (management accounting/controlling department, finance, accounting, budgeting and analysis etc.); most of the time was given, in particular, to people responsible for the use of the ABC system;

  • report writing – the last stage of the research was report writing which lasted about six months.

  It is relevant to characterize the role of the researcher in four case studies conducted – in the first three (ALPHA, BETA, GAMMA) the role of the researcher could be classified as "visitor". The researcher visited the case companies and interviewed management accountants and operational managers and did not get involved in the issues that were researched (it should be stressed, however, that the questions and commentaries of the researcher could influence the actions of individuals interviewed). In one company (OMEGA) the role of the researcher was completely different – he acted as a consultant and a part of the design and implementation team.

  Four case studies concentrated on the changes in the costing systems of the analyzed companies (i.e. implementation of activity-based costing) and management accountants' and managers' perceptions of why these changes happened, what the factors promoting and obstructing the change process were, what created the momentum for change and what the role of leaders in overcoming the barriers and the change implementation was. Conducting research based mainly on perceptions of managers and management accountants is an important limitation of this study although other sources of information like internal reports and so on were used. The research, like all research in the form of case studies, is a partial one because it concentrated on the costing system of the analyzed companies which is only one part of the overall system of organizational control (Otley, 1980). While conducting case studies the author made an effort to consider the costing systems of the analyzed companies in the wider internal and external context of the organizations (no attempt was made, however, to build a contingency model of the costing systems in the analyzed companies).

5.4. Case studies of activity-based costing implementation

5.4.1. ALPHA case

ALPHA was established over twenty years ago in central Poland. It was originally a trading company which supplied intestines, seasonings and other additives to meat processing plants. Gradually the scope of goods offered by ALPHA widened, the number of clients increased and the company began developing dynamically. Several years ago, a decision was made to expand the business and the company started to manufacture flexible netting used in the meat industry. At that time, the company's strategy was to give up purchasing ready-made products and gradually replace them with their own goods. ALPHA continued development of their products, carried on implementing new technologies, began building up a network of sales branches across the whole of Poland and expanded its sales abroad.

ALPHA employed more than 100 people. The business in which it operated is characterized by average competitiveness. The company's capital was entirely Polish and its sales were mainly domestic (approx. 70%). The company had a functional structure with basic functions, among them logistics, production, sales and finance (in this structure, the Controller was subordinate to the Chief Accountant). Prior to ABC implementation, ALPHA used traditional full absorption costing. It had been decided by the Board to implement it and, from then on, it was used in the company despite any external influences. In the company's cost structure, one could distinguish the following: (a) direct materials (60%), (b) direct labor cost (15%), (c) indirect costs (25%).

Before the implementation of activity-based costing in ALPHA, the Controller branded the decision making process as "management by trial and error". The lack of information (about the costs and profitability) and relying extensively on intuitive decision making was the most characteristic aspect of the company. Since the financial situation of ALPHA was satisfactory, no one had realized the need to improve the product costing system. The approach changed after the company underwent an internal course on cost accounting and management accounting. During the course, the CEO (Chief Executive Officer) of the company realized that "product cost accounting in the company leaves much to be desired, that this area has been neglected, and the company could benefit from implementing improvements." Subsequently, the CEO of ALPHA selected a group of several employees who could potentially deal with the problem, and afterwards he appointed one as the Controller to lead the group. The Controller, in order to complement and broaden his knowledge on cost and management accounting, was directed to attend post-graduate studies in management accounting and controlling.

The implementation of activity-based costing in ALPHA was influenced by numerous factors. Changing the management's information needs, cost reduction, improving business results and improving control were considered crucial. Yet, the implementation of ABC was mainly caused by dissatisfaction with the existing cost accounting system and the need to alter the company's organizational structure as well as the firm's strategy. A change in the top management and the implementation of new technologies moderately influenced the introduction of ABC. The rise of competitiveness, the aim to enter new markets, favorable atmosphere or access to relevant financial and human resources were of little significance.

Originally, in ALPHA's cost accounting system only a breakdown of costs by type functioned, which was mainly used for financial reporting. During the implementation of activity-based costing, new dimensions in the company's chart of accounts was created: (a) cost centres (divisions, departments, regions etc.), (b) activities (groups of related actions taken in the relevant cost centres, i.e. activities such as warping, weaving, braiding, weft winding, and packaging were isolated in the production department).

The activity-based costing model in ALPHA functions in an EXCEL spreadsheet and the Cost Calculation module, supported by information received from other modules. In the activity-based costing system in ALPHA all the resources may be assessed in standard costs as well as in actual costs and it is possible to draw up a cost variance analysis for each product (thus the activity-based costing is interconnected with elements of the standard costing).

Activity-based costing implementation in ALPHA was considered by the workers to be a 'moderate success'. During the implementation process several minor and major problems occurred. The most serious ones were the enormous amount of labor required to implement and maintain ABC (major problem) and other priorities (significant problem). Other common problems such as the high cost of ABC implementation and maintenance, insufficient knowledge of ABC among employees and difficulties with the model itself (selection of activities, drivers etc.) were listed. In the implementation process and the subsequent system maintenance, there were in fact no problems with the management's support nor with the IT resources (slight problem).

ALPHA's activity-based costing system did not accurately follow the Kaplan and Cooper cost accounting notion which focuses on tracing all direct costs on the basis of the source information to the products, and tracing all indirect costs firstly to resources, then allocating them to activities and lastly allocating the costs of activities to products. ALPHA's model is close to the above, yet with a few exceptions:

• the costs of machine and production unit repairs with all other machine costs are not collected on the resources of 'machine X' or 'machine Y' but they are directly allocated to activities, for example 'packaging';

• direct employee remuneration costs are not traced in the cost accounting system to products, but they are allocated on the basis of source information (timesheets) to activities performed by the employees for particular groups of products;

• the costs of raw materials are not directly traced to products but first they go to activities in which they are used, however, there is no indication what product they are used for. Subsequently, the raw material costs accumulated on a particular activity are accounted for, proportionally to established standards, for goods produced in a given activity;

• there are activity costs only at the level of a unit product activity (there are no activities at the level of product groups or a type of products). The lack of activities at the level of product groups or type of products, as the CFO in ALPHA put it, "is the only thing in the ABC system which has not been taken into consideration yet";

• indirect costs are only accounted for in relation to products and their groups (the client's profitability is calculated as a variation between the client's revenue and the cost of products sold to a particular customer – no activity costs are directly accounted for clients).

One should mention that, in the researched company, nobody used the term of a 'cost driver', instead they talked about an 'allocation base'. However, the allocation base used in ALPHA was equivalent to a cost driver from the ABC model. The company did not seek to implement the exact activity-based costing system with all its terminology and concepts presented in the academic literature, but they sought to improve considerably the quality of product costing. The CFO defined it as follows, "it was not about dividing by number or value of products sold or produced".

The generation and implementation of the activity-based costing in ALPHA enabled the creation of better information regarding costs and profitability for the internal customers in order to make accurate decisions for the production, sales and controlling results of these decisions. The implemented activity-based costing enabled the drawing up of profitability analysis of products, groups of products, customers and groups of customers, and selection of sales areas in the enterprise. All the information was used in ALPHA to explain the process of generating costs and allowed the cause-and-effect analysis, using benchmarking and outsourcing, undertaking activities aiming at cost reduction, and providing accurate information regarding costs and profitability of products, customers etc.

As far as usage of the information received from the activity-based costing in ALPHA is concerned, it should be emphasized that:

• the main users of the activity-based costing system in ALPHA were the junior and senior managers of the company, i.e. Junior Managers of Production (four people) and Senior Managers (Senior Production Manager and Senior Sales Manager). The President of the company did not use the information received from the activity-based costing. He was interested in more general information, namely costs and profitability of the whole company and production departments as well as controlling of the income and the expenses and the ownership transformations within the group of managed companies;

• the information from ABC was mainly used for decisions regarding prices, the optimization of the sales plan and performance measurement and improvement (the information from ABC was significant for making these decisions). The information from activity-based costing was relatively important in areas such as: cost reduction, product design, customer profitability analysis, cost tailoring and inventory valuation for financial reporting;

• the information received from activity-based costing was primarily used for taking decisions on the groups of products and products. These decisions concerned withdrawing unprofitable products and groups of products, limiting expenses for unprofitable products and groups of products, facilitating sales of profitable products and groups of products, and investing in new, potentially profitable products and groups of products;

• the information from ABC was also 'frequently' used for the measurement and evaluation of particular activities and processes and 'frequently' for performance measurement and evaluation of particular managers and employees, particular responsibility centres and the whole company.

All the people engaged in the implementing of ABC in ALPHA manifested a positive approach towards the system. All the effort put into the implementation of the activity-based costing became a new challenge for the people involved, diverted them from the daily routines, and were a chance for displaying their own skills in front of the superiors and enabled them to strengthen their position in the company. The whole group emphasized that the managers, as the main recipients of the information from ABC (especially those working in production units), presented a positive approach towards the implementation of the activity-based costing. They were, along with the management accounting specialists, the main beneficiaries of the implementation of the activity-based costing (the production managers eagerly used the ABC model as their bonuses greatly depended upon the results worked out by their departments, and these results were measured in the ABC system).

It should be mentioned however, that the development and the maintenance of the ABC systems can be jeopardized and the most important problems include:

- the key person responsible for the ABC project leaving the company, i.e. the Controller (it is not certain if other employees will be capable of taking the substantive supervision over the functioning of the ABC system, updating the system and involving other areas such as budgeting);

- implementing activity-based costing with the use of an EXCEL spreadsheet (apart from the numerous advantages like small cost and widespread use, the spreadsheet has its limitations – it's a highly individualized problem-solving system and there is a lack of capacity for unauthorized modifications. In brief, the model prepared by one user can be used with great difficulty by another user who may not be knowledgeable enough and may "spoil" the model in the process);

- the loss of interest in the ABC system by the President.

In the light of the above mentioned problems, the statement that development of the management methods in the company may describe a circle, and change "from the management by trial and error into the management based on the reliable information and then from the management based on the reliable information back to the management by trial and error" made by the former Controller in ALPHA may seem prophetic.

5.4.2. BETA case

BETA is a big telecommunications company. Sales of BETA are totally (100%) domestic. The structure of the company comprises: a Sales and Marketing Section, a Technical Section, an IT Section, a Legal Section and the Section of Finance and Administration. In the cost structure of the company the following costs can be enumerated: direct remuneration costs – approximately 3%, other direct costs (mainly the operator interconnection costs) – 37%, indirect costs – approximately 60%. The basic processes outlined in BETA comprise: product development, product management, marketing, product sales, operator interconnections cost clearing, billing, debt collecting, customer service, telecommunication network creation, access network development, telecommunication network maintenance, financial management, strategic management, buying, company assets management, IT systems maintenance, and human resources.

The changes in the cost accounting system in BETA which eventually resulted in activity-based costing creation (occurring within several years), date back to the late 1990s. At that time the attempts to create an interconnection costs allocation model were undertaken. In the subsequent years a sales costs allocation model was formed – primarily regarding commissions and remaining personal costs of the sales section employees. Subsequently, the costs division into the telecommunication network elements were worked out (the telecommunication network elements are not only the costs of depreciation but also personal costs and costs of external services). No reliable information regarding costs of products and customers was contained in the previous cost accounting system. According to the words of the Controlling Department Manager, "on the basis of the information from this system nobody would risk saying that the profitability of products or customers calculated with this system would mean anything".

The activity-based costing implementation in BETA was the direct initiative of the Management Board. According to the opinions of the Controlling Department and the managers of the operation sections two factors influenced ABC implementation in BETA: the change of the managers' information needs and determination of costs reduction and performance improvement (according to the Controlling Department there are three more, equally important factors for the implementation: facilitating the control process, the change of strategy, and the implementation of new technologies). In the analysis of the factors influencing activity-based costing implementation it is emphasized that the Controlling Department enumerates other factors significant for the process of implementation, such as: parent company requirements and the ABC implementation in competing companies, while the managers of operation sections do not acknowledge these factors (ABC implementation in competing companies) or they belittle their importance (parent company requirements).

The activity-based costing implementation in BETA took almost a year. The subsequent steps of implementation were as follows: (a) implementation planning and distribution of implementation duties, (b) defining bills of resources, activities and objects for ABC, (c) defining drivers of resources and activities for ABC, (d) creation of activity-based costing model, (e) tests of activity-based costing model.

The activity-based costing system in BETA specifies: approximately three hundred resources, a dozen or so resource drivers, a hundred and fifty activities, several dozen activity drivers and several thousand cost objects (products, customers etc.). The costs in the activity-based costing were divided into fixed and variable costs. Also, the costs of unused capacity were outlined but only at the level of resources connected with the network infrastructure. The activities at the level of a product unit, product batch, product type and the company as a whole were also specified.

Including the costs of the technical infrastructure of the telecommunication company in the ABC model required several basic elements in the model to be specified, and in BETA they were:

- resources (remuneration, telephones, cars, offices, computer network, type approval costs, interconnection costs etc.);
- supplementary activities, basic and general – hosting systems development, CRM system development, wholesale customers clearing, debt collecting, financial assets management, operational reporting etc.;
- the elements of the telecommunication network – several dozen groups of fixed assets into which the whole telecommunication network was divided (e.g. light pipes, radio lines, the Internet services servers, network safety systems, subscriber devices etc.);
- technical layers of network (technical products[1]) – several dozen groups consisting of the elements of telecommunication network used by specific technology (transmitting and commuting) to providing voice services and data transmission services (i.e. access layer, layer of data transmission services, hosting services layer etc.);
- final cost objects: (a) motion fractures (local connections, interurban connections, international connections etc.), (b) products (analogue line, wholesale voice termination, hosting services, collocation services etc.), (c) company (all the costs not connected to any other cost object – incurred in connection with the general company management or resulting from law regulations).

In the basic activity-based costing model described by Kaplan and Cooper there are resources, activities and cost objects – these elements are also a part of the ABC system in BETA. In this system, however, two more elements function, i.e. the telecommunication network elements and the technical network layer (technical products) – the description of these objects was necessary for an appropriate reflection of the processes occurring in the activity-based costing system in BETA. Thanks to the allocation of a considerable part of the costs of the telecommunication network elements, these costs can be relocated to the technical network layers and then the costs of the technical network layers can be relocated to final cost objects (motion fractions and products) – relocating these costs directly to products and motion fractions with the omission of the previous allocation of telecommunication network elements and technical network layers would be impossible.

The activity-based costing in BETA is carried out to estimate budget data to compare it with real data. This model (with budget data) basically does not make activity cost allocation of the company on particular objects of calculation

---

[1] Technical products mean the elements of indirect costs allocation connected with the telecommunication network. Later these costs are allocated to motion fractures and products. Technical products can be described as platforms and transmission and access network layers.

– however, such allocation is possible if, apart from the model itself, the way it is carried out is assumed. In the ABC model in the company, the allocation of the costs of unused capacity (these costs were estimated at the level of network resources) can be perceived in two different ways. It is possible to calculate the whole model with costs of unused capacity (then these costs are not demonstrated separately but they will be allocated to products or customers) or without costs of unused capacity (in that case these costs are not allocated to products or customers) – depending on the current needs, BETA uses both methods.

The activity-based costing implementation was unambiguously acknowledged as a success by the Controlling Department Manager (the person responsible for the heart of the implementation). The management of operation sections (business) perceived the implementation as a moderate success. During the process several problems of varying degrees of importance were detected (see Table 5.2).

Table 5.2. Problems in ABC implementation and maintenance in BETA

Problem	According to Controlling Department	According to operation sections
Extremely significant	• A lot of work included in ABC implementation and maintenance	• A lot of work included in ABC implementation and maintenance • Other priorities (i.e. ISO implementation, TQM, ERP etc.) • Problems with the model (i.e. choice of activities, drivers etc.)
Significant	• Insufficient knowledge of ABC among employees • Considerable costs of the ABC system implementation and maintenance • Problems with model construction • Lack of sufficient financial resources	• Insufficient knowledge of ABC among employees
Average	–	• Lack of support on the management side (the management board, the parent company etc.) • Considerable costs of ABC implementation and maintenance
No problem	–	• Lack of sufficient IT resources

The ABC system implementation in BETA enabled the creation of reliable information about the costs and results received mainly from products and product groups (reliable information regarding the costs in these aspects was not accessible in the previous cost accounting system in the company). This information is used in BETA to: explain the process of cost generation, enable cause and effect analysis, use benchmarking and outsourcing, undertake cost-reducing activities and provide reliable information regarding costs and profitability for different cost objects in the company. The following analyses are managed and carried out in BETA: (a) the profitability of the customer segment and product, (b) the profitability of the product and customer segment, (c) the profitability of the customer segment, product and types of connections, (d) the profitability of the segment and type of installation.

As for the information generated by activity-based costing in BETA it is worth emphasizing that:

• very often the information from ABC is used by marketing and sales specialists, operational sections and management accounting specialists. It is also frequently used by technical management, sporadically by senior management, and accountants do not use it at all;

• the information generated by activity-based costing is extremely important in the following areas: cost-reduction, customer profitability analysis and measurement and improvement of achievements. The information is also significant in price decision-making and cost-modelling. Less frequently the information provided by activity-based costing is used in sales planning and product design (the information is quite important). This information is not used for the purpose of financial reporting and budgeting;

• the information generated by the activity-based costing in BETA is used to make decisions regarding increasing costs for products, investments in new products and product groups reducing costs for customers and customer group. The activity-based costing system is not used to make decisions regarding the region sales, distribution channels, organizational units of the company or the projects because suitable information for this purpose is not generated in the current ABC in BETA;

• as for relations with customers, the activity-based costing in BETA influences the control of customer service costs (to a great extent), gives directions for working out marketing strategy (to a great extent), is a base for the resignation from the customers (to some extent), and provides information for forming the price policy (not frequently). The information from the ABC is also not used for forming customer policy or for renegotiating cooperation conditions with the customers.

After several years of using the ABC model in the company, a few quite significant changes in the financial section of the company occurred – there were different causes for the resignation from the post of almost all employees in the Controlling Department, including the Manager. The people who were employed in particular posts had come from other companies and did not have sufficient knowledge regarding either a telecommunications company or the use of activity-based costing (particularly its unique character in a telecommunications company). The consequences of this were the changes in the ABC model which made the whole model simpler. This led to the company abandoning allocations of personal costs based on employees' work cards in the supporting sections (the costs of these sections increased the general costs of the company which were not allocated to the final objects).

5.4.3. GAMMA case

GAMMA was one of the leaders on the Polish insurance market. It employed several thousand workers and it specialized in providing mass products to numerous clients (cost strategy); the area it operated in was characterized by high competitiveness. The sales of GAMMA were entirely (100%) domestic. The operations of GAMMA embraced three basic areas: the technical operation (operational), the investment operation and the reinsurance operation. The technical operation (operational) meant sales of insurance, among them such activities as direct sale of insurance but also activities indirectly related to insurance sales (active reinsurance).

Full absorption costing was the cost accounting system used in GAMMA before ABC implementation – it was decided by the Board to implement it and it was used despite any external influences (actuaries had a significant influence on its shape). The system was almost completely used for the means of external reporting, it was simplified and it was not used in terms of supporting business decisions in the company (according to one of the employees of the Management Accounting Department "it was hard to reconcile the requirements of external reporting with the requirements of management accounting"). Another employee of the Management Accounting Department claimed that in terms of business decisions support, the current cost accounting "was in some situations too detailed, and in some instances too general", whereas information about the costs and profitability of insurance products "was so distorted that no one wanted to trust it".

Activity-based costing operating in GAMMA had been implemented more than a year before carrying out this research and the decision about the implementation came directly from the Board of the capital group to which the company belonged. Interviewed employees of GAMMA noticed that the implementation of activity-based costing was influenced by various factors. The ABC implementation was triggered by the demands of the head office, dissatisfaction with the current cost accounting system, the necessity to alter the management's information needs and cost reduction with an improvement of business results. The implementation was moderately influenced by growing competitiveness, a change of strategy and the drive to improve control. The activity-based costing implementation in GAMMA was barely influenced by factors such as: the change of organizational structure, the change in top management, the implementation of new technologies, aiming to enter new sales markets, favorable attitude of workers towards changes, or availability of financial and human resources.

The implementation of activity-based costing in GAMMA lasted for two years (although it was initially planned to take 18 months), and the stages of work on ABC implementation were as follows: (a) development of the concept of activity-based costing, (b) study of data availability needed for ABC, (c) creation of the activity-based costing system, (d) generation of data needed for ABC, (e) tests of the activity-based costing system.

Implementation of the activity-based costing in GAMMA was an extremely complex process – in order to create the system the right way, cooperation between financial departments and operational ones were necessary. To make the cooperation more formal, a Steering Committee was founded; it consisted of representatives of the business units, financial units, IT, actuaries and representatives of the consulting company, which aided the process of implementation. In terms of contents, the shape of activity-based costing in GAMMA was substantially influenced by the Management Accounting Department (representatives of this department spent the most amount of time on tasks which involved implementation of the ABC). After implementation of ABC, the Steering Committee was dissolved, however it transformed into a regular committee which supervised the functioning of the system (maintenance and modifications of the system).

In the activity-based costing system in GAMMA, several dozen resources, several resource drivers, a few hundred activities and a few dozen activity drivers, and more than five hundred cost objects (products, clients etc.) were isolated. In the activity-based costing system of the company, the costs of unused capacity have been defined, although no fixed or variable costs nor activity hierarchy (activities at the level of unit of product, batch of products, type of products and type of company) have been isolated. Within the system a wide range of profitability analyses, in various cross-sections are carried out – more than five hundred analyses are made for products, whereas between a few and a few dozen analyses are prepared for such objects as groups of products, clients, groups of clients, sales regions, internal organizational units, distribution channels or projects.

In the activity-based costing in GAMMA, the costs of individual activities may be, when needed, allocated to different cost objects i.e. the costs of one activity can be, in terms of product profitability analysis, accounted for by one driver for products, whereas in the case of customer profitability analysis it can be accounted for by a different driver for customers. The portion of general activities in GAMMA is not allocated to costs objects by individual drivers but done proportionally to income.

Having implemented activity-based costing, GAMMA did not quit the previously used cost accounting system – ABC was used for internal purposes whereas the previous cost accounting provided a basis for external reporting.

The activity-based costing implementation was considered by the Head of the Management Accounting Department (the one who was responsible for the implementation in terms of merits) as a complete success. However, during the implementation process numerous problems of different significance were noticed, among them the high labor input in the implementation and operation of ABC were considered significant. Among the problems of a moderate scale one could enumerate the high costs of the implementation and operation of ABC, insufficient knowledge of ABC among employees, difficulties in the system's construction and lack of adequate data analysis resources. Priorities other than ABC implementation were a slight problem. However, there was no problem with the top management's support of the activity-based costing implementation project.

Implementation of the activity-based costing system in GAMMA enabled them to generate reliable information about the costs and results in the field of products and groups of products (competent information about costs in those dimensions was not available in the previous cost accounting system used in the company). The information was used in GAMMA to explain the process of cost formation, it enabled cause-and-effect analysis, it enabled benchmarking and outsourcing, as well as undertaking steps to lower costs; it also provided competent data about costs and profitability for various cost objects in the company. With reference to information generated by the activity-based costing system in GAMMA, it should be emphasized that:

• the ABC information was really frequently used by the management accounting specialists as well as experts from the operational departments. It was quite often used by marketing and sales specialists and the top management, whereas accountants made use of it sporadically;

• among the areas in which information generated from activity-based costing was crucial, were product design, customer profitability analysis as well as measurement and improvement of performance. ABC information was important in initiatives related to cost reduction and quite significant in pricing decisions, sales plan optimization and cost modelling. There was little significance for budgeting (ABB) and it was completely irrelevant in the case of financial reporting;

• information generated from activity-based costing in GAMMA was used to make decisions about the restriction or increase of inputs. Those decisions related to the restriction/increase of product input, restriction of input in the case of groups of clients, increase of input in terms of sales regions and distribution channels, and restriction of input in case of organizational units (e.g. departments);

• when client relations are considered, activity-based costing in GAMMA provided the information needed to shape customer policy (to a major extent), influenced the costs control involved in customer service (significant extent), helped to make decisions about quitting a client (significant extent), provided advice necessary for preparation of a marketing strategy (moderate extent), provided a basis for a renegotiation of terms and conditions of cooperation with customers (moderate extent) and it also provided information which was useful in the process of shaping pricing policy (minor extent).

5.4.4. OMEGA case

OMEGA was a manufacturing and trading company which mainly purchased nuts, dried fruits and vegetables, portioned and packed them and subsequently sold them under its own brand name or other private labels within, as well as outside the country. The company's head office and logistics center were in central Poland while its production plant was in the east of the country. When the study was carried out, the company employed a few hundred people and it specialized in providing mass products to numerous customers (cost strategy), while the business line it operated in was characterized by average competition. The sales of OMEGA were nearly entirely domestic, the export sales constituting only 4% of the whole sales. In the cost structure in OMEGA, direct material costs took up to approximately 74% of total costs. Indirect costs came second, and their share in the total costs of the company equalled 22%. Direct compensation and other direct costs each constituted approximately 2% of the company's costs.

Prior to activity-based costing implementation in OMEGA, full absorption costing functioned in the company. The system enabled real estimation of financial results for the company as a whole, however: (a) it did not generate fully accurate information about costs and income of sold products and groups of products, (b) it prevented profitability evaluation of isolated types of operation, organizational units, customers and groups of customers, (c) it did not provide reliable information about the costs of processes taking place in the company e.g. logistics processes, production processes, infrastructure maintenance processes etc.

The decision about the implementation of activity-based costing in OMEGA came from the Board (the role of the Board Member responsible for finance was crucial in the decision-making process). The decision about the implementation of the ABC system was mainly influenced by the change in the management's information needs, the willingness to reduce costs and improve results as well as the willingness to improve control.

The analysis of OMEGA lasted for about a month and it was carried out by five consultants from an external company (around 30 working days) and twenty people from the Board and top management (around 15 working days). The first stage of work on the ABC model in OMEGA comprised an analysis of the processes, especially the process of internal logistics, production, marketing and sales, external logistics, maintenance of the organization, product development, quality, and support process. At the same time, the analysis of the procedures of the previous cost accounting system used in OMEGA was carried out. In particular, attention was paid to the system of collecting and processing information in the IT systems (inter alia in the integrated IT system of the company and in the system of budgeting, which functioned in an EXCEL spreadsheet) in terms of the usefulness of information generated by the systems in the light of the planned activity-based costing and profitability management.

This stage of the analysis closed with the assessment of the correctness of the information about costs in the area of the following structures: by type, organizational unit and cost object (products and their groups, customers and groups of customers, distribution channels, sales regions) from the company strategy point of view. The assessment helped to formulate a proposal of changes in the area of costs accounting so that the system met the information needs of the Board and the top management of the company. The proposal presented by the consultants underwent an analysis and the compromise reached between the consultants and the management of OMEGA became the starting point for the preparation of the activity-based costing draft in the following stage. For the purpose of the project and effectiveness of the ABC implementation process, the top management (around 25 people) took part in a two-day training session on ABC/M.

In the construction of the ABC system, which lasted for about 2 months, three outside consultants (approx. 30 working days) and fifteen people from the Board and top management of OMEGA (approx. 20 working days) took part. The modelling of activity-based costing was divided into the following stages: (a) cost objects identification, (b) resource identification, (c) activity identification, (d) resource cost drivers identification, (e) activity cost drivers identification, (f) defining changes within the integrated IT system.

The activity-based costing system which functions in OMEGA is a system where one can distinguish: a few dozen resources, a dozen or so resource cost drivers, a few dozen activities, between ten and twenty activity cost drivers, and more than a thousand cost objects (products, groups of products, brands, recipients, distribution channels, groups of distribution channels, sales representatives, regions etc.).

The creation of the profitability management system on the basis of ABC lasted for about 2 months. Three consultants from an external company (approx. 20 working days) and five people from the Board and the top management of OMEGA (approx. 10 working days) participated in the project. At this stage it was possible to construct tabular profitability reports, which constituted an elementary method of internal reporting. The reports were issued monthly (or more frequently if needed) and they were prepared in two versions i.e. on a monthly basis, for a particular month, and on a year-to-date basis – from the beginning of the calendar year to the end of a given month (the data was accumulated from the start of the year). The reports mirrored the operation of OMEGA and provided information about costs, revenues and gross margin in different sections, which was especially useful when making decisions was concerned. Distribution of the data in the report allowed them to assess the profitability of particular: (a) products, groups of products, brands, (b) recipients, payers, distribution channels, groups of distribution channels, (c) sales representatives, sales regions, countries.

The purpose of those profitability reports was to provide economic information (planned and actual) to the management of OMEGA (the Management Board, Trading Department, International Sales Department, Financial Department, Production and Logistics Department). The profitability reports, which were issued within the framework of the management accounting system, constituted a source of information necessary to carry out: analyses of profitability in various sections (planned and actual), analyses of break-even point, analyses of the sensitivity of financial results, scenario analyses (what happens if) for OMEGA as a company but also for its various elements (e.g. regions, groups of products etc.).

The information generated by the activity-based costing system in OMEGA was important for the managers in terms of the valuation of products, making pricing decisions and product and customer profitability analyses (in particular, the profitability analyses prepared on the basis of activity-based costing were used to make decisions about the increase of expenses on products, groups of products, customers, groups of customers, sales regions, distribution channels and organizational units). The information from the ABC system in OMEGA was frequently used to measure and evaluate the performance of individual managers and employees, individual responsibility centres, activities and processes.

The activity-based costing was additionally used in terms of relations with customers. It basically provided information which was useful in the case of shaping customer policy, it supplied information needed to shape the pricing policy, it had an influence on the control of costs of customer service, it guided the marketing strategy, it provided a basis for dropping a customer and it also provided a basis for the renegotiation of the terms and conditions of customer cooperation.

After implementation of the activity-based costing system in OMEGA, one employee was involved in the maintenance of the system, however, it was just one responsibility among his other regular ones. The company did not abandon the previous cost accounting system which had functioned prior to the implementation, they used it for financial reporting, whereas the ABC system was used for management. The implementation of activity-based costing in the company was perceived by their employees as a moderate success.

A lack of resources (of both people and money) is the main reason behind the fact that so few small and medium-sized companies make the decision to implement ABC. As far as financial resources are concerned, they were not a problem in the case of OMEGA. Both remuneration for the consulting company and other costs were insignificant for the company. In terms of human resources, the problem occurred (but it was not impossible to overcome):

• the data needed for valuation and calculation of some activities was not collected at all – it happened with reference to some activities in the sales process (some sales representatives did not fill out the specially designed activity sheets which made precise cost calculation of those activities on cost objects impossible). The main reason underlying the problem was the fact the manager, who was in charge of sales representatives, changed his job at the beginning of the implementation process;

• the ABC analytics, which were implemented in the financial and accounting system of the company in the first version of the ABC, caused prolonged posting of accounting documents (the company attempted to modify the method of data gathering so that it was less time-consuming for the employees, however, it had to bear in mind the fact that all the important data for the ABC system must be available at hand);

• some of the information generated by the ABC system was not sufficiently used. For example, the management of the company was focused on the information about the profitability of products, groups of products, brands, customers, distribution channels etc., however they did not pay much attention to the operational and financial information about activities or resources.

All of the above problems occurred during the process of implementing activity-based costing in the analyzed company. The problems, however, did not eclipse the success of its implementation. It means that the process of implementation of activity-based costing is difficult and it is not easy to foresee all the problems which might arise during the implementation and, subsequently, during the usage of the implemented system. When this case study was prepared, the activity-based costing system in OMEGA was undergoing redefinition in terms of yearly experience and in terms of the necessity to adapt it to the current conditions of the company's operation. The Management Board was convinced that the modified version of the system would appear to be a better tool used for supporting the process of company management. Better than the first version of the ABC system.

5.5. Discussion

Three types of positive factors (motivators, catalysts, facilitators) and one type of a negative factor (barriers) influenced the process of implementing the innovations within the area of management accounting. These factors had a joint influence on the process of innovation implementation, thus promoting the process of change (the number of positive factors outweigh the number of negative factors).

According to Innes and Mitchell (1990), motivators are factors that influence the management accounting change process in a general manner. They stated that the main motivators were production technology, product cost structure and the level of competition in the market (these factors were also identified in Kasurinen's (2002) research along with the problems with financially oriented control systems and the mature stage of the products' lifecycle). In current research, similar motivators have been identified, namely the differentiation of products and an increase in competitiveness. The analyzed companies were under pressure of the environment, with costing systems which did not match the changed information needs of the managers. This created a pressure for change (motivator). More specific general factors motivating the change process in the analyzed companies which were not specified in Kasurinen's (2002) model were inaccuracy of cost data and the need for better information. In the case of particular companies some more factors motivating the change process were identified:

• ALPHA – the increase of competitiveness and market strategy; production strategy (the increase of diversity and complexity of products – the customers began to demand unconventional products, in small batches); the need for information reported by the managers and inaccuracy of data received from the present cost accounting,

• BETA – extremely high level of competition; strategy (increase of differentiation and complexity of products); the need for information reported by operational sections managers (technical sections, sales sections, supporting sections); lack or inaccuracy of the important information in the previous cost accounting system,

• GAMMA – the need for information reported by operational sections manager; lack of the important information useful in the process of management in the previous cost accounting system; high level of competition in business and increase of differentiation and complexity of products,

• OMEGA – the need for information reported by the Board and managers of sales, production and logistics departments; lack or inaccuracy of the important information in the previous cost accounting system.

Facilitators are factors necessary for the realization of the management accounting change, although these factors are not sufficient for the change to occur. Innes and Mitchell (1990) identified accounting staff resources, computing resources and the degree of autonomy from the parent company as main facilitators in the change process (in Kasurinen's (2002) research two factors facilitating change were identified, namely earlier balanced scorecard introduction and strategically well-structured situation). In current research similar facilitators have been identified, namely sufficient resources and management board support (Innes, Mitchell, 1990; Cobb *et al.*, 1995; Pimentel, 2008). More specific general factors facilitating the change process in the analyzed companies were knowledge transfer, susceptibility to fashions and trends, and change-oriented organization. In the case of particular companies some other factors facilitating the change process were identified:

• ALPHA – the management board's support (the president's "blessing" and giving "carte blanche"); knowledge transfer into the company (in-company training); Controller's level of knowledge in the area of new cost accounting systems; susceptibility to fashions and trends; sufficient resources; medium-sized company, medium level of complexity of processes, "everybody does everything," it is difficult to find people involved in the controlling implementation who would be proficient solely in the narrow part of the activity; good general condition of the company, the usage of the productive capacity up to 100%,

• BETA – the management board's support (all key people who were important for ABC implementation in the organization knew that the implementation must be successful); change-oriented organizational culture in the operational sections (mainly in technical sections, sales and support sections); knowledge transfer regarding ABC to the company (in-house training carried out by consultants, the participation of selected people from the financial section in the open training sessions); technical knowledge transfer – in-house training regarding the processes implemented in BETA carried out by the technical sections for the Controlling Department employees); susceptibility to fashions and trends (the conviction that a company such as BETA simply must have a system like ABC); sufficient resources (human, technical and financial),

• GAMMA – the management board's support (making managers aware of the benefits resulting from ABC implementation and making them involved in the process of implementation); change-oriented organizational culture in operational sections (managers got involved in the process of implementation of the new cost accounting system because they believed it would provide information which could be used in the decision-making process); knowledge transfer regarding ABC to the company e.g. in-house training carried out by the consultants; susceptibility to fashions and trends (many companies from the financial sector use activity-based costing); sufficient resources (human, technical and financial); the huge dedication of the Management Accounting Department (as the Head put it – "fierceness during implementation"),

• OMEGA – strong management board support (as the Controller put it, "the Board is for the implementation of activity-based costing all the way"); knowledge transfer regarding ABC to the company – in-house training carried out by the consultants, participation of the CFO in an open management accounting training session which mainly dealt with the issue of ABC; susceptibility to fashions and trends (the conviction of the CFO that "it is simply attractive for the company to have a system such as ABC"); sufficient resources (human, technical, financial).

Catalysts are factors that can be directly associated with the change. In their study Innes and Mitchel (1990) identified poor financial performance, loss of market share and launch of new competing products as a possible catalysts for change (in Kasurinen's (2002) research two catalysts were identified, namely the business unit general manager's experience in strategy work and conducted strategic analyses). In current research more specific catalytic factors have been identified, namely the acknowledgement of ABC's superiority, imitation of competitors and in company training. In the case of particular companies some more catalytic factors in the change process were identified:

- ALPHA – in-company training in the area of cost accounting; post-graduate studies undertaken by the Controller,
- BETA – the management board's acknowledgement of activity-based costing as the system which the telecommunication company "should have because other companies already have this system" (Financial Director);
- GAMMA – the management board's acknowledgement of ABC as the system which could provide for the first time information useful for managers,
- OMEGA – the CFO's acknowledgement of ABC as the system which may significantly improve the quality of information about costs and profitability.

According to the Cobb et al. (1995) model there are two more factors apart from motivators, facilitators and catalysts advancing the process of change – these are momentum of change and the role of leaders in the implementation process. Momentum of change is the continuing expectation of change, something that "keeps things moving" in the case of innovation implementation in the organization. Leadership is the crucial role of certain individuals in the change process. Brown et al. (2004) argued that leader support is the case when an individual (champion) from the company significantly promotes the cause of innovation. A champion will educate managers in the area of innovation (e.g. ABC, BSC) and create among managers awareness about the need to implement innovation. Motivators, catalysts and facilitators (both external and internal for the companies), are necessary to create the potential for change, but the determination of individuals is needed to overcome barriers to change – even if the potential for change is sufficient but there are no leaders in the company then the change process might be stopped– the momentum for change is necessary. In Kasurinen's study the strategy analysis process which was sponsored by the division general manager and the partnership project with Helsinki School of Economics were identified as the momentum of change while the division general manager played the role of the leader in the change process.

In the present study, factors such as the management board's support for the project or the president's "blessing" served to carry on the expectation of change – the momentum of change. Management accounting change would not be possible without certain individuals who played a crucial role in the implementation process. It was observed in the case companies that the role of individuals was twofold – they acted as catalysts for the management accounting change process and also they were leaders of the process. The catalytic role of individuals relied on their role in the change initiation and their leadership was essential in creating momentum for change and in overcoming the barriers to change. What these case studies showed is that leadership in a project of change matters. In the four companies studied, this role (leadership) was fulfilled by people from the management accounting sections of the companies and in one case also by the CFO. In two cases, not long after the implementation process, the individuals leading the process of change left the companies for different reasons. These resignations caused some problems with activity-based costing used in the companies (e.g. simplification of the system and decrease in the importance of information created by the system) and also increased uncertainty related to the future role of the ABC system.

Barriers disturb the process of change and examples of barriers in the study of Cobb *et al.* (1995) are resistance towards change, a great amount of labor, changing priorities, and accounting staff turnover. In terms of analyzing the barriers to change, the model of Kasurinen (2002) is an extended version of the Cobb *et al.* (1995) model, identifying three types of factors obstructing the process of change: confusers, frustrators and delayers. Kasurinen's study specified that the main confusers were uncertainty about the project's future role in the organization and different views on change. The main frustrators were existing reporting systems and the organizational culture, and the main delayers were the lack of clear-cut strategies and inadequate information systems. In current research similar barriers have been identified, namely the culture not favoring changes, the obstruction of IT department, a change of the IT system and high labor input. More specific general barriers to the change process in the analyzed companies were insufficient knowledge of the management and the company's complicated activity. In the case of these particular companies, some more factors obstructing the change process were identified:

• ALPHA – corporate culture objecting any changes (according to the employees of the company: "nobody has the time to get involved in tasks needed to have been done yesterday", "the company has no time and money for facilitating the process of time and money management", "in the initial state – management by trial and error – the financial situation is good but no one knows why"); insufficient level of knowledge of the senior management of the company,

• BETA – the company's very complicated and differentiated activity – it is difficult to find a person who knows all its aspects; insufficient knowledge of the technical processes of the financial section's employees; the organizational culture not favoring changes in other non-operational sections (mainly administrative sections, IT supporting sections, legal sections, etc.); insufficient level of knowledge of medium and senior management (regarding both cost accounting knowledge and the knowledge of the complexity of processes occurring in the company),

• GAMMA – the company's very complicated and differentiated activity and its size – the company operates in several regions all over the country, it has hundreds of organizational units and employs a few thousand people (there are 14 million cost objects used in the ABC system); insufficient knowledge of processes taking place in a big insurance company among the financial section's employees (some employees of the Management Accounting Department had worked there for a short time); insufficient level of knowledge of activity-based costing among employees from the financial and operational sections; lack of understanding of the importance of activity-based costing by the IT Department,

• OMEGA – the organizational culture not favoring changes (apart from ABC, the company did not use any of the modern methods of management and management accounting); changes in the integrated IT system used for management of the company (it led to revisions of procedures connected with data collection and transfer to the ABC system); high labor-consumption of recording documents in terms of the activity-based costing system in its first version; the departure of the manager who was in charge of sales representatives.

In conclusion, it should be stated that in all the companies surveyed a similar pattern was detected. In the companies, managers as well as management accounting specialists were ready to question the existing costing system and to plan and implement a new, better system in response to the changing internal and external environment of the companies. Managers questioned the quality of information provided by the current cost accounting system, and management accounting specialists reacted to that need by implementing activity-based costing. The role of the leaders in the process of management accounting change could probably not be exaggerated – without determined individuals from the financial sections the change in costing systems of the companies could not happen. Individuals in the analyzed companies contributed to creating the momentum for change and actively participated in overcoming the barriers to change. Management accounting specialists were on the one hand aware of the changes taking place on the market and inside their own company, and on the other hand they were also aware of the new cost accounting and cost management methods. As a result, they adapted the latest tool of cost accounting to solve problems within their company.

The change process in the analyzed companies resulted in both methodological and organizational changes in the companies. As far as the methodological changes are concerned, the main ones were an improvement of cost accuracy, better product cost calculations, an improvement of profit calculation and better information for decision making in general. From the point of view of organizational changes, the most important were bringing management accounting closer to an operational function making better information for decisions, more frequent use of management accounting information and promotion for people dealing with ABC. Bearing in mind all major methodological and organizational changes observed in the analyzed companies it should be stressed that probably the most important one was the intensification of contacts (both formal and informal) between management accountants and managers from the operational departments – the boundaries of costing systems expanded into the operational areas of the analyzed companies. What is more, the positive change in the attitudes of the operational managers to management accountants was observed – operational managers noticed that management accountants could provide them with useful information. The methodological and organizational changes following ABC implementation are presented in Table 5.3.

Table 5.3. The changes in management accounting in the analysed companies after ABC implementation

Company	Area of changes	Before ABC implementation	After ABC implementation
ALPHA	Methodological changes	· Decision-making through "management by trial and error" · Low accuracy of direct costs traced to products · Full absorption costing with indirect cost allocation "using the method of direct costs + x" · Costs established only for groups of products · Profitability analysis of the whole company and very inaccurate analysis of product profitability · No planning of the production capacity in order to determine its influence on the unit price (costs of unused resources not specified)	· Decision-making based on numerical data from the ABC system · High accuracy of direct costs traced to products · Activity-based costing with indirect cost allocation according to various costs drivers · Costs established for products as variable costs according to activities and resources plus fixed costs according to activities and resources · Profitability analysis of the whole company, products, groups of customers and customers etc., established based on activity-based costing · Costs of products calculated for normal production capacity (costs of unused resources allocated to profit and loss account)
	Institutional changes	· Controller supervised by chief accountant · Management accounting function distant from production and sales function · Low approach to information delivery needed for decision-making · No specified responsibility centres · Information from the management accounting rarely used by the managers of production, sales and other positions in the company	· Controller not supervised by chief accountant, directly supervised by president · Management accounting function close to production and sales function · Higher approach to information delivery needed for decision-making · Specified centres responsible for costs and profits · Information from management accounting frequently used by the managers of production, sales and other positions in the company

Table 5.3. (cont.)

Company	Area of changes	Before ABC implementation	After ABC implementation
BETA	Methodological changes	· Intuitional decision-making ("if the competing company does this so we must do it as well" – the manager of the controlling department) · Very low accuracy of calculating direct costs of products (mainly IC costs) · Profitability analysis at the whole company level and very inaccurate, in fact useless, profitability analysis of products · Lack of specified unused capacity costs (costs of products were charged with the costs of unused capacity)	· Taking numeral data from ABC in decision-making into consideration (data from ABC were not the only data considered in decision-making, neither were they the most important source of information – still they were used) · Very high accuracy of calculating direct costs of products (as a result of ABC implementation the accuracy of measures increased significantly therefore the costs of IC could be allocated on products) · Reliable profitability analysis at the whole company level, groups of products, products, groups of customers and customers, etc. based on activity-based costing · The possibility of cost calculating without costs of unused capacity (these costs are not allocated to products but they are allocated directly to the company as a whole)
	Institutional changes	· Lack of significant specification of people responsible for the cost accounting system in the controlling department structure	· Specified post of the person in the controlling department whose main task was to manage the ABC system; two other people were responsible for managing the ABC but it was only one of their regular duties; additionally, during the yearly modification of the system, if required, other employees of the controlling department participated in the work

Company	Area of changes	Before ABC implementation	After ABC implementation
BETA	Institutional changes	· Low importance of the controlling department · The function of management accounting remote from operational functions (technical sections, sales and supporting sections) · Poor attitude to information delivery for decisions · The information from management accounting was not used to evaluate activities · The information from management accounting was basically useless for the decision making of the managers of the operational sections	· Increase of the importance of the controlling department in the opinion of the operational sections · The use of management accounting close to operational functions (technical sections, sales and supporting sections) · Better attitude to information delivery for decisions · The information from management accounting was used for evaluating activities for the whole company and their basic sections · The information from management accounting is more frequently used for decision making by the managers of the operational sections
GAMMA	Methodological changes	· Making decisions without taking into account information about costs and profitability · Very low accuracy of calculating costs of products and lack of calculation of costs for other objects · Profitability analysis at the whole company level and very inaccurate (in fact useless) profitability analysis of products · Traditional budgeting was used · Lack of reporting system	· Taking into consideration the numeral data from abc in decision-making · Very high accuracy of calculating costs of regions, distribution channels, groups of customers, customers, lines of business, business segments, products · Profitability analysis at the whole company level, regions, distribution channels, groups of customers, customers, lines of business, business segments, products etc. on the basis of activity-based costing · Traditional budgeting still functions however the implemented abc, according to the head of management accounting department, "will support budgeting" · Creation of a reporting system on the basis of activity-based costing

Table 5.3. (cont.)

Company	Area of changes	Before ABC implementation	After ABC implementation
GAMMA	Institutional changes	· The function of management accounting remote from operational functions · Poor attitude to information delivery for decisions · The information from management accounting was not used by the operational managers at all · Lack of significant specification of people responsible for providing information about costs, income and results in the management accounting department structure for the needs of operational departments	· The function of management accounting close to operational functions (acquisition, liquidation, administration) · Better attitude to information delivery for decisions · The information from management accounting is more frequently used by the operational managers · Specified post of the person in the management accounting department whose main task was to manage the ABC system; two other people were responsible for managing ABC but it was only one of their regular duties
OMEGA	Methodological changes	· Making pricing decisions without any relation to the information provided by the cost accounting system · Low accuracy of calculating indirect costs · Costs precisely calculated only at the level of the whole company · Profitability analysis at the whole company level, and very inaccurate, in fact useless, profitability analysis of products, customers and other cost objects · Information from the cost accounting system was not used to make customer-related decisions	· Taking numeral data from abc into consideration in pricing decision-making · High accuracy of calculating indirect costs on different cost objects · Real costs precisely calculated at the level of products, customers, distribution channel, regions etc. · Reliable profitability analyses at the whole company level, sales regions, distribution channels, groups of customers, customers, brands, groups of products, products etc. Prepared on the basis of activity-based costing · High significance of abc information in the case of making pricing decisions, decisions which shape customer policy, decisions about the marketing strategy, decisions about renegotiation of terms and conditions of customer cooperation and decisions about quitting customers

Company	Area of changes	Before ABC implementation	After ABC implementation
OMEGA	Institutional changes	· The function of management accounting remote from operational functions (production section, sales section, logistics section etc.) · Poor attitude to information delivery for decisions · The information from management accounting was not used to evaluate performance · The information from management accounting was basically useless in terms of the decision-making of the managers of the organizational sections	· The function of management accounting close to operational functions (production section, sales section, logistics section etc.) · Better attitude to information delivery for decisions about pricing, discounts etc. · The information from management accounting is used to evaluate the performance of individual managers and employees, responsibility centres and activities and processes · The information from management accounting is more frequently used for decision-making by the board and the managers of the operational sections (it is also used by the management accounting specialists)

The research has made a contribution to Kasurinen's (2002) model of management accounting change – on the one hand it has proved the general validity (usefulness) of the model in explaining management accounting change in four companies which implemented ABC, and on the other hand it developed the model by proposing several new factors positively and negatively influencing the change process (it should be stressed, however, that some of the factors from Kasurinen's model were not observed in the present research). Current research has shown that, among the factors influencing the change process there are some which were not mentioned in Kasurinen's model. Those are:

- motivators – the need for information (observed in 4 out of 4 companies) and inaccuracy of cost data (observed in 4 out of 4 companies),
- facilitators – knowledge transfer (observed in 4 out of 4 companies), susceptibility to fashions and trends (observed in 4 out of 4 companies) and a change-oriented organization (observed in 2 out of 4 companies),
- catalysts – acknowledged ABC superiority (observed in 3 out of 4 companies), imitation of competitors (observed in 1 out of 4 companies) and in-company training (observed in 1 out of 4 companies),
- confusers – insufficient knowledge of managers (observed in 3 out of 4 companies) and the company's complicated activities (observed in 2 out of 4 companies).

The other significant difference between the present research results and Kasurinen's (2002) model was the position of the leaders. In Kasurinen's model the general manager played the key role in the implementation (was the leader) whereas in the present research, controllers (in 3 out of 4 companies) and the CFO (in 1 out of 4 companies) were the leaders of the process. The developed model of management accounting change is presented in Figure 5.2 (factors underlined are new in comparison to Kasurinen's model and the number of pluses means in how many companies a particular factor was observed).

It is important to mention that this study suffers from the limitations of empirical research grounded in case studies. The results were based on case studies of four companies only, therefore they should be interpreted with great caution (they are not representative of business diversity). This limitation, however, creates opportunities for further study. It would be interesting and potentially fruitful to test the model (in the form of case studies and questionnaires) on a sample of a few other companies which implemented activity-based costing (or other innovations). On the basis of that research it would be possible to further examine the quality and usefulness of the model in explaining the process of activity-based costing implementation and contribute to broaden the general knowledge about the implementation process of management accounting innovations.

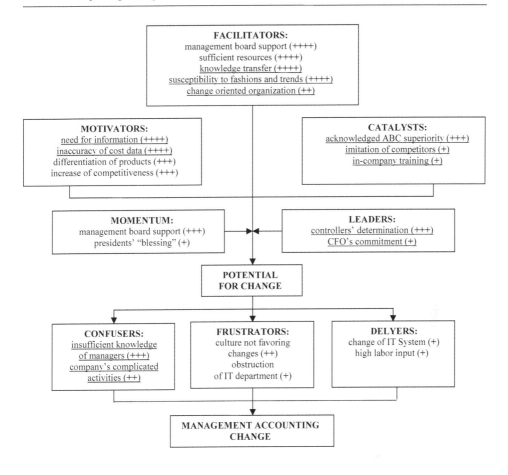

Figure 5.2. Developed management accounting change model

More research is needed in order to obtain an understanding of why and how management accounting innovations e.g. ABC, are implemented in practice and to get insights into the use of these innovations by managers, and also to analyze the implementation process of ABC in the more general context of management accounting change.

5.6. Summary and conclusions

The developed model of management accounting system change could be beneficial for identifying potential forces influencing change, especially at the early stages of the project. Using the model, barriers of the change process could be identified which could possibly result in at least some of the problems the company could encounter being taken into account. Use of the model, especially analysis of confusers, frustrators and delayers could help companies implementing management accounting innovations pay more attention to the context of change. This could lead to a proper evaluation of the structural barriers of change (such as organizational culture) and help organizations in making good decision whether to implement innovation or not, and if the decision about implementation is positive the model could be beneficial in avoiding or overcoming the influence of the negative factors. This knowledge may facilitate better decision making and may increase the likelihood of a successful implementation process. This study enables the formulation of findings as far as the implementation of activity-based costing in companies is concerned: (a) factors which foster activity-based costing implementation are: rise of competition, change of strategy and the need for more accurate information, (b) the moment of decision-making about innovation implementation should be dependent on the occurrence of one or more catalysts specified in the model, (c) in order to improve the effectiveness of a successful implementation of activity-based costing the company should be certain that the facilitators specified in the model occur and obstructors are minimized (also specified in the model), (d) momentum for change and leaders of the change process (determined individuals) are necessary to create potential for change, (e) implemented ABC should be modified in order to follow the changing conditions of the company's operations, so that it corresponds to the management's needs.

On the basis of the research carried out in four companies, the following conclusions on the hypothesis tested shall be drawn:

1. The research enabled the distinction of three types of factors positively influencing activity-based costing implementation and one type of negative factors. The factors affect the process of implementation collectively, promoting the process of change (positive factors dominate negative factors in that respect). The research identified the following positive factors:

a) the most important motivators, which have a continuous and long-term influence on implementation of the innovation, were: management's need for information (4 companies), inaccuracy of data from the current costing system (4 companies), increase of differentiation of products and customers' demand (3 companies) and increase of competitiveness (3 companies);

b) among the catalysts which directly influence the implementation of the innovation, the following were distinguished: the management board's acknowledgement of activity-based costing as the system which could provide significant information useful for management (2 companies), the management board's acknowledgement of activity-based costing as the system which 'is attractive' to have (1 company), in-service training in the area of cost accounting and post-graduate studies undertaken by the Controller (1 company);

c) four facilitators were identified in each company (without them, the process of implementation would be impossible): the management board's support, knowledge transfer, availability of sufficient resources, and susceptibility to fashions and trends. Additionally, in two companies, there was another facilitator i.e. a change-oriented organizational culture.

2. The key factors which negatively influenced the process of implementation of management accounting innovation in the researched companies included: organizational culture not favoring changes (2 companies) and insufficient knowledge of medium and senior management of the company (3 companies). In two out of the four analyzed companies there were also other obstructors impeding the process of implementation i.e. the company's very complicated and differentiated activities and insufficient knowledge of the technical processes among the financial section's employees. Sporadically (one case only), other negative factors were identified, including: lack of understanding of the importance of activity-based costing by the IT Department, change of the IT system, and the high labor input into activity-based costing procedures.

3. Changes triggered by the implementation of activity-based costing in the analyzed companies were evident in two areas – methodological and institutional/ organizational. The research revealed that in all four companies, the following methodological changes took place: improvement in the accuracy of cost calculations (direct and indirect), improvement in the cost of product calculation, improvement in the accuracy and wider use of profitability analyses, as well as the use of ABC information for making decisions. What is more, in two companies, the implementation of activity-based costing enabled the costs of unused capacity to be isolated, and in one of the companies it improved the system of budgeting and reporting.

4. The case studies also revealed institutional/organizational changes which resulted from activity-based costing implementation. The basic institutional changes in all the four companies included: bringing management accounting function closer to other operational functions, a better attitude to information delivery for decisions, and more frequent use of management accounting information by managers. In two companies, implementation of activity-based costing triggered off the creation of a specified post for the person in the Controlling Department whose main task was to manage the ABC system, and additionally, in the third company, the Controller was no longer supervised by the Chief Accountant but directly by the President. In one case, a significant increase in the importance of management accounting in the company was identified.

CHAPTER 6

SATISFACTION AND BENEFITS OF ACTIVITY-BASED COSTING IMPLEMENTATION IN POLISH COMPANIES

6.1. Introduction

At the turn of the 20th and 21st centuries, a substantial percentage of companies in different countries undertook the laborious task of activity-based costing implementation; the companies experienced numerous problems in the process of implementation and in some cases the implementation success was questionable. One of the first works which aimed to identify factors influencing the success of ABC implementation was the research by Shields (1995). The research was carried out on a group of 143 companies using activity-based costing and it proved that the degree of satisfaction of ABC was greatly varied (activity-based costing implementation was seen as a moderate success and companies using ABC evaluated the implementation as financially profitable). The study proved that the success of ABC implementation depends on behavioral and organizational factors, among them: board support, relation to competitive strategy, relation to systems of performance appraisal and reward and the fact of having enough resources for the implementation. Shields (1995) concluded that success of ABC implementation does not significantly depend on such technical variables as: type of software, consultants' participation in the process of implementation or implementation as a part of ERP or other system.

Swenson (1995) completed his study in the same year as Shields (1995). The research aimed to analyze financial and operational managers' satisfaction resulting from activity-based costing functioning in their companies (the research was carried out on a group of 25 companies). In general, the study showed that the level of ABC satisfaction was higher than the satisfaction of traditional systems. However the author stressed that one should interpret the results cautiously since the respondents came from a group of people which, in the analyzed companies, were responsible for activity-based costing implementation process. The measurement of success of ABC implementation was improved in the research by Foster and Swenson (1997), who suggested four measures of success i.e. the use of ABC information in the decision making process, making decisions and taking actions based on ABC information, the perceived financial consequences of ABC implementation and the evaluation of success of ABC implementation by managers[1].

In another piece of research on the factors determining the success of activity-based costing implementation, McGowan and Klammer (1997) analyzed the relation between the factors which determined ABC implementation and employees' satisfaction of the system. The main result of the study stated that the degree of satisfaction of the ABC system was dependent on most of the factors which had been identified earlier in the research by Shields (1995) i.e. support of the board, the degree of involvement in the implementation process, and relation to the system of performance appraisal and training. The research (McGowan, Klammer, 1997) proved that employees generally found the implementation of activity-based costing as a positive phenomenon, however, the level of satisfaction was higher with people who oversaw on a daily basis the functioning of ABC system (preparers) than those who only used ABC information (users). The involvement of employees in the process of ABC implementation and assessment of information quality generated by activity-based costing were positively correlated to ABC implementation success.

Research conducted by Anderson and Young (1999) concentrated on the analysis of relations between the employees' satisfaction of activity-based costing and the factors determining the implementation. The study based on an example of two companies helped to form the statement that the general evaluation of activity-based costing is mainly dependent on the quality of traditional costing system and the precision of ABC information generally depends on the necessity of changes and involvement of adequate resources in the design process perceived by respondents, whereas the use of information generated by the ABC system was mainly dependent on the support of the board, accessibility of adequate resources, the respondent's involvement in the project and the organization of the implementation. The fundamental variables used in the key studies of activity-based costing satisfaction and ABC implementation success are presented in Table 6.1.

---

[1] Foster and Swenson's study (1997) aimed to analyze the factors which influence the success of the implementation of activity-based management methods. The research was based on a sample of 166 ABC implementations in 132 companies. It agreed with earlier studies that the two key factors which determine implementation success are support of the board and relation to the system of performance appraisal. The analysis showed that there was a positive relation between the success of ABC implementation, the length of time it was used, and the number of various applications of the system.

Table 6.1. Variables used to analyze satisfaction and ABC implementation success

Research	Method	Variables used
Anderson (1995)	Case study of one company	Success as transition to another phase of implementation
Shields (1995)	Survey of 143 companies which use ABC	Perceived implementation success Financial effects of implementation
Swenson (1995)	Telephone interviews with 50 people from 25 companies	Satisfaction of previous product costing Satisfaction of ABC product costing
Innes, Mitchell (1995)	Survey of 21 manufacturing and non-manufacturing companies	Success as transition to another phase of implementation
Gosselin (1997)	Survey of 161 business units in manufacturing companies	Success as transition to another phase of implementation
McGowan, Klammer (1997)	Study of 53 employees from 4 companies	Perceived ABC implementation success
Foster, Swenson (1997)	Survey of 166 ABC users from 132 companies, 15 companies visited	Use of ABC information in decision making and taking actions based on ABC information Perceived financial effects of ABC implementation ABC implementation success seen by managers Composite measure
McGowan (1998)	Survey of 4 companies (67 respondents, both preparers and users)	User attitude Technical characteristics of information Perceived usefulness in improving job performance Organizational process impact
Anderson, Young (1999)	Survey and case studies of 21 ABC projects in 2 companies	Perceived ABC value Perceived ABC accuracy Perceived usage of ABC information
Swenson, Barney (2001)	Survey of 15 best practice ABC companies	Quantifiable financial improvements Perceptions of success of key managers
Kennedy, Affleck-Graves (2001)	Survey of UK firms	Increase in firm value
Fortin et al. (2007)	Survey of 15 government organizations (25 respondents)	ABC uses and frequency of use changes made Financial improvements Managers' and personnel's evaluation of ABC success Composite measure
Byrne et al. (2009)	Survey of 7 companies (65 Respondents, both preparers and users)	User attitude Technical characteristics of information Perceived usefulness in improving job performance Organizational process impact

To sum up the analysis of the research into the evaluation of activity-based costing implementation success, it should be stressed that it was mainly based on the opinions of management and employees (generally managers and employees were asked for a subjective assessment of success in the five-point Likert scale). As a result, evaluation the success of ABC implementation in the analyzed research may be difficult to assess in terms of subjectivity. The measurement of success resulting from activity-based costing implementation is not simple, although in subsequent researches (Shields, 1995; Anderson, Young, 1999) better measures were used.

The literature on activity-based costing contains a long list of potential benefits companies may derive from ABC implementation. Despite the fact that many publications bring up examples of potential benefits of ABC implementation, one may notice an insufficient number of studies on the actual benefits of the companies, in which activity-based costing has been implemented. The research into the benefits of ABC implementation primarily used one general measure of success i.e. 'respondent's satisfaction' (Swenson, 1995; Shields, 1995; McGowan, Klammer, 1997)[2]. Only a few pieces of research provided more detailed proof of the perceived benefits of ABC implementation[3]. McGowan (1998), for example, researched the the benefits of ABC implementation in four dimensions: (a) general satisfaction of ABC, (b) quality of ABC information, (c) perceived usefulness of ABC, (d) influence of ABC on the organization (the same approach was replicated by Byrne *et al.* (2009)).

Questions about the benefits of activity-based costing are interesting not only for academics. The answers may be even more interesting for practitioners who decide or will decide on the implementation of ABC – it is important for them to verify the real usefulness of ABC in their company; it will help them to make a decision which is not only based on 'the possible benefits' but on the opinions of people whose companies have already implemented and use ABC. The results of the research may provide the people who prepare and those who use the ABC information with data about the potential influence of the implementation on their work; the results also emphasize the need to consider behavioral issues which may contribute to the improvement of the implementation effectiveness and maximizing of benefits of the ABC system. In the light of presented facts, it is important to fill in the identified research gap

---

[2] It should be stressed that although such measures of ABC success as *increase in firm value* or *financial effects of implementation* are theoretically appealing, they are very difficult to control – it is extremely difficult to prove that there is a direct link between the implementation of ABC and *increase in firm value* or *financial effects of implementation*. Consequently the most often used measure of ABC success is perceived satisfaction. It could be argued that satisfaction with ABC could be a proxy for system success (McGowan, Klammer, 1997; McGowan, 1998) – a measure of overall user attitude toward ABC is an appropriate substitute for assessing the success of the system.

[3] The literature on management information systems shows that evaluation based on the criterion of usefulness for users is the most important criterion used in the assessment of an information system's effectiveness (Lucas, 1975).

i.e. to analyse satisfaction and to identify the benefits of activity-based costing implementation in Polish companies.

The research in this chapter (questionnaire C) aims to analyse the satisfaction and benefits of ABC implementation in companies operating in Poland, in particular it aims to analyse the attitudes of preparers and users of ABC information, the quality of ABC information, its usefulness and its influence on the company[4]. In order to realize the aim of this research, it has been divided into two parts. The first part characterizes the research methodology i.e. it presents a tested sample, analysed variables and research hypotheses. The second part presents the research results i.e. analysis of the results of carried out works and conclusions. The chapter ends with a summary, the limitations of this research and directions for further studies.

6.2. Research method

In order to examine the benefits of activity-based costing implementation in companies operating in Poland, it was necessary to identify companies which have already implemented the ABC system. To determine the biggest possible population of companies using ABC, the author made use of all information sources known to him i.e. (a) results of his previous surveys (questionnaires A and B), (b) projects and cases of implementation of cost accounting (including ABC) carried out by the author under his consulting activity, (c) all known publications which described companies using ABC, (d) conference publications and didactic aids which enlisted companies using ABC, (e) information from IT and consulting companies which implemented ABC systems.

Generally, 71 companies which used activity-based costing were identified (46 companies were identified on the basis of the author's own survey research (questionnaires A and B) and 25 came from other sources). The author contacted the companies in person or by telephone and sent them detailed questionnaires via e-mail. The companies back 28 completed surveys (from a statistical point of view the sample was small). The author made sure that the people who completed the surveys had practical knowledge of ABC – they were responsible in their companies for the construction and modification of activity-based costing or used ABC information. In 5 out of 7 companies the ABC system was mature (fully implemented) and in 2 companies the implementation process was advanced in about 60%. There were more companies in the sample tested (7) and they came from broader cross-section of industries then in the McGowan (1998) study (still, study of Byrne et al. (2009) included even more (30) companies from more (8) industry sections).

---

[4] The research carried out in this paper is modelled on McGowan's research (1998), particularly, the questionnaire developed by McGowan, has been used (McGowan's research was replicated in 2009 by Byrne et al. on the sample of Australian companies).

The respondents came from seven companies, among them a mid-size manufacturing and trading company (5 questionnaires), a large manufacturing company (8 questionnaires), a very large company from the financial sector (2 questionnaires), a big manufacturing and trading company (4 questionnaires), a large service company (5 questionnaires), a very large company from the telecommunications sector (2 questionnaires) and a big manufacturing company (2 questionnaires). The respondents in each of the companies were categorized into two groups – people preparing the ABC information (the group was defined as 'preparers' – 12 people) and those who made use of the information (the group was defined as 'users' – 16 people). As the respondents were asked to compare two costing systems, to participate in the study they had to have experience with both a traditional (old) costing system and the ABC (new) system. The average work experience of the respondents varied from 2.5 years to 18.5 years with the mean being at the level of 8.5 years. Most of the respondents were relatively young (24 out of 28 respondents were under 45).

The research into benefits of ABC implementation in companies operating in Poland was preceded by intensive literature studies. The studies embraced literature on activity-based costing and activity-based management, in particular research into measurement of ABC implementation successes and benefits of it. To analyze the benefits of ABC implementation in Polish companies, four basic groups of variables were used (to make country comparisons easier, the items were the same as those used by McGowan (1998) and Byrne et al. (2009)):

1. General satisfaction of ABC implementation – generally, implementation is perceived as a success if the implemented system is accepted and used (Lucas, 1975; Robey, 1979) or if the user's satisfaction improves (Bailey, Pearson, 1983; Ives et al., 1983; Doll, Torkzadeh, 1988). The first of the enlisted measurements i.e. acceptation and use of the system cannot be used in this research, since the study was carried out in companies which implemented and use ABC (in this context, in all of the tested companies ABC is 'accepted and used'). In this case, as a measurement of success, a general attitude towards the functioning of activity-based costing can be implemented. So far, the research clearly proved that activity-based costing is generally well-received. Both managers (Bailey, 1991; Innes, Mitchell, 1991; Nicholls, 1992; Swenson, 1995) and employees of companies using ABC (Foster, Gupta, 1990; McGowan, Klammer, 1997) expressed positive opinions about the implementation and found this system better than the previous one.

2. Quality of ABC information – virtually all Polish and foreign practical publications from the last twenty years stress the fact that traditional cost accounting does not provide sufficient information needed to manage the company in the competitive, global and rapidly changing environment. New methods e.g. ABC were an answer to companies' new needs in the new conditions of operation. Most of the researchers confirm that activity-based costing provides

better information compared to the previously used traditional costing system (Raffish, Turney, 1991; Brimson, 1991). Those common positive opinions about the quality of ABC information are mixed with critical viewpoints[5]. Does activity-based costing really provide information of a better quality in comparison to the traditional cost accounting systems? The literature enumerates many characteristic features of information, important from the users' point of view (Delone, McClean, 1997). The difference in satisfaction of ABC implementation perceived by managers and employees may be dependent not only on the fact that the old cost accounting system was replaced by a new one, but on the quality of information the new system provides compared to the previous one. Qualitative characteristics of information, which influence the satisfaction of the system used, are mentioned in the literature: for example (a) general high quality of information (Lucas, 1975), (b) accessibility of information (Kraemer *at el.*, 1993), (c) accuracy and adequacy of information (Fuerst, Cheney, 1982).

3. Usefulness of ABC information – one answer to the question about the reasons underlying the satisfaction of activity-based costing may be that it depends on its usefulness at work. In numerous publications, one may find the opinion that activity-based costing leads to better knowledge of the causes of costs or that ABC may respond to managers' and employees' needs in a more flexible manner compared to traditional systems (Turney, 1992; Brimson, 1991; Pemberton *et al.*, 1996; Geishecker, 1996). Hamilton and Chervany (1981) notice that general usefulness of the information system may be different depending on the manger and employee's position in a company[6]. When considering ABC, it may indicate that, depending on the fact whether the person prepares or uses ABC information, the usefulness of activity-based costing may be perceived differently.

4. ABC influence on the company – the influence of any implemented innovation on a company is critical at the assessment of the success and effectiveness of the implementation of a given innovation. Every implemented innovation should be well-received by the managers and employees but it simultaneously should match the organization (it should be compatible with the organization). In this context, it is worth examining the analyzed implementations of activity-based costing. ABC perceives organization not through the prism of divisions and departments but through the prism of processes and activities – it helps to overcome functional barriers existing in the company. Bhimani and Pigot (1992) claim, on the basis of carried out studies, that the success of ABC implementation is closely related to such variables as: decision making, interpersonal relations, communication and involvement in the realization of the aims of the company.

---

[5] For example Piper and Walley (1990) question fundamental ABC principles, including the one that activities generate costs. They also claim that the internal logic of activity-based costing is wrong.

[6] Hamilton and Chervany's (1981) research proved that implemented system improved the quality of decisions but lengthened the time needed to make them.

5. Characteristics of preparers and users of ABC information – studies on the satisfaction of ABC clearly prove that activity-based costing is evaluated in a positive manner (Bailey, 1991; Innes, Mitchell, 1991; Nicholls, 1992; Swenson, 1995; Foster, Gupta, 1990; McGowan, Klammer, 1997). Are satisfaction of implemented activity-based costing and its positive evaluation common? Is it influenced by such variables as: (a) the respondent's education and experience (Lucas, 1975), (b) the respondent's age (Fuerst, Cheney, 1982), (c) the respondent's personality and character traits (DeSanctis, 1984) or (d) the respondent's position in the company (Zmud, Cox, 1979; McKeen et al., 1994; Anderson, 1995)? The implementation of the new cost accounting system may influence, to a large degree, a change of roles in the company, it may alter the level of freedom of individual people or departments, and it may influence the procedures of decision making. The impact of those changes on individual people may influence their perception of ABC. It is possible that managers and employees see activity-based costing in a different way, depending an whether they prepare the information for ABC or whether they are users of the information. This research concentrates on the two groups – preparers and users of ABC information (McKeen et al., 1994; Leonard-Barton, 1988):

a) users of ABC information – individuals (employees and managers) for whom activity-based costing has been created and who use ABC information at work (e.g. in the process of decision making). From their point of view, the system is evaluated in a positive manner if it provides information useful in their work;

b) preparers of ABC information – individuals such as analysts, accountants, programmers, management accounting and controlling specialists, who are responsible for the development, modification and maintenance of ABC. From their point of view, the system is evaluated in a positive manner if tasks (aims) set up for the system are realized and the system functions well.

To summarize, individuals who prepare the information will pay more attention to the quality of the information, whereas individuals who make use of the information will pay more attention to the information's usefulness in their everyday work[7].

All major worldwide research on activity-based costing prove that both managers and employees share a positive attitude towards ABC implementation. With reference to the characteristics of managers' and employees' attitude in Polish companies, the following hypothesis has been suggested: hypothesis 1 – managers and employees are positively oriented towards ABC implementation.

One of the main reasons which underlies the laborious task of ABC implementation is the pursuit of improvement of the information obtained from

---

[7] It should be noted that people responsible for the development, modification and maintenance of ABC may identify with the system and are more prone to determine the implementation as a success (Anderson, 1995). On the other hand, those people may see some limitations of the system in a given company; it may result from the fact that they are involved in the implementation process and have knowledge of ABC, therefore they are aware of the possible shortcomings of activity-based costing in a particular company (e.g. they know which assumptions of the model are likely to fail).

activity-based costing in comparison with the traditional cost accounting system. With respect to the characteristics of information from activity-based costing, the following hypothesis has been formulated: hypothesis 2 – managers and employees rank the information from ABC higher than from the traditional cost accounting system. In order to verify the hypothesis, it was decided to specifically verify whether managers and employees perceive the information from ABC as: (a) more accurate, (b) more accessible, (c) more reliable, (d) timely to obtain and (e) more understandable in comparison with the traditional cost accounting system.

Benefit assessment resulting from the ABC implementation may be viewed through the usefulness of activity-based costing in the everyday work of a given person. With reference to the usefulness of information generated from activity-based costing, the following hypothesis has been suggested: hypothesis 3 – managers and employees evaluate positively the usefulness of the ABC information. To verify the hypothesis, it was decided to specifically verify whether managers and employees see the ABC implementation as a process which: (a) has improved the quality of their work, (b) has improved the control over their work, (c) has enabled tasks to be accomplished more quickly, (d) has supported the critical aspects of their job, (e) has improved job productivity, (f) has enabled improvement of job performance, (g) has enabled them to perform a bigger number of tasks, (h) has increased effectiveness of their job, (i) has facilitated easier accomplishment of work-related tasks and (j) has generally been useful at work.

Every new initiative in a company, especially as significant as the implementation of a new cost accounting system, influences the organization's functioning. With reference to the influence of activity-based costing on a company, the following hypothesis has been formulated: hypothesis 4 – managers and employees are convinced that ABC implementation influenced their company in a positive way. In order to verify the hypothesis, it was decided to specifically verify whether managers and employees see the ABC implementation as a process which influenced: (a) the improvement of quality of decisions, (b) waste reduction (c) the rise of innovativeness, (d) the improvement of relationships across functions, (e) the improvement of communications across functions and (f) the increase of focus on the goals of the entity.

Individual innovations implemented in a company may be evaluated differently, depending on the point of view of the person who is evaluating – generally the evaluations of people involved in the implementation and responsible for the preparation of information (preparers) may be different from those who make use of that information (users). With reference to the standpoints on ABC of preparers and users, the following hypothesis has been suggested: hypothesis 5 – the opinions of preparers and users of ABC information on implementation benefits will differ considerably.

6.3. Analysis of the research results

To carry out an examination of the perceived benefits of ABC implementation, descriptive analysis and test of significance for mean values and variations were used (to see if the observed relations are statistically significant). To allow comparisons with both American (McGowan, 1998) and Australian (Byrne et al., 2009) studies parametric statistical methods were used. Below one can find detailed results of research which enable the verification of formulated hypotheses i.e. general satisfaction resulting from the ABC implementation, the quality of information from ABC in comparison with the traditional cost accounting system, usefulness of information from ABC, the influence of ABC on the company, and differences in ABC assessment made by preparers and users of the ABC information.

6.3.1. General satisfaction resulting from ABC implementation

The results presented in Table 6.2 support hypothesis 1. The value of satisfaction assessment resulting from the activity-based costing implementation is significantly smaller (statistical significance 0.01, $t = -16.20$) than the test value of 3 (3 – average satisfaction of ABC implementation). The results are statistically significant and point out that on average respondents are definitely positive towards ABC implementation (mean = 1.43).

Table 6.2. General satisfaction ensuing from ABC implementation

Dependent variable[a]	Mean	Standard deviation	t-value	McGowan (1998) mean	Byrne et al. (2009) mean
General satisfaction of ABC implementation	1.43	0.50	-16.20^b	1.98	1.83

[a] In this question a scale from 1-very high evaluation to 5-very low evaluation was used.
[b] Significant at level 0.01.

The results of this research, with respect to hypothesis 1, confirm the results of McGowan (1998) and Byrne et al. (2009), who, in the researched sample, also got confirmation of the respondents' generally positive attitude towards ABC implementation. However, the average satisfaction in this research was assessed at a higher level (1.43) than in the studies by McGowan (1.98) and Byrne et al. (1.83).

6.3.2. Quality of ABC information with respect to traditional system

In order to verify the hypothesis about better quality of information from ABC in comparison with traditional cost accounting system, tests enabling the comparison of the two means in the case of related pairs of samples were carried out. The respondents were asked to evaluate the traditional cost accounting system and the newly implemented ABC system in terms of five features i.e. accuracy, accessibility, reliability, timeliness and understandability of information provided by both systems. The results presented in Table 6.3 support hypothesis 2. The respondents assess accuracy (statistical significance 0.01, t = –8.42), accessibility (statistical significance 0.01, t = –5.89), reliability (statistical significance 0.01, t = –3.18), timeliness (statistical significance 0.01, t = –4.30) and understandability (statistical significance 0.01, t = –5.65) of the information from the newly implemented ABC system significantly higher than the information generated from the traditional cost accounting system.

Table 6.3. Quality of ABC information with respect to traditional system

Dependent variable[a]	Traditional system		ABC		t-value	McGowan (1998) ABC mean	Byrne et al. (2009) ABC mean
	mean	standard deviation	mean	standard deviation			
Accuracy	3.29	1.05	1.43	0.63	–8.42[b]	2.27	2.20
Accessibility	3.36	0.99	1.64	0.73	–5.89[b]	3.57	2.38
Reliability	2.86	1.48	1.86	0.76	–3.18[b]	2.49	2.35
Timeliness	3.36	1.25	1.71	0.81	–4.30[b]	2.58	2.45
Understandability	2.93	1.05	1.64	0.62	–5.65[b]	2.47	2.31

[a] In this question a scale from 1-very high evaluation to 5-very low evaluation was used.
[b] Significant at level 0.01.

The research results of information quality from the new activity-based costing, with respect to the information from the traditional cost accounting system (Table 6.3), are confirmed by the McGowan (1998) and the Byrne et al. (2009) studies; however: (a) in this research the information quality from the new ABC, in relation to the traditional cost accounting system, was ranked much higher (all averages below 2) than in the McGowan (1998) and the Byrne et al. (2009) studies (where none of the averages was lower than 2), (b) in McGowan's research (1998) the accessibility of information from the current system and ABC was evaluated by respondents at a similar level (3.50 and 3.57 respectively), although the difference was not statistically significant.

The results obtained in this research are mirrored in the work of Swenson et al. (1996), who examined the level of satisfaction of managers from 25 companies (where activity-based costing was used) resulting from the implementation of product valuation methods. The average satisfaction level was much higher in the case of ABC than in the case of traditional cost accounting systems (managers' satisfaction with ABC in companies which implemented ABC in the Swenson, Flescher (1996) study, was similar to the satisfaction of managers in Howell's *et al.* research (1987)). Similar results were also reported in the study of Swenson and Barney (2001), who examined 15 best practice companies using ABC. The overall attitude towards ABC was in this study quite favourable, especially when compared with traditional costing systems[8]. One respondent in this research noted that "ABC/M is, and has been our only cost management tool. Compared to what we had before, it's excellent". Swenson and Barney (2001) noted, however, that for many companies the positive perceptions were based not on actual but projected benefits.

6.3.3. Usefulness of ABC information

In order to evaluate the usefulness of activity-based costing, ten variables were used (while variable ten tested the overall perception of ABC usefulness and variable six the job performance, the rest of the variables related generally to the usefulness of ABC information in the respondents' work). The results presented in Table 6.4 support hypothesis 3. The respondents confirm the positive and statistically significant influence of ABC (much lower mean than the average value of 3) on their work, especially its influence on the improvement in the quality of their work (mean 1.57 and $t = -8.88$ at statistical significance 0.01), its influence on control over work-related procedures (mean 1.50 and $t = -10.46$ at statistical significance 0.01), the ability to accomplish tasks quickly (mean 2.21 and $t = -4.27$ at statistical significance 0.01), aiding of critical aspects of their job (mean 1.43 and $t = -11.01$ at statistical significance 0.01), its influence on the improvement of their job productivity (mean 1.86 and $t = -7$ at statistical significance 0.01), the ability to improve their job performance (mean 1.64 and $t = -8.54$ at statistical significance 0.01), accomplishing more work than under the old system (mean 2.07 and $t = -4.93$ at statistical significance 0.01), improvement of their job effectiveness (mean 1.93 and $t = -6.85$ at statistical significance 0.01), and easier accomplishment of work-related tasks (average 1.64 and $t = -9.65$ at statistical significance 0.01). The respondents point out that ABC is generally useful in their work – they rank its influence on their work usefulness as definitely positive and the influence is statistically significant (mean 1.43 and $t = -11.01$ at statistical significance 0.01).

---

[8] Swenson and Barney (2001) reported that ABC/M was perceived as 'good' or 'excellent' in respect of information reliability (by 88% of respondents), timeliness of information (by 64% of respondents) and information accessibility (by 47% of respondents).

Table 6.4. Usefulness of ABC information

Dependent variable[a]	Mean	Standard deviation	t-value	McGowan (1998) mean	Byrne et al. (2009) mean
Improvements in the quality of work	1.57	0.84	−8.88[b]	2.30	2.42
Greater control over work-related procedures	1.50	0.75	−10.46[b]	2.49	2.23
Accomplishing tasks more quickly	2.21	0.96	−4.27[b]	2.56	2.74
Support for the critical aspects of the job	1.43	0.74	−11.01[b]	2.33	2.14
Increased job productivity	1.86	0.85	−7.00[b]	2.30	2.46
Increased job performance	1.64	0.83	−8.54[b]	2.13	2.40
Accomplishing more work than under the old system	2.07	0.98	−4.93[b]	2.62	2.80
Enhanced effectiveness on the job	1.93	0.81	−6.85[b]	2.28	2.31
Makes it easier to accomplish work-related tasks	1.64	0.73	−9.65[b]	2.77	2.48
Overall, I find ABCM useful in my job	1.43	0.74	−11.01[b]	2.03	2.09

[a] In this question a scale from 1-definitely yes to 5-definitely not was used.
[b] Significant at level 0.01.

The results of the research which examined the usefulness of information generated from the newly implemented activity-based costing are confirmed by the results of the McGowan (1998) and Byrne et al. (2009) studies, however: (a) this research found the usefulness of ABC information higher (eight means below 2) than the McGowan (1998) and Byrne et al. (2009) studies (none of the means was lower than 2), (b) in this research the respondents assessed that the implementation of ABC makes it easier to accomplish work-related tasks in a considerably positive and statistically significant manner, whereas respondents in the McGowan study (1998) did not see such a relationship.

6.3.4. Influence of ABC on the company

The results presented in Table 6.5 partly support hypothesis 4. The respondents confirm that ABC implementation had a considerably positive and statistically significant impact (much lower than the average value of 3) on the increase of quality of decisions (mean 1.48 and t = −13.61 at statistical significance 0.01) as well as on the increase of the overall focus on the goals of the entity (mean 1.50

and t = −15.31 at statistical significance 0.01). According to the respondents, ABC implementation had a slightly positive (slightly lower than the average value of 3) yet statistically significant influence on the boost of innovativeness (mean 2.14 and t = −5.89 at statistical significance 0.01) and an improvement of communications across functions (mean 2.50 and t = −3.10 at statistical significance 0.01). The research proves that ABC implementation had no statistically significant influence on the improvement of relations across functions (insignificant and unimportant positive impact) or on waste reduction (insignificant and unimportant negative impact).

Table 6.5. Influence of ABC on company

Dependent variable[a]	Mean	Standard deviation	t-value	McGowan (1998) mean	Byrne et al. (2009) mean
Quality of decisions	1.48	0.58	−13.61[b]	2.32	2.05
Waste reduction	3.29	1.18	1.26	2.01	2.26
Innovation	2.14	0.76	−5.89[b]	2.10	2.51
Relationships across functions	2.86	0.76	−0.98	2.29	2.40
Communications across functions	2.50	0.84	−3.10[b]	2.21	2.39
Overall focus on the goals of the entity	1.50	0.51	−15.31[b]	2.23	2.92

[a] In this question a scale from 1-definitely yes to 5-definitely not was used.
[b] Significant at level 0.01.

The results of this research on the influence of a newly implemented ABC on a company (Table 6.5) are partly confirmed by the McGowan (1998) and Byrne et al. (2009) studies. However, their studies claimed that the influence of ABC implementation on a company was insubstantial yet statistically significant in the case of all dependent variables. The research carried out in Poland claims that ABC implementation had: (a) a substantially positive and statistically significant influence on the improved quality of decisions and the increase of concentration on the company's aims, (b) a slightly positive and statistically significant impact on the boost of innovativeness and improvement of communication across functions, and (c) a statistically insignificant and unsubstantial influence on the improvement of relations across functions (positive influence) and waste reduction (negative influence).

The results are confirmed by the Swenson and Flescher research (1996). The authors of the study noticed that the general satisfaction assessment resulting from ABC implementation (which was very positive in their study) was a rather subjective measure of benefits derived from the process of ABC implementation. They also claimed that ABC information may be of little importance if it is not used in the decision-making process. After close examination of the use of ABC information, they stated that 92% of companies used it to improve the processes, 72% to set product prices and to make decisions about products, 48% used it in the process of product design and 24% in making decisions about components[9]. The respondents emphasized the necessity to integrate ABC with all other areas of the company's functioning and they stressed the fact that the systems were not implemented in isolation. In all companies, without exception, representatives of different departments took part in the process of implementation, and ABC systems were designed with the application of a new philosophy – people who made use of ABC information were seen as ABC system *clients* while accounting departments attempted to satisfy the needs of internal *clients*, just in the same way as the companies tried to satisfy the needs of their external clients.

6.3.5. Differences in ABC evaluation by preparers and users

The results presented in Table 6.6 mostly do not support hypothesis 5. In particular:

1) general satisfaction of ABC implementation does not significantly differ between preparers and users of ABC information (in the study by McGowan (1998), the satisfaction of people preparing the information was statistically more significant than the people who used it);

2) evaluation of accuracy, reliability and understandability of information does not differ between preparers and users of ABC information, however, accessibility (F = 5.44 at statistical significance 0.01) and timeliness of ABC information (F = 3.68 at statistical significance 0.01) was evaluated higher by preparers than users (in McGowan's research (1998) there were no statistically significant discrepancies);

3) evaluation of the influence of ABC implementation on the aiding of critical aspects of the respondents' work (F = 3.21 at statistical significance 0.1) and its general usefulness in their work (F = 5.04 at statistical significance 0.1) is ranked substantially higher by preparers than users; the evaluation of the remaining variables which influence the quality of information does not differ significantly between the preparers and users of ABC information (in McGowan's study (1998) statistically significant differences were noticed in the perception of improvement of work quality, improvement of work control and boost of work effectiveness);

4) evaluation of the influence of ABC implementation on the improvement of decision quality (F = 2.61 at statistical significance 0.1) is ranked substantially

---

[9] The results of the current research were also supported by the findings of Swenson and Barney (2001), who observed that 97% of respondents from 15 best ABC practice companies assessed ABC/M information as 'good' or 'excellent' in decision support and 73% as 'good' or 'excellent' from the point of view of cross-functional needs.

higher by preparers than users; the evaluation of the remaining variables does not differ significantly between the two groups (in McGowan's study (1998) there were no statistically significant discrepancies).

Table 6.6. Differences in ABC evaluation by preparers and users

Dependent variable	Mean (preparers)	Mean (users)	F-value
A. Satisfaction			
General satisfaction of ABC implementation	1.50	1.38	1.12
B. Information quality			
Accessibility	2.00	1.75	1.37
Accuracy	1.33	2.00	5.44[a]
Reliability	1.83	0.38	1.50
Timeliness	1.17	2.00	3.68[a]
Understandability	2.17	0.63	2.47
C. Information usefulness			
Improvements in the quality of my work	1.50	1.63	1.20
Greater control over work-related procedures	1.50	1.50	1.23
Accomplishing tasks more quickly	2.50	2.00	1.28
Support for the critical aspects of my job	1.33	1.50	3.21[b]
Increased job productivity	1.67	2.00	1.29
Increased job performance	1.50	1.75	1.12
Accomplishing more work than under the old system	1.83	2.25	2.39
Enhanced effectiveness on the job	2.00	1.88	2.46
Makes it easier to accomplish work-related tasks	1.33	1.88	2.61
Overall, I find ABCM useful in my job	1.17	1.63	5.04[b]
D. Influence on company			
Quality of decisions	1.50	1.38	2.61[b]
Waste reduction	2.67	3.75	1.27
Innovation	2.00	2.25	1.60
Relationships across functions	2.67	3.00	1.17
Communications across functions	2.50	2.50	1.22
Overall focus on the goals of the entity	1.92	1.13	1.36

[a] Significant at 0.01.

[b] Significant at 0.1.

In the research by Swenson and Flescher (1996) one may find different results of satisfaction evaluation resulting from ABC implementation perceived by preparers and users of the information. In that research, the satisfaction of the preparers (3.30) was statistically more significant than the users (2.73) (where 1 meant 'lack of satisfaction', 2 'the need for improvement', 3 'satisfaction' and 4 'great satisfaction'). The change of a cost accounting system is a complex and expensive process. It should take place to improve the satisfaction of information users. The respondents of Swenson *et al.* (1996) stressed the fact that they would have implemented ABC "even if they had to spend their own money on it." After ABC implementation, the people who used the information were substantially more satisfied with the information provided by management accounting specialists.

6.4. Summary and conclusions

Due to the fact that most activity-based costing implementations in developing countries, including Poland, took place in the first decade of the 21st century, the majority of empirical research on ABC diffusion in those countries has only appeared in recent years. Research issue related to the measurement of ABC implementation successes in developing countries is current, both for theoreticians, enabling them to compare the practices implemented in more developed countries, and for practitioners who seek to determine the degree of satisfaction and benefits connected with ABC implementation. The survey research carried out on satisfaction and benefits of activity-based costing implementation in Polish companies perceived by preparers and users of ABC information enabled the author to form the following, detailed conclusions and enabled him to verify hypotheses formulated at the beginning of the chapter:

1. In accordance with previous studies on the way activity-based costing is perceived (Foster, Gupta, 1990; Bailey, 1991; Innes, Mitchell, 1991; Nicholls, 1992; Swenson, 1995; McGowan, Klammer, 1997; McGowan, 1998; Byrne *et al.*, 2009), this research shows that respondents display a highly positive attitude towards ABC implementation and the results are statistically significant. In general, activity-based costing is regarded as being better than previously implemented systems, however the average satisfaction of ABC implementation in this study was higher (mean of 1.43) than in the research by McGowan (1.98) and Byrne *et al.* (1.83).

2. The conducted research proves that the quality of ABC information is better than that of the traditional cost accounting system. All studied qualitative characteristics of information i.e. accuracy, accessibility, reliability, timeliness and understandability were evaluated notably higher and the results were statistically significant (overall mean evaluation of those characteristics in the traditional cost accounting system was 'neutral' –3.16, and in the case of ABC it was 'good' to 'very good' –1.66). The results are compliant with both formulated in the literature (e.g. Rafish, Turney, 1991; Brimson, 1991) and the results of earlier studies e.g. by McGowan (1998) and Byrne *et al.* (2009). However, in this research the quality of ABC information in comparison to the traditional cost accounting system was evaluated considerably higher than in the McGowan and Byrne *et al.* research

(accessibility of ABC information and information from the traditional cost accounting was evaluated likewise in McGowan's research).

3. Many publications (Turney, 1992; Brimson, 1991; Pemberton *et al.*, 1996; Geishecker, 1996) claim that ABC is useful in the work of both managers and employees – this claim is confirmed by the research results. It means that the respondents agree with the statement that ABC has a considerably positive and statistically significant influence on their work, in particular: it improves work quality, improves control over work-related procedures, helps to accomplish more tasks, aids critical aspects of their work, improves productivity, helps to improve job performance, helps to accomplish more work than before, boosts the effectiveness of their work and makes it easier to accomplish work-related tasks. The respondents point out that ABC is extremely useful in their job (average of 1.43). The results are confirmed by the McGowan's (1998) and Byrne *et al.* (2009) researches. The elementary difference between the studies is the fact that usefulness of ABC information was ranked higher (eight out of ten means were below 2) in this research than in the research by McGowan and Byrne *et al.* (none of the means was below 2).

4. The respondents positively evaluate the influence of the ABC implementation on the improvement of the quality of decisions and the increase of concentration on the company's aims (a considerably positive impact) and on the boost of innovativeness and improvement of communications across functions (minor positive impact). The results, however, do not confirm the influence of activity-based costing implementation on the improvement of relations across functions or on waste reduction. The results are partly confirmed by the results of the McGowan (1998) and Byrne *et al.* (2009) studies. However, in their research, the influence of ABC implementation on the company was minor but statistically significant for all dependent variables (in this research on four out of six variables).

5. In accordance with the literature (Zmud, Cox, 1979; McKeen *et al.*, 1994; Anderson, 1995) the evaluation of an implemented innovation may be influenced by the respondent's role in the organization. As the research shows, general satisfaction of activity-based costing implementation does not significantly differ between preparers and users of ABC information (in McGowan's research (1998), satisfaction of preparers was considerably higher than users). Yet, the research helped to draw alternation on the fact that preparers evaluate ABC implementation better in terms of accessibility and timeliness, aiding critical aspects of their work and general ABC usefulness at work than the users. An inverse pattern (better evaluation among users than preparers) was registered in the case of influence of ABC implementation on the improvement of quality of decisions.

The conclusions of this research (questionnaire C) bear both theoretical and practical significance. From the practical point of view, companies considering implementation of ABC in the future should be aware of the problems with the implementation and the benefits it may bring for the organization. Managers thinking of ABC implementation must be aware of the fact that activity-based costing may provide information of better quality, in terms of all features characterizing the quality of information, than the traditional cost accounting system. They may additionally use the knowledge of usefulness of ABC information in preparers' and users' job as well as the knowledge of ABC implementation's influence on the company (the characteristics of ABC do suggest consideration by companies operating in global, competitive and changing environment). This finding of the research carried is an important contribution to the literature on ABC because it suggests that the slow diffusion and low adoption rates are not the effect of a perceived lack of satisfaction with ABC (the research done in a developing country, Poland, confirms the findings in the United States and Australia). This knowledge may facilitate better decision making in the case of implementations of ABC systems, and when the decision has been made, it may increase the likelihood of a successful implementation process.

From the theoretical point of view, the conducted research may facilitate the defining of a general tendency: modifications of cost accounting systems in companies in developing countries (e.g. Poland) and the implementation of modern management accounting methods e.g. ABC, although delayed in comparison to more economically developed countries, head in a similar direction as the practice of management accounting in the world, and newly implemented innovative cost accounting systems, such as ABC, are evaluated positively. The carried out research also stresses the necessity to systematically analyze what better cost accounting system means, how satisfaction from a new cost accounting system should be measured and what problems are specific for these measurements. This study also addresses a need to articulate the measure of success for innovative management accounting techniques to achieve comparability between different studies and therefore help the advancement of the theory.

Previous research on the implementations of various projects analysing the practice of numerous companies around the world allow the author to state that there is a relation between the evaluation of the implementation's success and factors characteristic of specific organizations. The factors are e.g. size of the company, type of business, organizational structure and the environment the organization operates in (McKeen et al., 1994). The increase in satisfaction of the information provided by ABC and traditional cost accounting depends on the quality of the former system (e.g. it is hard to, on the basis of the conducted research, state how 'good' the implemented ABC system since it is not known how 'good' the previous system was – only the difference in quality of information provided by both systems examined). The factors, in quite a clear way, influence the fact that all generalizations made on the basis of this research must be careful. Evaluation of the satisfaction of the implemented system (e.g. ABC) is influenced by specific factors, characteristic of a particular company. Analysis of the factors is interesting and worth taking into account in the future, however it falls outside of the framework of this research.

The results of this study may also be influenced by the characteristics of respondents e.g. their education and experience (Lucas, 1975), age (Fuerst, Cheney, 1982), personality (DeSanctis, 1984) or position in the company (Anderson 1995). Out of the specified characteristics, only one was taken into consideration in this research – respondents' answers were analyzed on the basis of whether the respondents prepared or used ABC information.

The means of measurement of the elementary variable which characterizes the satisfaction of ABC implementation is another limitation of this research. Since it was a subjective opinion formed by the respondents, the results mirror their viewpoint and not necessarily the real success of the implementation[10]. Even if the results are not fully objective in terms of implementation success, they may be interesting and significant because a generally positive attitude towards the implemented activity-based costing reflects, to some extent, the benefits of the implementation for the company (satisfaction may be an important implementation success indicator, since it leads to more frequent use of ABC information for example in decision making).

Measurement of the satisfaction and the benefits of ABC implementation is a part of a more general tendency which measures the success of implementation of all innovative methods of management accounting. Many authors of publications, both for students and practitioners, promote 'new' tools of management accounting, emphasizing their benefits, yet they base their opinion on anecdotes or unsystematic and fragmentary analysis of case studies from practice (knowledge of ABC functioning in developing countries is mostly normative and does not include information about the real degree of satisfaction and benefits of ABC implementation). According to the author, this research on the degree of satisfaction and perceived benefits resulting from ABC implementation, may lead to better and fuller recognition of the attitudes presented by the preparers and users of ABC information, and, at the same time, better and fuller recognition of the degree of satisfaction and benefits of ABC implementation, perceived by the people. Additionally, this research may facilitate analysis of attitudes towards ABC implementations by companies operating in developing countries and companies from developed countries. The large extent to which the results of this research conform to the results of studies carried out in more developed countries means that practice of management accounting in developing countries, although delayed, is developing in a similar way, and in the same direction as the practice of more developed countries.

---

[10] The applied means of the study claim that all respondents want to share their opinion on the degree of satisfaction resulting from ABC, however this may not be true. The respondents' answers may be influenced by the extent of satisfaction and their general attitude towards ABC (e.g. respondents who are highly satisfied with ABC implementation may tend to participate in the research more often).

CONCLUSIONS

In the first years of the 21st century, a growing number of Polish companies implemented modern systems of cost accounting. In general, the practice of management accounting in Poland is heading in the same direction as the practice of management accounting in the world. An increasing number of Polish companies uses methods which are used by companies in more developed countries – one of them is activity-based costing. Its first wider use in Polish companies was identified at the beginning of the 21st century when more and more manufacturing and non-manufacturing companies implemented or were implementing activity-based costing. Due to the growing interest in the method and its more frequent use among practitioners, the research objective was formulated; it aimed to analyze the development and diffusion of activity-based costing, and, additionally, to study and evaluate the use and extent of activity-based costing in Polish companies.

The presented research support the main thesis which claimed that the diffusion of activity-based costing in Polish companies, although delayed in comparison to the practice of more developed countries, is conditioned by the same factors and is heading in the same direction as in other countries.

The conducted questionnaire research (495 companies in questionnaire A, 33 companies in questionnaire B and 28 companies in questionnaire C) and research in the form of case studies (4 companies) cannot constitute a complete source of knowledge about the diffusion, structure and use, as well as evaluation of ABC implementation in Polish companies. With respect to the questionnaire research, there are two reasons for that. Firstly, the sample is not representative, thus it cannot be seen as the basis for the evaluation of activity-based costing functioning in all the companies operating in Poland. Secondly, the limitations of the questionnaire research itself must be taken into consideration; it is impossible to conduct a detailed and accurate analysis of the structure and use of ABC systems by means of this method. The case studies (including action research) which were applied to carry out a more detailed analysis of activity-based costing systems used in Polish companies also characterize some limitations, among them the small sample size. The limitations of the methods used have been reduced to some extent by triangulation of research methods and by comparing of the study to other research carried out by different authors and to subject literature.

The conclusions of the present research bear theoretical and practical significance. From the theoretical point of view, the research complies with the general tendency that activity-based costing modifications in Polish companies and implementation of modern methods of management accounting such as ABC, are heading in a similar direction as in other countries in the world. From the practical point of view, companies considering implementation of ABC in the future should be aware of the factors influencing ABC implementation, as well as problems which might occur during implementation. Managers who are considering implementation must be aware of the minuteness level, and how activity-based costing modelling and methods are used. They also may benefit from gaining knowledge about the factors which positively and negatively influence activity-based costing implementation, as well as about methodological and institutional/organizational changes resulting from the implementation of such a costing system. The knowledge may facilitate decisions about the implementation of ABC systems, and once the decision is made, it is more likely that implementation will be successful. The present research may also provide numerous recommendations for companies which use activity-based costing, as well as for those which are considering ABC implementation in the future:

1. The implementation of activity-based costing should be considered particularly by large companies with a varied scope of activity, in which indirect costs have a large share in total costs and their products are exposed to a high level of price competitiveness.

2. Activity-based costing may be used as a supplement to the traditional cost accounting system. Systems of activity-based costing do not have to embrace all indirect costs, they may exclusively focus on indirect costs of the primary activity e.g. distribution or marketing activities.

3. Companies which are considering the implementation of activity-based costing should know that ABC systems do not have to be extended (especially in the early stage of its use). Cost calculations and profitability analyses do not have to be prepared on the current or monthly basis but for example on quarterly or semiannual basis, and that considerably reduces the costs of collecting information and the system's maintenance.

4. The complexity of the ABC/ABM model depends on the purpose it is used for. If the system is implemented to facilitate economic processes then the model should be more detailed. If the system is implemented for the purpose of product or customer profitability analysis then the number of elements within the model can be reduced. A more complex and larger model is not always a better one. The optimal size and level of complexity depend on the purpose of the implementation and the company's own conditioning.

5. In order to overcome problems occurring in the implementation of activity-based costing, the company should: (a) make sure that the implementation process has management's support, (b) provide sufficient resources for the implementation and maintenance of the system, (c) spread the knowledge about activity-based costing among management, (d) clearly communicate the aims of the implementation, (e) involve managers from all areas of the company into the implementation, (f) appropriately outline the range and plan the implementation well, (g) not design models that are too complex, (h) integrate the system of activity-based costing with the existing IT infrastructure, (i) provide real results as quickly as possible.

6. In companies which use activity-based costing, the information generated by the system should be used for: (a) operational cost management through effective evaluation and control of the company's activity in a cross-section of activities and processes performed in the company, (b) product management through monitoring of product profitability, pricing policy as well as promotion and marketing strategy based on reliable information about costs of products, (c) customer management through analysis of profitability, customer and groups of customers service costs and through appropriate customization of products on offer and ways of servicing certain groups of customers, (d) strategic cost management through defining the value of activities and optimalization of resource use.

7. The implemented system of activity-based costing should be used for performance evaluation of the entire company, as well as individual responsibility centers, processes and activities, managers and employees. Linking activity-based costing to performance evaluation fosters the use of information from that system by managers from all levels of management.

8. Companies using activity-based costing should remember about its modifications, which will customize the system to the changing conditions the firms are operating in. The systems should be gradually improved so that they meet the needs of the company's management.

9. The system of activity-based costing can be integrated with other modern methods of management e.g. target costing, balanced scorecard or economic value added.

10. The implementation of activity-based costing does not directly improve the competitiveness of the company or its financial results. This is only possible when information generated by the system is used by managers in taking appropriate operational and strategic decisions.

11. Activity-based costing should not be implemented by all companies. It seems that smaller companies, in which the share of indirect costs is slight, products are highly profitable and not differentiated, and availability of resources, especially human resources is constrained, should wait with the implementation of activity-based costing.

On the basis of the present study, the following conclusions for further research can be formulated:

1. The conducted questionnaire research may be continued. A lot of Polish companies are considering implementating of ABC, a lot of international companies which use ABC may soon invest in Poland – both factors may increase the percentage of companies using ABC. Conducting the presented questionnaire research again, in its initial form, in a few-years time might be interesting. It would improve the representativeness of the sample, and additionally it would show how the practice of activity-based costing implementation and functioning, and the use of ABC information changes in time.

2. In order to analyze the construction of ABC systems and the use of ABC information in more detail, the case studies method (especially action research) should be extended. This method would enable a detailed analysis of how the systems were implemented, how they function and how they are used (within an individual company or companies), and how they are modified and how different people from the company evaluate ABC functioning (in particular the analysis of opinions of preparers and users). Analysis of ABC implementations in the form of case studies, despite their limitations, would enable better investigation into the above problems.

3. As mentioned before, a large number of companies are considering ABC implementation in the near future. Some of them will decide to undergo the difficult process of implementation and some of them will reject the implementation. The companies which abandom ABC implementation after analyzing its pros and cons will constitute an interesting group. The group may be analyzed and may provide reasons for the rejection of ABC implementation, the direction of change in the costing system of those companies, and an analysis of the results derived from the non-implementation of significant modifications in the costing system of those companies. In terms of further research, a comparison of companies which, after analysis, implemented ABC to companies which rejected ABC would be interesting.

4. Further research which would analyze and evaluate the satisfaction and benefits of activity-based costing implementation in Polish companies, in particular: financial benefits related to the process of implementation, satisfaction with calculation of cost of products, customers etc., use of information for decision-making and general evaluation of activity-based costing implementation might be intriguing.

5. At the beginning of the 20th century, a new generation of ABC emerged; it aimed to solve the fundamental problems connected to the process of implementating and using of activity-based costing – time-driven activity-based costing and resource consumption accounting. It would be interesting to investigate if, and how these methods are going to be used in Polish companies in the future.

6. Research on changes in the cost accounting systems in Polish companies should be further developed in order to analyze in more detail particular phenomena. Other research areas for further investigation are e.g. target costing, balanced scorecard, theory of constraints or value chain costing. These research areas may be, and should be, analyzed with the use of all the available methods like surveys, case studies and action research.

BIBLIOGRAPHY

Abrahamson E. (1991), "Managerial Fads and Fashions: The Diffusion and Rejections of Innovations", *Academy of Management Review*, 16(3), pp. 586–612.

Abrahamson E., Rosenkopf L. (1993), "Institutional and Competitive Bandwagons: Using Mathematical Modeling as a Tool to Explore Innovation Diffusion", *Academy of Management Review*, 21, pp. 254–285.

Alcouffe S. (2004), "Exploring the Communication Structures in Accounting Research: Some Evidence from the ABC Journal Literature in France", paper presented at the 27th European Accounting Association Annual Congress, Prague, 1–3 April.

Alcouffe S., Berland N., Levant Y. (2008), "Actor-Networks and the Diffusion of Management Accounting Innovations: a Comparative Case Study", *Management Accounting Research*, 19, pp. 1–17.

Al-Omiri M., Drury C. (2007), "A Survey of Factors Influencing the Choice of Product Costing Systems in UK Organizations", *Management Accounting Research*, 18(4), pp. 399–424.

Anand M., Sahay, B.S., Saha S. (2005), "Activity-Based Management Practices in India: an Empirical Study", *Decision (Social Science Research Network)*, 32(1), pp. 123–152.

Anderson S.W. (1995), "Framework for Assessing Cost Management System Changes: The Case of Activity-Based Costing Implementation at General Motors 1986–1993", *Journal of Management Accounting Research*, 7, pp. 1–51.

Anderson S.W., Lanen W.N. (1999), "Economic Transition Strategy and the Evolution of Management Accounting Practices: the Case of India", *Accounting, Organizations and Society*, 24, pp. 379–412.

Anderson S., Young S. (1999), "The Impact of Contextual and Process Factors on the Evaluation of Activity-Based Costing Systems", *Accounting, Organizations and Society*, 24(7), pp. 525–559.

Argyris C., Kaplan R.S. (1994), "Implementing New Knowledge: the Case of Activity-Based Costing", *Accounting Horizons*, 8, pp. 83–105.

Armitage H.M., Nicholson R. (1993), "Activity Based Costing: a Survey of Canadian Practice", Issue Paper No. 3, Society of Management Accountants of Canada.

Armstrong P. (2002), "The Costs of Activity-Based Management", *Critical Perspectives on Accounting*, 11(4), pp. 383–406.

Ask U., Ax C. (1992), "Trends to the Development of Product Costing Practices and Techniques – a Survey of Swedish Manufacturing Industry", paper presented at the 15th European Accounting Association Annual Congress, Madrid, 22–24 April.

Askarany D., Yazdifar H. (2007), "Why is ABC Not Widely Implemented?", *International Journal of Business Research*, 7(1), pp. 93–98.

Babad Y., Balachandran B. (1993), "Cost Driver Optimization in Activity-Based Costing", *The Accounting Review*, 68(3), pp. 563–575.

Bailey J. (1991), "Implementation of ABC Systems by U.K. Companies", *Management Accounting*, February, pp. 30–32.

Bailey J.E., Pearson S.W. (1983), "Development of a Tool for Measuring and Analyzing Computer User Satisfaction", *Management Science*, May, pp. 530–545.

Baines A., Langfield-Smith K. (2003), "Antecedents to Management Accounting Change: a Structural Equation Approach", *Accounting, Organizations and Society*, 28, pp. 675–698.

Baird K., Harrison G., Reeve R. (2004), "Adoption of Activity Management Practices: a Note on the Extent of Adoption and the Influence of Organizational and Cultural Factors", *Management Accounting Research*, 15(4), pp. 383–399.

Bellis-Jones R., Hand M. (1989), "Seeking out The Profit Dissipators", *Management Accounting* (UK), September, pp. 48–50.

Berliner C., Brimson J.A. (1988), *Cost Management for Today's Advanced Manufacturing: the CAM-I Conceptual Design*, Harvard Business School Press, Boston.

Bescos P.L., Cauvin E., Gosselin M. (2002), "Activity-Based Costing and Activity-Based Management: Comparison of the Practices in Canada and in France", *Comptbilitè, contrôle et audi*, 8, pp. 229–244.

Bescos P.L., Cauvin E., Gosselin M., Yoshikawa T. (2001), "The Implementation of ABCM in Canada, France and Japan: A Cross National Study", paper presented at the 24th European Accounting Association Annual Congress, Athens, 18–20 April.

Bescos P.L., Mendoza C. (1995), "ABC in France", *Management Accounting* (US), 76(10), pp. 33–35, 38–41.

Bhimani A., Pigott D. (1992), "Implementing ABC: a Case Study of Organizational and Behavioural Consequences", *Management Accounting Research*, 3, pp. 119–132.

Björnenak T. (1997), "Diffusion and Accounting: the Case of ABC in Norway", *Management Accounting Research*, 8(1), pp. 3–17.

Björnenak T., Mitchell F. (2000), "A Study of the Development of the Activity Based Costing Journal Literature 1987–1998", paper presented at the 23rd European Accounting Association Annual Congress, Munich, 29–31 March.

Björnenak T., Mitchell F. (2002), "The Development of Activity-Based Costing Journal Literature. 1987–2000", *The European Accounting Review*, 11(3), pp. 28–56.

Booth P., Giacobbe F. (1998), "Activity-Based Costing in Australian Manufacturing Firms: the 'State of Play'", *Contemporary Perspectives on Management Accounting*, pp. 35–61.

Bright J., Davies R.E., Dovnes C.A., Sweeting R.C. (1992), "The Deployment of Costing Techniques and Practices: a UK Study", *Management Accounting Research*, 3, pp. 201–211.

Brimson J. (1991), *Activity Accounting*, John Wiley and Sons, New York.

Brimson J., Fraser R. (1991), "The Key Factors of ABB", *Management Accounting* (UK), January, pp. 42–43.

Bromwich M. (1998), "Editorial: Value Based Financial Management Systems", *Management Accounting Research*, 9, pp. 387–389.

Bromwich M., Bhimani A. (1989), *Management Accounting: Evolution not Revolution*, Chartered Institute of Management Accountants, London.

Brown D., Booth P., Giacobble F. (2004), "Technological and organizational influences on the adoption of activity-based costing in Australia", *Accounting and Finance*, 44, pp. 329–356.

Byrne S., Stower E., Torry P. (2009), "Is ABC Adoption a Success in Australia?", *Journal of Applied Management Accounting Research*, 7(1), pp. 37–51.

Cagwin D., Bouwman M.J. (2002), "The Association between Activity-Based Costing and Improvement in Financial Performance", *Management Accounting Research*, 13, pp. 1–39.

CAM-I (1992), Raffish N., Turney P.B.B. (ed.), *The CAM-I Glossary of Activity-Based Management*, Arlington.

Cardinaels E., Labro E. (2008), "On the Determinants of Measurement Error in Time-Driven Costing", *Accounting Review*, 83(3), pp. 172–191.

Carmona S., Gutierrez I. (2003), "Vogues in Management Accounting Research", *The Scandinavian Journal of Management*, 19(2), pp. 213–231.

Chenhall R. (2008), "Accounting for the Horizontal Organization: a Review Essay", *Accounting, Organizations and Society*, 33, pp. 517–550.

Chenhall R., Langfield-Smith K. (1998), "Adoption and Benefits of Management Accounting Practices: an Australian Study", *Management Accounting Research*, 9(1), pp. 1–19.

Chow C.W., Duh R-R., Xiao J.Z. (2007), "Management Accounting Practices in the People's Republic of China", [in:] Chapman Ch.S., Hopwood A.G., Shields M.D. (eds.), *Handbook of Management Accounting Research*, Elsevier, Amsterdam, Vol. 2, pp. 923–967.

Cinquini L., Collini P., Marelli A., Quagli A., Silvi R. (1999), "A Survey of Cost Accounting Practices in Italian Large and Medium Manufacturing Firms", paper presented at the 23rd European Accounting Association Annual Congress, Bordeaux, 5–7 May.

Cinquini L., Collini P., Marelli A., Tenucci A. (2008), "An Exploration of the Factors Affecting the Diffusion of Advanced Costing Techniques: a Comparative Analysis of Two Surveys (1996–2005)", paper presented at the 31st European Accounting Association Annual Congress, Rotterdam, 23–25 April.

Clarke F., Dean G., Lowry J., Wells M. (1997), "Financial and Management Accounting in Australia", [in:] Baydoun N., Nishimura A., Willet R. (eds.), *Accounting in the Asia – Pacific Region*, Wiley, Singapore.

Clarke P.J., Hill N.T., Stevens K. (1999), "Activity-Based Costing in Ireland: Barriers to, and Opportunities for Change", *Critical Perspectives in Accounting*, 10, pp. 443–468.

Clarke P.J., Mullins T. (2001), "Activity Based Costing in the Non-Manufacturing Sector in Ireland: a Preliminary Investigation", *The Irish Journal of Management*, July, pp. 1–18.

Clinton B.D., Webber S.A. (2004), "RCA at Clopay – Here's Innovation in Management Accounting with Resource Consumption Accounting", *Strategic Finance*, 84(4), pp. 20–26.

Cobb I., Helliar C., Innes I. (1995), "Management Accounting Change in a Bank", *Management Accounting Research*, 5, pp. 155–175.

Cobb, I., Mitchell F. (1993), "Activity-Based Costing Problems: the British Experience", *Advances in Management Accounting*, pp. 68–83.

Cobb J., Mitchell F., Innes J. (1992), *Activity Based Costing: Problems in Practice*, Chartered Institute of Management Accountants, London.

Cohen M.D., March J.G. & Olsen A. (1972), "A Garbage Can of Organizational Choice", *Administrative Science Quarterly*, 17, pp. 1–25.

Colson R.H., MacGuidwin M. (1989), "The Rossford Plant", [in:] Robinson M.A. (ed.), *Cases from Management Accounting Practice*, Vol. 5: *Instructors Manual. National Association of Accountants*, pp. 1–8.

Cookins G. (2001), *Activity-Based Cost Management. An Executives Guide*, Wiley, New York.

Cooper R. (1985), *Schrader Bellows (B), Case No: 9-186-051*, Harvard Business School Publishing, Boston.

Cooper R. (1986), *Mueller-Lehmkuhl GmbH, Harvard Business School, Case 9-189-032*, Harvard Business School Publishing, Boston.

Cooper R. (1987a), "The Two-Stage Procedure in Cost Accounting: Part One", *Journal of Cost Management*, Summer, pp. 43–51.

Cooper R. (1987b), "The Two-Stage Procedure in Cost Accounting: Part Two", *Journal of Cost Management*, 1(3), pp. 39–45.

Cooper R. (1988a), "The Rise of Activity-Based Costing – Part One: What is an Activity-Based Costing System?", *Journal of Cost Management*, Summer, pp. 45–54.

Cooper R. (1988b), *Siemens Electric Motor Works, Harvard Business School, Case 9-189-089*, Harvard Business School Publishing, Boston.

Cooper R. (1989a), "The Rise of Activity-Based Costing – Part Three: How Many Cost Drivers do You Need and How do You Select Them?", *Journal of Cost Management*, Winter, pp. 34–46.

Cooper R. (1989b), "The Rise of Activity-Based Costing – Part Four: What do Activity-Based Cost System Look Like?", *Journal of Cost Management*, Spring, pp. 38–49.

Cooper R. (1989c), "ABC: Key to Future Costs", *Management Consultancy*, October, pp. 1–3.

Cooper R. (1990), "Cost Classifications in Unit-Based Activity-Based Manufacturing Cost Systems", *Journal of Cost Management for the Manufacturing Industry*, 4(3), pp. 4–14.

Cooper R. (1994), "Activity Based Costing for Improved Product Costing", [in:] Brinker B., (ed.), *Handbook of Cost Management*, Warren, Gorham & Lamont, New York.

Cooper R. (1996a), "Look Out Management Accountants (Part 1)", *Management Accounting*, May, pp. 20–26.

Cooper R. (1996b), "Look Out Management Accountants (Part 2)", *Management Accounting*, June, pp. 35–41.

Cooper R., Kaplan R. (1987a), *Winchell Lighting, Inc. (A), Case No: 9-187-074, 1.16*, Harvard Business School Publishing, Boston.

Cooper R., Kaplan R. (1987b), *Winchell Lighting, Inc. (B), Case No: 9-187-075, 1.16*, Harvard Business School Publishing, Boston.

Cooper R., Kaplan R.S. (1988a), "Measure Costs Right: Make Right Decision", *Harvard Business Review*, September–October, pp. 96–103.

Cooper R., Kaplan R.S. (1988b), "How Cost Accounting Distorts Product Costs", *Management Accounting* (US), 69(10), pp. 20–27.

Cooper R., Kaplan R. (1991), *The Design of Cost Management Systems. Text, Cases and Readings*, Prentice-Hall International Edition, Englewood Cliffs.

Cooper R., Kaplan R.S. (1992), "Activity-Based Systems: Measuring the Costs of Resource Usage", *Accounting Horizons*, September, pp. 1–19.

Cooper R., Montgomery J. (1985a), *Schrader Bellows (D-1), Case No: 9-186-053*, Harvard Business School Publishing, Boston.

Cooper R., Montgomery J. (1985b), *Schrader Bellows (E), Case No: 9-186-054*, Harvard Business School Publishing, Boston.

Cooper R., Turney P. (1988), *Tektronix: Portable Instruments Division (A), Case No: 9-188-142, 1.14*, Harvard Business School Publishing, Boston.

Cooper R., Weiss A. (1985), *Schrader Bellows (A), Case No: 9-186-050*, Harvard Business School Publishing, Boston.

Cotton W.D.J., Jackman S.M., Brown R.A. (2003), "Note on a New Zealand Replication of the Innes et al. UK Activity-Based Costing Survey", *Management Accounting Research*, 14, pp. 67–72.

Covaleski M., Dirsmith M., Samuel S. (1996), "Managerial Accounting Research: the Contributions of Organizational and Sociological Theories", *Journal of Management Accounting Research*, 8(1), pp. 1–35.

Czakon W. (2004), "Interpretacja rachunku kosztów działań w przedsiębiorstwie handlowym", *Controlling i Rachunkowość Zarządcza* (dodatek), 11, pp. 1–12.

Datar S., Gupta M. (1994), "Aggregation, Specification and Measurement Errors in Product Costing", *The Accounting Review*, 69(4), pp. 567–591.

Davies R., Sweeting B. (1991), "Management Accounting: Industrial Revolution?", *Certified Accountant*, 45, pp. 44–46.

Dillon R.D., Nash J.F. (1978), "The True Relevance of Relevant Costs", *The Accounting Review*, pp. 11–17.

Dolinsky L.R., Vollman T.E. (1991), "Transaction-Based Overhead Considerations for Product Design", *Journal of Cost Management*, 5, pp. 7–19.

Delone W.H., McLean E.R. (1992), "Information Systems Success: the Quest for the Dependent Variable", *Information System Research*, 3(1), pp. 60–95.

DeSanctis G. (1984), "A Micro Perspective of Implementation", *Management Science Implementation* (Supplement 1), pp. 1–27.

DiMaggio P.J., Powell W.W. (1983), "The Iron Cage Revisited: Institutional Isomorphism and Collective Rationality in Organizational Fields", *American Sociological Review*, 48, pp. 147–160.

Dolinsky L.R., Vollman T.E. (1991), "Transaction Based Overhead Considerations for Product Design", *Journal of Cost Management*, Summer, pp. 7–19.

Doll W.J., Torkzadeh G. (1988), "The Measurement of End-User Computing Satisfaction", *MIS Quarterly*, June, pp. 259–273.

Domagała J., Wnuk-Pel T. (2011), "Badanie rozwoju publikacji z zakresu rachunku kosztów działań na podstawie artykułów opublikowanych w polskich czasopismach w latach 1994–2009", *Acta Universitatis Lodziensis. Folia Oeconomica*, 249, pp. 123–147.

Drury C. (2000), *Management and Cost Accounting*, Business Press, Thomson Learning, London.

Drury C., Tyles M. (1994), "Product Costing in UK Manufacturing Organisations'", *European Accounting Review*, 3(3), pp. 443–469.

Dyhdalewicz A. (2000), "Kierunki usprawnień rachunku kosztów w wybranych przedsiębiorstwach produkcyjnych", referat na konferencję *Rachunkowość podmiotów gospodarczych w XXI wieku*, Spała.

Dyhdalewicz A. (2001), "Wykorzystanie rachunku kosztów w zarządzaniu przedsiębiorstwem – wyniki badań", [in:] *Zarządzanie kosztami w przedsiębiorstwach w aspekcie integracji Polski z Unią Europejską*, Prace Wydziału Zarządzania Politechniki Częstochowskiej, Częstochowa, pp. 33–38.

Firth M. (1996), "The Diffusion of Managerial Accounting Procedures in the People's Republic of China and the Influence of Foreign Partnered Joint-Ventures", *Accounting, Organizations and Society*, 21(7/8), pp. 629–654.

Foster G., Gupta M. (1990), "Activity Accounting: an Electronics Industry Implementation", [in:] Kaplan R.S. (ed.), *Measures for Manufacturing Excellence*, Harvard Business School Press, Boston, pp. 225–268.

Foster G., Swenson D.W. (1997), "Measuring the Success of Activity-Based Cost Management and its Determinants", *Journal of Management Accounting Research*, 9, pp. 109–141.

Fortin A., Haffaf H., Viger Ch. (2007), "The Measurement of Success of Activity-Based Costing and its Determinants: a Study within Canadian Federal Government Organizations", *Accounting Perspectives*, 6(3), pp. 231–262.

Friedman A.F., Lyne S.R. (2000), "Implementation, Interaction and Activity-Based Techniques", The Bristol Centre for Management Accounting Research, Working Paper 00-01, March.

Fuerst W., Cheney P. (1982), "Factors Affecting the Perceived Utilization of Computer-Based Decision Support Systems in the Oil Industry", *Decision Sciences*, 13, pp. 554–569.

Garner S.P. (1954), *Evolution of Cost Accounting to 1925*, University of Alabama Press, Alabama.

Geishecker M.L. (1996), "New Technologies Support ABC", *Management Accounting*, March, pp. 42–48.

Gervais, M., Levant Y., Ducrocq Ch. (2009), "Time Driven Activity Based Costing: New Wine, or Just New Bottles?", paper presented at the 32nd European Accounting Association Annual Congress, Tampere, 12–15 May.

Gierusz J., Kujawski A., Kujawski L. (1996), "Stan obecny oraz kierunki ewolucji rachunku kosztów i rachunkowości zarządczej w przedsiębiorstwach Polski północnej", *Zeszyty Teoretyczne Rady Naukowej SKwP*, 35, pp. 41–47.

Gietzmann M. (1991), "Implementation Issues Associated with the Construction of an Activity-Based Costing System in an Engineering Components Manufacture", *Management Accounting Research*, 1, pp. 189–199.

Goetz B. (1949), *Management Planning and Control: A Managerial Approach to Industrial Accounting*, McGraw-Hill, New York.

Goldratt E.M. (1990), *The Haystack Syndrome. Shifting Information Out of the Data Ocean*, North River Press, Great Barrington.

Gosselin M. (1997), "The Effect of Strategy and Organizational Structure on the Adoption and Implementation of Activity Based Costing", *Accounting, Organizations and Society*, 22(2), pp. 105–122.

Gosselin M. (2007), "A Review of Activity-Based Costing: Technique, Implementation and Consequences", [in:] Chapman Ch.S., Hopwood A.G., Shields M.D. (eds.), *Handbook of Management Accounting Research*, Elsevier, Amsterdam, Vol. 2, pp. 641–671.

Gosselin M., Mevellec P. (2004), "Development of a Cladogram of Cost Management Systems", working paper, Université Laval.

Granlund M., Lukka K. (1998), "It's a Small World of Management Accounting Practices", *Journal of Management Accounting Research*, 10, pp. 153–179.

Grasso L.P. (2005), "Are ABC and RCA accounting systems compatible with Lean Management", *Management Accounting Quartely*, 7(1), pp. 12–17.

Groot T.L.C.M. (1999), "Activity Based Costing in US and Dutch Food Companies", *Advances in Management Accounting*, 7, pp. 47–63.

Groot T., Lukka K.L. (2000), *Cases in Management Accounting. Current Practices in European Companies*, Pearson Education.

Hamilton S., Chervany N.L. (1981), "Evaluating Information System Effectiveness: Comparing Evaluator Viewpoints", *MIS Quarterly*, December, pp. 79–86.

Hauer G. (1994), "Hierarchische kennzahlenorientierte Entscheidungsrechnung – Ein Beitrag zum Investitions und Kostenmanagement", D. Phil. Thesis, Regensburg, [in:] Scherrer G., *Management Accounting. A German Perspective*, [in:] Bhimani A. (1996), *Management Accounting. European Perspectives*, Oxford University Press, Oxford.

Hicks, D.T. (1999), *Activity-Based Costing. Making it Work for Small and Mid-Sized Companies*, John Wiley and Sons, New York.

Ho S., Kidwell L. (2000), "A Survey of Management Techniques Implemented by Municipal Administrators", *The Government Accountants Journal*, Spring, pp. 46–53.

Hopper T., Otley D., Scapens. R. (2001), "British Management Accounting Research: Whence and Whither: Opinions and Recollections", *British Accounting Review*, 33, pp. 263–291.

Hopwood A.G. (1983), "On Trying to Study Accounting in the Contexts in which it Operates", *Accounting, Organizations and Society*, 8, pp. 287–305.

Hopwood A.G. (1987), "Archeology of Accounting Systems", *Accounting, Organizations and Society*, 12(3), pp. 1–20.

Horngren C.T. (1990), "First Discussant", *Journal of Management Accounting Research*, 2, pp. 21–24.

Horvath P., Gleich R., Seidenschwarz W. (1998), "New Tools for Management and Control in German Organizations – Report on the Stuttgart Study", paper presented at the 21st European Accounting Association Annual Congress, Antwerp, 6–8 April.

Hoque Z. (2000), "Just-in-Time Production, Automation, Cost Allocation Practices and Importance of Cost Information: an Empirical Investigation in New Zealand – Based Manufacturing Organizations", *British Accounting Review*, 32, pp. 133–159.

Howell R.A., Brown J.D., Soucy S.R., Seed III A.H. (1987), *Management Accounting in the New Manufacturing Environment*, Institute of Management Accountants (previously National Association of Accountants), Montvale, New York.

IFAC (2009a), *Sustainability Framework – Internal Management* http://web.ifac.org/sustainability-framework/imp-improvement-of-information (retrieved 25 May 2009).

IFAC (2009b), *International Good Practice Guidance*, International Federation of Accountants Professional Accountants in Business Committee.

Innes J., Mitchell F. (1990), "The Process of Change in Management Accounting: Some Field Study Evidence", *Management Accounting Research*, 1, pp. 3–19.

Innes J., Mitchell F. (1991), "Activity Based Costing: a Survey of CIMA Members", *Management Accounting* (UK), 69, pp. 28–30.

Innes J., Mitchell F. (1995), "A Survey of Activity-Based Costing in the U.K.'s Largest Companies", *Management Accounting Research*, 6, pp. 137–153.

Innes J., Mitchell F. (1997), "The Application of Activity-Based Costing in the United Kingdom's Largest Financial Institutions", *The Service Industries Journal*, 17(1), pp. 190–203.

Innes J., Mitchel F. (1998), *A Practical Guide to Activity-Based Costing*, CIMA, London.

Innes J., Mitchell F., Sinclair D. (2000), "Activity-Based Costing in the U.K.'s Largest Companies: a Comparison of 1994 and 1999 Survey Results", *Management Accounting Research*, 11, pp. 349–362.

Institute of Management Accountants (IMA) (1993), *Cost Management Update*, Montvale.

Institute of Management Accountants (IMA) (1995), *Cost Management Update*, Montvale.

Institute of Management Accountants (IMA) (1996), *Cost Management Update*, Montvale.

Institute of Management Accountants (IMA) (1997), *Cost Management Update*, Montvale.

Ittner C.D., Lanen W.N., Larcker D.F. (2002), "The Association Between Activity-Based Costing and Manufacturing Performance", *Journal of Accounting Research*, 40, pp. 711–726.

Ives B., Olson M., Baroudi J. (1983), "The Measurement of User Information Satisfaction", *Communications of the ACM*, 26(1), pp. 785–793.

Januszewski A. (2004a), "Stan, potrzeby i możliwości wdrożenia rachunku kosztów działań w dużych przedsiębiorstwach województwa kujawsko-pomorskiego", *Zeszyty Teoretyczne Rachunkowości*, 21(77), pp. 112–125.

Januszewski A. (2004b), "Ocena celowości i możliwości wdrożenia rachunku kosztów działań w przedsiębiorstwach produkcyjnych w Polsce", *Zeszyty Teoretyczne Rachunkowości*, 22(78), pp. 5–24.

Januszewski A. (2005), "Stosowanie rachunku kosztów działań w polskich przedsiębiorstwach – wyniki badań empirycznych", *Controlling i Rachunkowość Zarządcza*, 1, pp. 35–39.

Januszewski A., Gierusz J. (2004), "Możliwości wdrożenia rachunku kosztów działań – wyniki badań empirycznych", *Rachunkowość*, 7, pp. 19–23.

Jaruga A.A. (2001), "Koszty i efekty: zarys koncepcyjny", [in:] Jaruga A.A., Nowak W.A., Szychta A., *Rachunkowość zarządcza. Koncepcje i zastosowania*, WSPiZ, Łódź.

Jaruga A., Nowak W.A., Szychta A. (2001), *Rachunkowość zarządcza. Koncepcje i zastosowania*, SWSPiZ, Łódź.

Jarugowa A., Skowroński J. (1982), *Rachunek kosztów w systemie informacyjnym przedsiębiorstwa*, PWE, Warszawa.

Jarugowa A., Skowroński J. (1994), "O wierny obraz rachunku kosztów", *Rachunkowość*, 4, pp. 166–172.

Jaruga A.A., Szychta A. (1994), "Rozwój rachunku kosztów działań", *Rachunkowość*, 10, pp. 429–437.

Johnson H.T. (1988), "Activity-Based Information: a Blueprint for World-Class Management Accounting", *Management Accounting* (US), June, pp. 23–30.

Johnson H.T. (1991), "Activity-Based Management: Past, Present and Future", *The Engineering Economist*, 36(3), pp. 219–238.

Johnson H.T. (1992), "It's Time to Stop Overselling Activity-Based Concepts: Start Focusing on Customer Satisfaction Instead", *Management Accounting* (US), September, pp. 26–35.

Johnson H.T., Loewe D.A. (1987), "How Weyerhauser Manages Corporate Overhead Costs", *Management Accounting* (US), August, pp. 20-26.

Johnson H.T., Kaplan R.S. (1987), *Relevance Lost. The Rise and Fall of Management Accounting*, Harvard Business School Press, Boston.

Jones C.T., Dugdale D. (2002), "The ABC Bandwagon and the Juggernaut of Modernity", *Accounting, Organizations and Society*, 27(1–2), pp. 121–163.

Jonez J.W., Wright M.A. (1987), "Material Burdening: Management Accounting Can Support Competitive Strategy", *Management Accounting* (UA), August, pp. 27–31.

Joshi P.L. (2001), "The International Diffusion of New Management Accounting Practices: the Case of India", *Journal of International Accounting, Auditing & Taxation*, 10, pp. 85–109.

Kallunki J-P., Silvola H. (2008), "The Effect of Organizational Life Cycle Stage on the Use of Acivity-Based Costing", *Management Accounting Research*, 19, pp. 62–79.

Kaplan R.S. (1984), "The Role of Empirical Research in Management Accounting", *Accounting, Organization and Society*, 11(415), pp. 429–452.

Kaplan R.S. (1985), "Accounting Lag: the Obsolescence of Cost Accounting Systems", [in:] Clark K.B., Hayes R.H., Lorenz C. (eds.), *The Uneasy Alliance: Managing the Productivity-Technology Dilemma*, Harvard Business School Press, Boston.

Kaplan R.S. (1986), "The Evolution of Management Accounting", *The Accounting Review*, July, pp. 390–418.

Kaplan R.S. (1987a), *John Deere Component Works (A), Case No: 9-187-107, 1.19*, Harvard Business School Publishing, Boston.

Kaplan R.S. (1987b), *American Bank, Case No: 9-187-194*, Harvard Business School Publishing, Boston.

Kaplan R.S. (1988), "One Cost System isn't Enough", *Harvard Business Review*, 88(1), pp. 61–66.

Kaplan R.S. (1989), *Kanthal (A) i Kanthal (B), Case No: 9-190-002/3*, Harvard Business School Publishing, Boston.

Kaplan R.S. (1992), "In Defense of Activity-Based Cost Management", *Management Accounting* (US), November, pp. 58–63.

Kaplan R.S. (1994a), "Flexible Budgeting in Activity-Based Costing Framework", *Accounting Horizons*, June, pp. 104–109.

Kaplan R.S. (1994b), "Management Accounting (1984–1994): Development of New Practice and Theory", *Management Accounting Research*, 5(3–4), pp. 247–260.

Kaplan R.S., Anderson S. (2004), "Time-Driven Activity-Based Costing", *Harvard Business Review*, 82(11), pp. 131–138.

Kaplan R.S., Anderson S. (2008), *Rachunek kosztów działań sterowany czasem TDABC*, Wydawnictwo Naukowe PWN, Warszawa.

Kaplan R.S., Cooper R. (1998), *Cost & Effect. Using Integrated Cost Systems to Drive Profitability and Performance*, Harvard Business School Press, Boston.

Kaplan R.S., Cooper R. (2000), *Zarządzanie kosztami i efektywnością*, Dom Wydawniczy ABC: Oficyna Ekonomiczna, Kraków.

Karmańska A. (2001), *Modelowanie rachunkowości zarządczej ubezpieczyciela na podstawie rachunku kosztów działań*, Monografie i Opracowania, nr 482, Szkoła Główna Handlowa, Warszawa.

Karmańska A. (2003), *Rachunkowość zarządcza ubezpieczyciela. Modelowanie na podstawie rachunku kosztów działań*, Wydawnictwo Naukowe PWN, Warszawa.

Kasurinen T. (2002) „Exploring Management Accounting Change: the Case of Balaced Scorecard Implementation", *Management Accounting Research*, 13(3), pp. 323–343.

Kennedy T., Affleck-Graves J. (2001), "The Impact of Activity-Based Costing Techniques on Firm Performance", *Journal of Management Accounting Research*, 13, pp. 19–45.

Kennett D.L., Durler M.G., Downs A. (2007), "Activity-Based Costing in Large U.S. Cities: Costs & Benefits", *Journal of Government Financial Management*, Spring, pp. 20–29.

Keys D.E., van der Merwe A. (2002), "Gaining Effective Organizational Control with RCA", *Strategic Finance*, 83(11), pp. 41–47.

Khalid A. (2005), "Activity-Based Costing in Saudi Arabia's Largest 100 firms in 2003", *The Journal of American Academy of Business*, 2, pp. 285–292.

Kiani R., Sangeladji M. (2003), "An Empirical Study about the Use of the ABC/ABM Models by Some of the Fortune 500 Largest Industrial Corporations in the USA", *Journal of American Academy of Business*, 3, pp. 174–182.

Kinast A. (1993), "Modernizacja rachunku kosztów", *Rachunkowość*, 6, pp. 6–12.

Kludacz M. (2006), "Koncepcja budżetowania w przekroju działań jako instrument sterowania kosztami szpitala", *Rachunkowość*, 1, pp. 48–50.

Kovac E., Troy H. (1989), "Getting Transfer Prices Right: What Bellcore Did", *Harvard Business Review*, September–October, pp. 148–154.

Kraemer K., Danziger J., Dunkle D., King J. (1993), "The Usefulness of Computer Based Information to Public Managers", *MIS Quarterly*, June, pp. 129–148.

Krumwiede K.R. (1998), "The Implementation Stages of Activity-Based Costing and the Impact of Contextual and Organizational Factors", *Journal of Management Accounting Research*, 10, pp. 239–277.

Kujawski J., Ossowski M. (2000), "Przesłanki wdrożenia rachunku kosztów działań w Proelco Industrial", referat na konferencję *Rachunkowość podmiotów gospodarczych w XXI wieku*, Spała.

Laitinen E.K. (1999), "Management Accounting Change in Finnish Small Technology Companies", paper presented at the Conference on Accounting Perspectives on the Threshold of the 21st Century, Tartu.

Lapsley I., Wright E. (2004), "The Diffusion of Management Accounting Innovations in the Public Sector: a Research Agenda", *Management Accounting Research*, 15(3), pp. 355–374.

Lawson R.A. (2005), "The Use of Activity Based Costing in the Healthcare Industry: 1994 vs. 2004", *Research in Healthcare Financial Management*, 10(1), pp. 77–94.

Leonard-Barton D. (1988), "Implementation Characteristics of Organizational Innovations", *Communications Research*, 15(5), pp. 603–631.

Lere J.C. (1986), "Product Pricing Based on Accounting Costs", *The Accounting Review*, pp. 318–324.

Leszczyński Z., Wnuk-Pel T. (2004), *Controlling w praktyce*, ODDK, Gdańsk.

Love A.D., Brader W. (1994), "Activity Based Costing Sane: New Zealand Evidence", paper presented at the British Accounting Association Conference, Winchester.

Lucas H.C. Jr. (1975), "Behavioural Factors in System Implementation", [in:] Schultz R.L., Slevin D.P. (eds.), *Implementing Operations Research, Management Science*, American Elsevier, New York, pp. 203–216.

Lukka K., Granlund M. (1996), "Cost Accounting in Finland: Current Practice and Trends of Development", *European Accounting Review*, 5(1), pp. 1–18.

Lukka K., Granlund M. (2000), "The Asymmetric Communication Structure within the Accounting Academia: the Case of Activity-Based Costing Research Genres", paper presented at the 23rd European Accounting Association Annual Congress, Munich, 29–31 March.

Lukka K., Granlund M. (2002), "The Fragmented Communication Structure within the Accounting Academia: the Case of Activity-Based Costing Research Genre", *Accounting, Organizations and Society*, 27(1–2), pp. 165–190.

Lukka K., Shields M. (1999), "Innovations in Management Accounting Focus", *Management Accounting* (UK), 77(3), pp. 33–34.

Macintosh N.B. (1998), "Management Accounting Europe: a View from Canada", *Management Accounting Research*, 9, pp. 495–500.

Malmi T. (1997), "Towards Explaining Activity-Based Costing Failure: Accounting and Control in a Decentralized Organization", *Management Accounting Research*, 8, pp. 459–480.

Malmi T. (1999), "Activity-Based Costing Diffusion Across Organizations: an Exploratory Empirical Analysis of Finnish Firms", *Accounting, Organizations and Society*, 24(8), pp. 649–672.

Markus M.L., Pfeffer J. (1983), "Power and the Design and Implementation of Accounting and control systems", *Accounting, Organizations and Society*, 8, pp. 205–218.

McGowan A.S. (1998), "Perceived Benefits of ABCM Implementation", *Accounting Horizons*, 12(1), pp. 31–50.

McGowan A.S., Klammer T.P. (1997), "Satisfaction with Activity-Based Costing Cost Management Implementation", *Management Accounting Research*, 9, pp. 217–237.

Mecimore Ch.D., Bell A.T. (1995), "Are We Ready for Fourth-Generation ABC?", *Management Accounting*, January, pp. 8–13.

McKeen J.D., Guimaraes T., Wetherbe J.C. (1994), "The Relationship between User Participation and User Satisfaction: an Investigation of Four Contingency Factors", *MIS Quarterly*, December, pp. 427–451.

Michalak J. (2006), *Wpływ globalizacji na pomiar wyników ekonomicznych w rachunkowości zarządczej* (PhD thesis).

Mielcarek J. (2008), *Teoretyczne podstawy rachunku kosztów i zasobów – koncepcji ABC i ABM*, Wydawnictwo Akademii Ekonomicznej, Poznań.

Miller J.A. (2000), *Zarządzanie kosztami działań*, WIG-Press, Warszawa.

Mitchell F. (2002), "Research and Practice in Management Accounting: Improving Integration and Communication", *The European Accounting Review*, 11(2), pp. 277–289.

Nair M. (2000), "Activity-Based Costing: Who's Using it and Why?", *Management Accounting Quarterly*, Spring, pp. 1–5.

Nanjing University International Accounting Department Project Group (2001), "A Survey and Analysis of the Adoption of Cost Management Methods and Their Effects in Chinese Firms", *Accounting Research*, 7, pp. 46–55, [in:] Chow C.W., Duh R-R., Xiao J.Z. (2007), "Management Accounting Practices in the People's Republic of China", [in:] Chapman Ch.S., Hopwood A.G., Shields M.D. (eds.), *Handbook of Management Accounting Research*, Elsevier, Amsterdam, Vol. 2, pp. 923–967.

Nassar M. (2012), "The Diffusion of Activity Based Costing in Jordanian Industrial Companies", paper presented at the 35th Annual Congres of the European Accounting Association, Ljubljana, 9–11 May.

Nassar M., Mah'd O., Morris D., Thomas A. (2010), "Activity Based Costing Diffusion across the Jordanian Industrial Shareholding Companies", paper presented at the 33rd Annual Congres of the European Accounting Association, Istanbul, 19–21 May.

National Association of Accountants (NAA) (1991), *Cost Management Update*, Montvale.

Nicholls B. (1992), "ABC in the U.K. – a Status Report", *Management Accounting* (UK), 70, pp. 22–28.

Noreen E. (1987), "Commentary on H. Thomas Johnson and Robert S. Kaplan's Relevance Lost: The Rise and Fall of Management Accounting", *Accounting Horizons*, December, pp. 110–116.

Noreen E. (1991), "Conditions Under Which Activity-Based Costing Systems Provide Relevant Costs", *Journal of Management Accounting Research*, 3, pp. 159–168.

Novák P. (2009), "Cost Management Changes in the Economic Resort of Czech and Slovak Republic", *Global Business and Management Research: An International Journal*, 1(2), pp. 70–77.

Ohl I. (1995), "Rachunek kosztów działań – stan badań", *Zeszyty Teoretyczne Rachunkowości*, 33, pp. 102–119.

Ossowski M. (2009), "Rachunek kosztów działań w publicznych szkołach wyższych", *Controlling i Rachunkowość Zarządcza*, 2, pp. 20–28.

Ostrenga M.R. (1990), "Activities: the Focal Point of Total Cost Management", *Management Accounting* (US), February, pp. 42–47.

Otley D. (1980), "The Contingency Theory of Management Accounting: Achievement and Prognosis", *Accounting, Organizations and Society*, 4, pp. 413–428.

Otley D. (1995), "Management Control, Organizational Design and Accounting Information Systems", [in:] Askton D., Hopper T., Scapens R. (eds.), *Issues in Management Accounting*, Prentice Hall, London, pp. 45–63.

Ozgowicz R. (2008), "Wpływ rachunku kosztów działań na działalność administratora budynków", *Controlling i Rachunkowość Zarządcza*, 8, pp. 3–5.

Parkinson A. (2009), "The Implementation and Use of Activity-Based Costing in China: Perceptions of Managers in China Regarding Theory and Reality", paper presented at the 32nd European Accounting Association Annual Congress, Tampere, 12–15 May.

Pemberton N., Arumugam L., Hassan N. (1996), "ABM at Dayton Technologies: from Obstacles to Opportunities", *Management Accounting*, March, pp. 20–27.

Piechota R. (2005), *Projektowanie rachunku kosztów działań*, Difin, Warszawa.

Pierce B. (2004), "Activity Based Costing: The Irish Experience: True Innovation or Passing Fad?", *Accountancy Ireland*, October, pp. 28–31.

Pimentel L.V. (2008), "Management Accounting Change in a Portuguese Service Company", paper presented at the 31th Annual Congres of the European Accounting Association, Rotterdam, 23–25 April.

Piosik A. (2002), *Budżetowanie i kontrola budżetowa w warunkach stosowania rachunku kosztów działań*, Wydawnictwo Akademii Ekonomicznej, Katowice.

Piper J., Walley P. (1990), "Testing ABC Logic", *Management Accounting* (UK), September, pp. 36–37.

Polak A. (2003), "Procesowy rachunek kosztów", *Controlling i Rachunkowość Zarządcza*, 3, pp. 41–44.

Prather J., Rueschoff N. (1996), "An Analysis of International Accounting Research in US Academic Accounting Journals 1980 through 1993", *Accounting Horizons*, 10, pp. 1–17.

Przytuła A. (2007), "Ewolucja rachunku kosztów działań", *Rachunkowość*, 8, pp. 27–31.

Radek M., Schwarz R. (2000), "Zmiany w rachunkowości zarządczej w polskich przedsiębiorstwach w okresie transformacji systemu gospodarczego (na podstawie badań empirycznych)", *Zeszyty Teoretyczne Rachunkowości*, 1(57), pp. 58–83.

Raffish N., Turney P. (1991), "Glossary of Activity-Based Management", *Journal of Cost Management*, Autumn, pp. 53–63.

Reeve J.M. (1996), "Projects, Models, and Systems – Where is ABM Headed?", *Cost Management*, 10, pp. 5–16.

Roberts M.W., Silvester K.J. (1996), "Why ABC Failed and How it May yet Succeed", *Journal of Cost Management*.

Robey D. (1979), "User Attitudes and Management Information System Use", *Academy of Management Journal*, 22(3), pp. 527–538.

Robinson M.A. (ed.) (1990), "Contribution Margin Analysis: No Longer Relevant. Strategic Cost Management: the New Paradigm", *Journal of Management Accounting Research*, 2, pp. 1–32.

Ryan B., Scapens R.W., Theobald M. (2002), *Research Method & Methodology in Finance & Accounting*, Thomson, London.

Scapens R.W. (1990), "Researching Management Accounting Practice: the Role of Case Study Methods", *British Accounting Review*, 22, pp. 259–281.

Scapens R.W. (2004), "Innovation in Management Accounting Practice and Research in the United Kingdom", paper presented at the 4th Conference on New Directions in Management Accounting: Innovations in Practice and Research, Brussels.

Scapens R.W., Roberts J. (1993), "Accounting and Control: a Case Study of Resistance to Accounting Change", *Management Accounting Research*, 4, pp. 1–32.

Shank J.K., Govindarajan V. (1988), "Transaction Based Costing for the Complex Product Line: a Field Study", *Journal of Cost Management*, Summer, pp. 31–38.

Shields M.D. (1995), "An Empirical Analysis of Firms' Implementation Experiences with Activity-Based Costing", *Journal of Management Accounting Research*, 7, pp. 148–166.

Shields M.D. (1997), "Research in Management Accounting by North Americans in the 1990s", *Journal of Management Accounting Research*, 9, pp. 3–61.

Sobańska I. (2002), "Jak się zmienia praktyka rachunkowości zarządczej na przełomie XX i XXI wieku? (część II – Polska)", *Controlling i Rachunkowość Zarządcza*, 1, pp. 6–11.

Sobańska I. (2009), "Rachunkowość zarządcza", [in:] Sobańska I., Czarnecki J., Wnuk-Pel T., *Rachunek kosztów. Podejście operacyjne i strategiczne*, C.H. Beck, Warszawa.

Sobańska I., Szychta A. (1995), "Management Accounting in Polish Companies in the Period of Structural Transformation", paper presented at the 18th European Accounting Association Annual Congress, Birmingham, 10–12 May.

Sobańska I., Szychta A. (1996), "Projektowanie systemów rachunkowości zarządczej. Uwarunkowania i możliwości", [in:] Rachunkowość zarządcza w teorii i praktyce, Akademia Ekonomiczna im. K. Adamieckiego, Katowice, pp. 111–122.

Sobańska I., Wnuk T. (1999), "Causes and Directions of Changes in Costing Systems in Polish Enterprises During 1991–1999", paper presented at the Conference on Accounting Perspectives on the Threshold of 21st Century, Tartu, pp. 217–221.

Sobańska I., Wnuk T. (2000), "Causes and Directions of Changes in Management Accounting Practice in Poland", paper presented at the Conference on Economics & Management: Actualities and Methodology, Kaunas.

Sobańska I., Wnuk T. (2001), "Management Accounting Practice in Poland", paper presented at the Conference on Accounting Changes in European Organizations, Kaunas.

Solomons D. (1968), "The Historical Developments in Costing", [in:] Solomons D. (ed.), *Studies in Cost Analysis*, Irwin, Homewood, pp. 3–49.

Spicer B.H. (1992), "The Resurgence of Cost and Management Accounting: a Review of Some Recent Developments in Practice", *Management Accounting Research*, 3, pp. 1–37.

Staubus G.J. (1971), *The Dark Ages of Cost Accounting*, Irwin, Boston.

Staubus G.J. (1990), "Activity Costing: Twenty Years on", *Management Accounting Research*, 1, pp. 249–264.

Strebel P. (1996), "Why do Employees Resist Change?", *Harvard Business Review*, May–June, pp. 86–92

Swenson D.W. (1995), "The Benefits of Activity-Based Cost Management to the Manufacturing Industry", *Journal of Management Accounting Research*, 7, pp. 167–180.

Swenson D.W. (1997), "Managing Costs Through Complexity Reduction at Carrier Corporation", *Management Accounting* (US), April, pp. 20–28.

Swenson D., Barney D. (2001), "ABC/M: Which Companies Have Success?", *The Journal of Corporate Accounting & Finance*, March–April, pp. 35–44.

Swenson D., Flesher D.W. (1996), "Are You Satisfied with Your Cost Management System?", *Management Accounting* (UK), March, pp. 49–53.

Szadziewska A. (2002), "Rachunek kosztów w przedsiębiorstwach produkcyjnych północnej Polski – stan i kierunki zmian", *Zeszyty Teoretyczne Rachunkowości*, 9(65), pp. 90–112.

Szadziewska A. (2003), "Wybrane zagadnienia z zakresu wykorzystania rachunku kosztów przedsiębiorstw działających na terenie Polski i Niemiec", *Zeszyty Teoretyczne Rachunkowości*, 12(68), pp. 54–65.

Szychta A. (2001), "Zastosowanie metod rachunkowości zarządczej w przedsiębiorstwach w Polsce", *Zeszyty Teoretyczne Rachunkowości*, 5(61), pp. 101–119.

Szychta A. (2002), "The Scope and Application of Management Accounting Methods in Polish Enterprises", *Management Accounting Research*, 13(4), pp. 401–418.

Szychta A. (2006), "Praktyka rachunkowości zarządczej w Polsce w świetle wyników badań ankietowych", [in:] Sobańska I., Nowak W.A. (eds.), *Międzynarodowe i krajowe regulacje rachunkowości i ich implementacja: wyzwania i bariery*, Wydawnictwo Uniwersytetu Łódzkiego, Łódź.

Szychta A. (2007a), *Etapy ewolucji i kierunki integracji metod rachunkowości zarządczej*, Wydawnictwo Uniwersytetu Łódzkiego, Łódź, pp. 222–250.

Szychta A. (2007b), "Time-Driven ABC w kontekście uwarunkowań implementacji rachunku kosztów działań", [in:] Sobańska I., Szychta A., *Wpływ międzynarodowych i krajowych regulacji sprawozdawczości finansowej i auditingu na zmiany praktyce rachunkowości*, Wydawnictwo Uniwersytetu Łódzkiego, Łódź, pp. 363–377.

Szyszłowski R. (2006), "Zastosowanie rachunku kosztów działań na potrzeby analizy opłacalności odbiorców (część I)", *Controlling i Rachunkowość Zarządcza*, 4, pp. 13–17.

Szyszłowski R. (2007), "Zastosowanie rachunku kosztów działań na potrzeby analizy opłacalności odbiorców (część II)", *Controlling i Rachunkowość Zarządcza*, 9, pp. 42–46.

Świderska G.K., Pielaszek M. (2001), "Rachunek kosztów działań w zarządzaniu przedsiębiorstwem w branży farmaceutycznej", [in:] Micherda B. (ed.), *Ewolucja polskiej rachunkowości na tle rozwiązań światowych*, Akademia Ekonomiczna, Kraków.

Świderska G.K., Pielaszek M. (2002), "Wpływ koncepcji obiektowego rachunku kosztów na proces budżetowania", [in:] Krawczyk W. (ed.), *Budżetowanie działalności jednostek gospodarczych – teoria i praktyka. Część III*, KNOiZ PAN, AGH, Kraków, pp. 261–266.

Świderska G.K., Rybarczyk K., Pielaszek M. (2002), "Obiektowy rachunek kosztów", *Zeszyty Teoretyczne Rachunkowości*, 8(64), pp. 223–228.

Tse M.S.C., Gong M.Z. (2009), "Recognition of Idle Resources in Time-Driven Activity-Based Costing and Resource Consumption Accounting Models", *Journal of Applied Management Accounting Research*, 7(2), pp. 41–54.

Turney P.B.B. (1992), "Activity-Based Management", *Management Accounting* (US), January, pp. 20–25.

Van Nguyen H., Brooks A. (1997), "An Empirical Investigation of Adoption Issues Relating to Activity-Based Costing", *Asian Accounting Review*, 5, pp. 1–18.

Wickramasinghe D., Alawattage Gh. (2007), *Management Accounting Change. Approaches and Perspectives*, Routledge.

Widera R. (2008), "Porównanie tradycyjnego rachunku kosztów i rachunku kosztów działań", *Controlling i Rachunkowość Zarządcza*, 9, pp. 17–20.

Wnuk T. (2000), "Rachunek kosztów działań – konsekwencje niespełnienia podstawowych założeń modelu (studium przypadku)", *Zeszyty Teoretyczne Rachunkowości*, 1(57), pp. 110–132.

Wnuk-Pel T. (2006a), "Struktura systemów ABC w przedsiębiorstwach działających w Polsce: analiza przypadków", [in:] Sobańska I., Nowak W.A. (eds.), *Międzynarodowe i krajowe regulacje rachunkowości i ich implementacja: wyzwania i bariery*, Wydawnictwo Uniwersytetu Łódzkiego, Łódź.

Wnuk-Pel T. (2006b), "Wdrożenie i wykorzystanie rachunku kosztów działań w firmie produkcyjno-handlowej", *Rachunkowość*, 10, pp. 26–34.

Wnuk-Pel T. (2006c) *Zarządzanie rentownością. Budżetowanie i kontrola. Activity-Based Costing/ Management*, Difin, Warszawa.

Wnuk-Pel T. (2008), "Wdrożenie rachunku kosztów działań w średniej wielkości firmie produkcyjnej", *Zeszyty Teoretyczne Rachunkowości*, 42(98), pp. 383–396.

Yin R.K. (2003), *Case Study Research: Design and Methods*, 3th edition, California, Sage Publications Inc.

Yoshikawa T., Innes J., Mitchell F. (1992), "Activity Based Cost Information: Its Role in Cost Management", *The Journal of Management Accounting* (Japan), Autumn, pp. 43–54.

Zieliński T. (2007), "As Easy As ABC' Rachunek kosztów działań prosty jak abecadło", *Controlling i Rachunkowość Zarządcza*, 5, pp. 36–40.

Zimmermann J.L. (1979), "The Costs and Benefits of Cost Allocation", *The Accounting Review*, pp. 504–521.

Zimmermann J.L. (2001), "Conjectures Regarding Empirical Management Accounting Research", *Journal of Accounting and Economics*, 1(32), pp. 411–427.

Zmud R.W., Cox J.F. (1979), "The Implementation Process: a Change Approach", *MIS Quarterly*, 3(2), pp. 35–43.

LIST OF TABLES

LIST OF FIGURES

REVIEWERS
Karim Charaf, Toomas Haldma, Monika Marcinkowska

EDITOR OF ŁÓDŹ UNIVERSITY PRESS
Ewa Siwińska

LANGUAGE EDITOR
Mark Muirhead

TYPESETTING
AGENT PR

COVER DESIGN
Barbara Grzejszczak

COVER PHOTO
Compass and computer keyboard (29697593)
© *andersphoto – Fotolia.com*

Author is especially grateful to Akademia Biznesu Sp.k.
for financial help in publishing this book

PRINT AND SETTING
Quick Druk